"Both a highly readable historical overview of public housing policy in Canada and in several western countries, including the US, and an ambitious longitudinal case study of the redevelopment of a large Toronto public housing project into mixed income, mixed tenure housing. With first-hand insights from 52 residents, we are given a unique perspective on the enormous complexity of such efforts ... a significant contribution to the literature on the opportunities and challenges of large-scale public housing redevelopment."

Rachel G. Bratt, Professor Emerita, Department of Urban and Environmental Policy and Planning, Tufts University; Senior Research Fellow, Joint Center for Housing Studies, Harvard University, USA.

"This public-private project is vitally important for its breathtaking scale and amenities, commitment to original residents and hard-learned solutions to physical and social transformation challenges that will be quite familiar to those tackling similar efforts in other cities. Johnson and Johnson's thorough and very accessible book will help end the Regent Park knowledge gap and should be required reading for policymakers, practitioners, researchers and students with an interest in the mixed-income approach to equitable urban redevelopment."

Mark Joseph, Ph.D, Co-author of Integrating the Inner City: The Promise and Perils of Mixed-Income Public Housing Transformation; *Founding Director, The National Initiative on Mixed-Income Communities, Case Western Reserve University, USA.*

Regent Park Redux

Regent Park Redux evaluates one of the biggest experiments in public housing redevelopment from the tenant perspective. Built in the 1940s, Toronto's Regent Park has experienced common large-scale public housing problems. Instead of simply tearing down old buildings and scattering inhabitants, the city's housing authority came up with a plan for radical transformation.

In partnership with a private developer, the Toronto Community Housing Corporation organized a twenty-year, billion-dollar makeover. The reconstituted neighbourhood, one of the most diverse in the world, will offer a new mix of amenities and social services intended to "reknit the urban fabric."

Regent Park Redux, based on a ten-year study of 52 households as they moved through stages of displacement and resettlement, examines the dreams and hopes residents have for their community and their future. Urban planners and designers across the world, in cities facing some of the same challenges as Toronto, will want to pay attention to this story.

Laura C. Johnson is Professor of Planning at the University of Waterloo, Canada. She has authored three books—on childcare, industrial homework, and teleworking—as well as numerous articles on related topics. She received the American Planning Association's 2004 National Women in Planning Award in honour of Diana Donald.

Robert E. Johnson is Professor Emeritus of History at the University of Toronto, Canada, and Senior Journalism Fellow of Massey College, Canada. His main research focus has been Russian and Soviet history, including a recent study of living space in Russian cities. He collaborated with Laura Johnson on *The Seam Allowance* (1983).

THE RTPI Library Series

Published by Routledge in conjunction with The Royal Town Planning Institute, this series of leading-edge texts looks at all aspects of spatial planning theory and practice from a comparative and international perspective.

Reviving Critical Planning Theory
Dealing with Pressure, Neo-liberalism, and Responsibility in Communicative Planning
Tore Øivin Sager

Planning for Growth
Urban and Regional Planning in China
Fulong Wu

Reconsidering Localism
Edited by Simin Davoudi and Ali Madanipour

Planning/Conflict
Critical Perspectives on Contentious Urban Developments
Edited by Enrico Gualini

Conflict, Improvisation, Governance
Lessons in Democratic Planning from the Netherlands
David Laws and John Forester

The Craft of Collaborative Planning
People Working Together to Shape Creative and Sustainable Places
Jeff Bishop

Future Directions for the European Shrinking City
Edited by Hans Schlappa and William J.V. Neill

Insurgencies and Revolutions
Edited by Haripriya Rangan, Kam Mee NG, Libby Porter, Jacquelyn Chase

Planning for Small Town Change
Neil Powe and Trevor Hart

Regent Park Redux
Reinventing Public Housing in Canada
Laura Johnson and Robert Johnson

Regent Park Redux

Reinventing Public Housing in Canada

Laura C. Johnson and Robert E. Johnson

LONDON AND NEW YORK

First published 2017
by Routledge

2 Park Square, Milton Park, Abingdon, Oxfordshire OX14 4RN
52 Vanderbilt Avenue, New York, NY 10017

Routledge is an imprint of the Taylor & Francis Group, an informa business

First issued in paperback 2020

Library of Congress Cataloging in Publication Data
Names: Johnson, Laura Climenko, author. | Johnson, Robert Eugene, 1943- author.
Title: Regent Park redux : reinventing public housing in Canada / Laura C. Johnson and Robert E. Johnson.
Description: New York, NY : Routledge, 2017. | Series: The RTPI library series | Includes index.
Identifiers: LCCN 2016028526 | ISBN 9781138812109 (hardback)
Subjects: LCSH: Public housing--Canada. | Housing policy--Canada. | Urban renewal--Canada.
Classification: LCC HD7305.A3 J59 2017 | DDC 363.5/850971--dc23
LC record available at https://lccn.loc.gov/2016028526

ISBN: 978-1-138-81210-9 (hbk)
ISBN: 978-0-367-66782-5 (pbk)

Typeset in Goudy Old Style
by Saxon Graphics Ltd, Derby

In memory of Barrie Cheval, who taught us the importance of neighbourhood

Contents

Illustrations

Figures

Charts

Acknowledgements

As co-authors, we followed different routes to the Regent Park story. Social planner Laura Johnson, with her graduate students, began in 2006 to track tenants' experiences with displacement from their Regent Park home in the face of redevelopment. Historian Robert Johnson began several years later to follow the story of history being repeated as Regent Park was—for a second time—being rebuilt. In *Regent Park Redux* we bring our two perspectives together to set the current residents' experiences within historical context. We owe thanks to our colleagues, friends, family, and neighbours who supported us through the various stages of research and writing.

The longitudinal study at the base of this research examines the TCHC tenants' experiences of redevelopment through the first of five projected phases. A most important debt of gratitude is owed to the many Regent Park residents who agreed to repeated interviews to discuss their personal experiences with displacement, relocation, and resettlement. The Regent Park redevelopment is a major project that has attracted much attention from academic researchers and the news media. The residents' participation in this research was granted in the context of many other competing requests for their time and their views. Their participation in this research process is acknowledged with sincere thanks.

During the course of this research, four University of Waterloo graduate students have worked under Laura Johnson's supervision to complete one doctoral dissertation and three masters' theses investigating various aspects of the redevelopment of Regent Park. Danielle Leahy Laughlin's Ph.D dissertation research used the photovoice technique to study young people's ideas about public spaces in Regent Park beginning in 2004, before the start of any redevelopment (Leahy Laughlin 2008). In 2007 Rick Schippling's MA thesis was a digital multimedia examination of the displacement of Phase 1 residents from their Regent Park homes. That thesis generated a half-hour documentary video, *Breaking Ground*, telling the story from the perspective of relocated residents. The video served as the basis of a "member check" (respondent validation)[1] of the research, bringing preliminary findings back to the community in the form of rough cut video which served as the basis of discussion about the start of the revitalization. The video and the thesis in text form are together on file in the University of Waterloo thesis library (Schippling 2007). Although he completed his master's degree requirements in 2007, Rick

Schippling has maintained to the present time an active interest and involvement in the Regent Park redevelopment. In 2014 Stephanie Fernandes, also a University of Waterloo graduate student in Planning, completed a master's thesis on social mix and public space in Regent Park (Fernandes 2014). That qualitative research involved interviews with samples of RGI tenants and condominium residents as well as key informants from the Regent Park community. The TD Centre of Learning convened a workshop in Regent Park to "member check" Fernandes's preliminary results through informal discussion with residents. In 2015, University of Waterloo Planning graduate student Navroop Singh Tehara completed a master's thesis on Regent Park residents' Right of Return in the redevelopment. Key informants and document review are the basis of this investigation, which compares the application of the Right of Return in the Toronto instance with previous applications of this policy (Tehara 2015). All of these four graduate students' research projects contributed significantly to the research reported in this volume. Each has investigated and documented a distinct component of the unique Regent Park redevelopment. These four key sources are referenced at various points in the pages that follow; the thesis documents appear in the list of References.

University of Waterloo Librarian Marian Davies provided valuable assistance in tracking down elusive and obscure historical documents for this research. Her creativity and detective skills are acknowledged with gratitude. An early meeting with archivist Sally Gibson suggested sources for the historical neighbourhood data we were seeking. Jack de Klerk, of Neighbourhood Legal Services, was generous with his time answering questions about the legal dimension of redevelopment. Friend and neighbour Jim Shedden played an important role in conceptualizing this project as the revitalization was about to begin. It was he who said that this redevelopment is destined to become an important event in Toronto's urban history; someone needs to document it—why not us? George Rust-D'Eye, our neighbour and Cabbagetown historian, provided important comments on a draft manuscript. Nicholas Humphries and Hilary Browning helped us to understand the real estate market in and around Regent Park. Jane Springer provided a careful review of the book manuscript in its penultimate draft. Don Duff McCracken assisted us in reformatting illustrations. We are especially grateful to Series Editor Jill Grant and the editorial staff of Routledge for their efficient and thoughtful handling of the manuscript. Errors and omissions, needless to say, are solely our own.

Over the years of this study, valuable research assistance was provided by a team of urban planning students, mostly from the University of Waterloo, as well as several from the University of Toronto. Acknowledgement of this important assistance is made to the following graduate students: Noreen Khimani, Chris Rahim, Tanisha Sri Bhaggayadatta, and Bryan Sherwood, and other student research assistants: Renée Mak, Minh Toan, Revital Weiss,

Rebecca Lau, Clarissa Nam, and Phung Lam. In 2015–2016 research assistance was provided by University of Toronto graduate students Amir Abdul Reda, Kevin Chan and Thilo Schaefer. Undergraduate students from University of Toronto Naveeda Hussain and Shalah Mohammed provided additional research assistance.

Jim Dunn, of McMaster University, was an important research collaborator. Early in this research, he and Laura held an informal and occasional seminar with our various graduate students; this was an important research highlight, providing opportunities to keep up to date with ongoing Regent Park redevelopment initiatives and to coordinate activities with a view toward minimizing the research burden on residents. We are also grateful to Penny Gurstein, Director of the UBC School of Community and Regional Planning, for including us in her May 2015 SSHRC-supported workshop on the future of public housing, which broadened our comparative context for our Toronto study.

Throughout the course of this research Toronto Community and Housing Corporation (TCHC) provided various kinds of informal and in-kind support, including shared project office space in the Regent Park Relocation Office at an early point in the Phase 1 relocation process. While not serving as a formal research partner in the conduct of the research, and while remaining at arm's length from this research process, housing authority staff at various levels in the organization and from numerous departments were important sources of assistance and information about the implementation of the redevelopment plans. While many people at TCHC provided assistance in this research, Abigail Moriah in the Development Department served as a key liaison with that organization.

Sincere thanks are also extended to the many key informants who generously gave their time to participate in this study, helping us to understand the community, its history, and the policy context for its redevelopment.

Finally, we would like to thank the research funders. The research received financial support in the form of grants to Laura Johnson from Social Sciences and Humanities Research Council of Canada (SSHRC), under their Standard Research Grant program, and Canada Mortgage and Housing Corporation, (CMHC), through a grant from their External Research program. The University of Waterloo provided additional support to Laura Johnson in the form of sabbatical leave to pursue research and writing for this book, and financial support for student research assistance. While the opinions expressed in this volume are solely those of the authors, that funding support made possible the research on which this book is based.

Notes

1 Member checking refers to "taking ideas back to research participants for their confirmation" (Charmaz 2014, 210).

References

Charmaz, Kathy. 2014. *Constructing Grounded Theory*. 2nd Ed. London, UK: SAGE.

Fernandes, Stephanie. 2014. "Informal relationships in a newly mixed income community: A Regent Park case study." School of Planning, University of Waterloo, Waterloo, Ontario, Canada. Master's thesis. uwspace.uwaterloo.ca/handle/10012/8535.

Leahy Laughlin, Danielle. 2008. "Defining and Exploring Public Space: Young People's Perspectives from Regent Park, Toronto." Ph.D. dissertation, University of Waterloo. hdl.handle.net/10012/3737.

Schippling, Richard M. 2007. "Public Housing Redevelopment: Residents' Experiences with Relocation from Phase 1 in Toronto's Regent Park Revitalization." Master's thesis, School of Planning, University of Waterloo, Waterloo, Ontario, Canada. The thesis includes a 30-minute documentary video, *Breaking Ground*. uwspace.uwaterloo.ca/handle/10012/3028.

Tehara, Navroop Singh. 2015. "Tenants' Right of Return: Early Experiences from Toronto's Regent Park Redevelopment." Master's thesis. School of Planning, University of Waterloo, Waterloo, Ontario, Canada. uwspace.uwaterloo.ca/handle/10012/9739.

Introduction[1]

In 2013, Toronto's City Council considered a proposal to develop high-rise, high-density housing along the city's scenic Lake Ontario waterfront. Designed as mixed income, mixed tenure housing, that project was to include some 75 units of subsidized housing targeted at low-income households. Rob Ford, the city's then-mayor, objected, saying the city had no business providing poor people with a water view (CBC 2013). Mayor Ford was advocating a "no-frills" model of public housing—one that provides shelter to the neediest populations but avoids "extras." Such housing often segregates the recipients from the rest of the urban population, even to the point of stigmatization.

Toronto's Regent Park, more than sixty years old, used to represent that kind of housing. But for the past decade it has been the site of an alternate plan that takes a radically different approach. Its twenty-year, billion-dollar[2] redevelopment features mixed-tenure housing for a mixed income population, settling middle-income residents alongside rent-geared-to-income (RGI) tenants in a diverse community that includes a large proportion of recent immigrants. Instead of separating RGI units from the rest of the population, the plan aims to create a "tenure blind" streetscape in which market-level and subsidized housing will be indistinguishable. Going forward as a public-private partnership, it addresses problems that municipalities around the world are facing. If Regent Park succeeds, it may offer lessons and models for many other cities. Its ten-year midpoint is a good time to assess its accomplishments and prospects.

Cities in North America, Europe, Britain and Australia are struggling to renew or replace ageing and deteriorated public housing stock. In many jurisdictions, "urban renewal" efforts of earlier times have left a legacy of fractured communities and social displacement—problems that are especially acute for populations of recent immigrants. Today, lacking the budgetary resources that renewal would require, cities in many jurisdictions are looking for new and effective housing redevelopment models. In many countries, municipal leaders are reviewing and reconsidering the design and purpose of state-supported housing. Some see full or partial privatization as the best alternative, using public-private partnerships to advance social housing development. These initiatives are typically characterized by income and tenure mix. Initiatives such as Britain's "Right to Buy" or the HOPE VI program in the United States have achieved mixed results. Critics fault them for failing to address the problems of the poorest residents. Some view these efforts as a covert form of gentrification aimed at freeing valuable real estate for other uses (Slater 2006).

Built in the late 1940s on a 69 acre (29 hectare) site in Toronto's downtown, the original Regent Park resembled large public housing projects in many other localities. Its older, northern half consisted of row-house and low-rise (three- and six-storey) apartment buildings in a Garden City design. The part to the south, built a decade later, was inspired by Swiss-French architect Le Corbusier's "Towers in the Park" modernist vision: It featured five 14-storey apartment buildings of prize-winning design. In superblock layout without through streets, Regent Park was intended to be an island of tranquillity separated from the ills of city life. Instead it became what one recent commentator termed a "gated community of poverty" (Kosny 2005)[3]: Isolated, stigmatized, and in profound disrepair. Regent Park seemed to symbolize all that was wrong with public housing.

Toronto, Canada's largest city, has turned to public-private partnership to redevelop this community. In an era of austerity, when government programs to build and renovate social housing have been drastically cut if not altogether eliminated, private sector residential and commercial development is being used to finance the rebuilding of social housing. Elements of this plan are familiar from other jurisdictions—for example, an emphasis on mixed land use and a street-oriented design in place of older "garden cities" and modernist superblocks. The influence of "New Urbanist"[4] planning principles is evident. But Toronto's planners have emphasized two particular features, derived from study of what has and hasn't worked elsewhere: resident participation in the planning process, and a firm guarantee that original tenants enjoy a Right of Return. Other jurisdictions have offered such a promise, but the track record suggests that it has not often been honoured. Instead of uprooting the original public housing community, the Regent Park plan aims to incorporate it into a broader, more diverse and better serviced neighbourhood.

The old Regent Park was known widely in Canada, and has been the focus of much media attention over its lifespan. Two National Film Board of Canada (NFB) documentary films have chronicled the project's changing fortunes and the changing public view of Regent Park. A 1953 NFB production, *Farewell Oak Street*, described the good fortune of residents whose slum housing was razed to make way for the modern Regent Park community. The voice of narrator Lorne Greene boomed "Down came the verminous walls..." as the old, decaying tenement houses were demolished and modern dwellings were constructed for the grateful poor families (NFB 1953). Those modernist public housing buildings were equated with cleanliness, and signalled an improved quality of life for the residents, whom the film portrayed as fortunate and grateful. In 1994 the NFB's documentary film, *Return to Regent Park*, directed by Bay Weyman, tells a very different story of Regent Park tenants' frustrations, including drug dealing, gangs, and poorly maintained premises (NFB 1994). Residents and urban experts interviewed on-camera pin the blame on bad urban planning.

Many speak of the "footprint" of Regent Park, distinguishing the territory within and outside its boundaries. Bounded on all sides by arterial streets, and built in architectural styles different from those on surrounding blocks, Regent Park had long had the reputation of being a community unto itself. Its separation from the surrounding neighbourhoods—which, at the time of construction, retained many of the qualities of the old "slum" neighbourhood that Regent Park had replaced—was not accidental. The project's designers intended it to be tranquil and family-friendly, and believed that these goals could best be accomplished by taking the neighbourhood "off the grid." They also believed that single-use zoning would enhance this goal, and as a result Regent Park was built without shops or services.

The design features that were originally celebrated were later blamed for the project's decline and, to some critics, failure. While initially lauded in the 1950s and 1960s as a successful urban environment, its deterioration and deferred maintenance resulted in its becoming stigmatized as crime-ridden and unsafe. Over the years Regent Park developed a reputation as a magnet for gang and criminal activity. News media from the 1970s onward fostered Regent Park's reputation as an isolated "no-go zone." But residents resisted this characterization, asserting their own claim to the city and emphasizing the many positive accomplishments of community organizations.

By 2002, as a consequence of the amalgamation of the Toronto metropolitan area, several local housing agencies were merged into a single consolidated housing authority. Designated the Toronto Community Housing Corporation (TCHC), it became North America's second largest public housing landlord (TCHC 2015), and the largest in Canada. Leaders of the new agency decided to mark its formation with a suitably ambitious project. With a projected fifteen- to twenty-year timeline, the phased Regent Park redevelopment was intended to address long-standing problems, including deterioration of physical plant. The plan would also establish Toronto's reputation as an innovator in the challenging area of replacing ageing social housing stock.

On the weekend of Saturday May 29 and Sunday May 30, 2004, the Regent Park community participated in its first public open house, inviting members of the general public to tour their community and review initial plans for its revitalization[5] (TCHC 2004). The invitation began with the announcement "We are opening our doors to the public…" printed below a photograph looking down one of Regent Park's tree-lined internal non-vehicular streets. For four hours in the afternoon of each of those days, Regent Park welcomed neighbours and others interested to a series of guided tours featuring displays on the history, the present, and the planned future of Regent Park. According to the flyer inviting the public into their neighbourhood, visitors would see a model of the proposed revitalization, and be given an opportunity to share their opinions of the redevelopment proposal with members of the project planning team. Project Team members were in attendance to answer questions and provide background information (ibid.). Co-hosted by the housing authority (TCHC), and the Regent Park Residents Council, the invitation was a part of the city-wide *Doors Open Toronto* program, in which a variety of public and private landmarks that are usually off limits to visitors open their doors to welcome the public. In the case of *Doors Open Regent Park*, the invitation had the symbolic value of a public pronouncement that this previously isolated and stigmatized community was embarking on a new initiative to which the rest of the city was invited.

In 2005 Toronto City Council voted to approve the planning permission required to redevelop the old Regent Park site into a mixed income, higher density, six-stage project (subsequently streamlined to five stages). This was to be accomplished under a public-private partnership between the municipality of Toronto, its non-profit public housing authority (TCHC), and a private developer. All housing on the site would eventually be razed and rebuilt. The TCHC was committed to replacing—not only unit-for-unit but room-for room—all of the 2,083 housing units that were occupied at the project start-up. These would be supplemented by the addition of approximately 3,000 market units (a number that would later be increased to over 5,000), in the form of condominium apartments and townhouses. Social and market housing would occupy separate buildings but those buildings would be intermixed in the various sections of the site. The original plan, as approved, had a 40–60 percent split of social to market housing. The original public housing tenants were granted a landmark Right of Return once their homes were rebuilt. The plans called for supplementing residential land use with on-site commercial development, parks, and a variety of social and community services.

To organize the redevelopment, the site was divided into geographic zones, to be redeveloped sequentially. This limited the number of households displaced at one time, and confined the demolition and the new construction to particular areas. Together, the phases of redevelopment were originally planned to take fifteen years, but this was later extended to twenty.

The first, in the area bounded by Dundas, Sackville, Oak and Parliament Streets, had housed a total population of approximately 400 low-income households (TCHC 2013). Demolition of the buildings in this quadrant was completed in 2006. New social housing units were completed by 2011. The new stock included ground-oriented townhouse units as well as apartments in tower buildings of varying height (the tallest being 22 storeys).

In 2013, with Phases 1 and 2 complete, the housing authority went back to city council with applications for a zoning change, to allow still more market units on site. As approved by council, the redeveloped Regent Park would now have a 25–75 percent split of social to market housing. The original low income tenants, while resettled in new housing in their rebuilt community, would occupy a smaller proportion of units. (Because their families are on average larger, they would still constitute between 40 and 50 percent of residents in the reconstituted community.) The original residents could still exercise the Right of Return that had been promised to them, but the community to which they returned would be in some ways very different from the one they left.

The Aim of This Book

This book evaluates the redevelopment process from the viewpoint of the first cohort of residents who were displaced, relocated and resettled. Residents' stories have been collected in repeated confidential interviews with a sample of some 52 households from the first of five planned redevelopment phases. The book looks at who returns, who does not—the reasons for residents' choices, and their satisfaction or dissatisfaction with outcomes. Our purpose is to compare these experiences, on the one hand, with those of earlier generations of inhabitants: to ask whether the past can offer lessons for the future, and whether today's residents and planners are taking proper account of the strengths and weaknesses of the old Regent Park. Second, we will try to place Regent Park into a comparative framework that learns from the successes and failures of public housing in other cities in the industrial world. Many features of today's redevelopment—public-private partnership, mixed-income development, Right of Return—have featured prominently in other localities' plans. Others—the Social Development Plan, the one-for-one replacement of demolished housing, the efforts to build a more diverse and integrated community based on the strengths of the older one—make Regent Park distinctive, and may be instructive to communities, planners and decision-makers elsewhere, who are facing similar problems and choices.

Chapter 1 examines the origin of the first Regent Park, the ideas behind its beginning in 1947, and the various stages through which the northern and then the southern parts of the community were turned into public housing. Chapter 2 examines and evaluates the subsequent evolution of Regent Park, including various lines of criticism put forward over the decades from 1960 to 2000. Chapter 3 looks at the housing policy context in a number of prosperous industrial states in Western Europe and the UK, comparing these to policies adopted in Canada and the United States and then to the specific approaches that, more recently, defined Regent Park's redevelopment. Chapter 4 lays out the context for the replanning and rebuilding of Regent Park starting in the new millennium. Chapter 5 looks at the old and new Regent Park through the eyes of residents: their feelings about living there before redevelopment, their apprehensions and hopes for the neighbourhood's transformation. Chapters 6, 7 and 8 trace the original Phase 1 residents through their experiences of redevelopment, following them through displacement, temporary relocation, and eventual resettlement back into a rebuilt community. Chapter 9 offers an overall assessment of what was accomplished in the first ten years of redevelopment. Chapter 10 generalizes from this experience: It reviews the ways in which Regent Park may or may not be a useful model for other jurisdictions, and speculates on issues that the community and the housing authority may face in the years ahead.

Notes

1 The research on which this book is based was funded, in part, by a Standard Research Grant from the Social Sciences and Humanities Research Council of Canada (SSHRC) and an External Research Program grant from Canada Mortgage and Housing Corporation (CMHC). In-kind support has also been provided by Toronto Community Housing (TCH) and by the University of Waterloo. The views expressed are those of the authors and do not represent official views of either funding agency, or the organizations providing research support.

2 Throughout this book, dollar sums are expressed in Canadian currency unless otherwise indicated.

3 The speaker, Mitchell Kosny, was at that time the newly-designated Chair of the Board of Directors of Toronto Community Housing Corporation.

4 New Urbanism is an urban design movement that has flourished, especially in the United States and Canada, since the 1980s. Drawing on the ideas of such figures as Andres Duany in responding to what is seen increasingly as the waste and excess of urban sprawl, New Urbanism promotes development of communities characterized by intensification of settlement, mixed use, walkability, diversity, and attractive, accessible open spaces. High quality design and a rich array of commercial amenities and services are among the defining features of these compact communities, along with mixed housing designs for households of varied means (Grant and Bohdanow 2008). Although its proponents advocate greater density of settlement than traditional suburbs have offered, they have also promoted "traditional" design features such as front porches and ground-oriented single-family dwellings, on the grounds that these may promote positive social interaction among neighbours. New Urbanist ideas have influenced the redevelopment of public housing in a number of localities including Toronto's Regent Park.

5 Toronto Community Housing, Public Open House: Regent Park Revitalization Plan. Flyer posted and distributed throughout the community. May 29 and May 30, 2004.

References

CBC (Canadian Broadcasting Corporation). 2013. "No affordable housing on the waterfront, says Rob Ford." October 29. www.cbc.ca/news/canada/toronto/no-affordable-housingon-the-waterfront-says-rob-ford-1.2287508. (Accessed September 5, 2015).

Grant, Jill L. and Stephanie Bohdanow. 2008. "New urbanism developments in Canada: A survey." *Journal of Urbanism: International Research on Placemaking and Urban Sustainability* 1(2): 109–127.

Kosny, Mitchell E. 2005. "Unlocking value in Toronto's East Downtown: The revitalization of Regent Park." An address to The Economic Club of Toronto. Toronto: Sutton Place Hotel. March 8.

NFB (National Film Board of Canada). 1953. *Farewell to Oak Street*. Grant McLean, Director. www.nfb.ca/film/farewell_oak_street. (Accessed January 10, 2017).

NFB (National Film Board of Canada). 1994. *Return to Regent Park*. Bay Weyman, Director. Co-produced by Close Up Film Productions Ltd., CBC Newsworld, and National Film Board of Canada.

Slater, Tom. 2006. "The Eviction of Critical Perspectives from Gentrification Research." *International Journal of Urban and Regional Research* 30(4): 737–757.

TCHC (Toronto Community Housing Corporation). 2004. Regent Park Residents Council. Doors Open, Regent Park. Co-hosted by Regent Park Resident Council. Toronto: TCHC.

TCHC (Toronto Community Housing Corporation). 2013. *Regent Park Revitalization, Housing Issues Report: Official Plan Amendment and Re-zoning Application for Phases 3, 4, 5, Lifting of the Holding Symbol Phase 3*. (September).

TCHC (Toronto Community Housing Corporation). 2015. Interim Report of the Mayor's Task Force on Toronto Community Housing. July 16. Statement by Greg Spearn, Interim President and Chief Executive Officer of TCHC. www.torontohousing.ca. (Accessed January 10, 2017).

1
Historical Background

> It seems to me that the only availing remedy in Toronto is a planned decentralization... [that] would permit workers to establish their homes convenient to their work in surroundings where their children would learn by experience that grass is a green, living and loving carpet, and that there are really and truly other and lovelier flowers than those of the lithographed calendar that hangs on the cracked, crumbling and soiled wall of a murky room into which the sun's rays have never penetrated... as we evacuate those factories and hovels, we must raze them and bury the distressing memory of them in fine central parks and recreational centres... devoted to the physical and mental improvement of our people.
>
> (Bruce Report 1934, 5)

The first Regent Park Housing was built on a site in east-central Toronto, barely a mile from where the town originally known as York was founded in 1793 (Figure 1.1). Here the Don River flows into Lake Ontario, creating a natural harbour that Lieutenant Governor John Graves Simcoe chose as the capital city of the new province of Upper Canada. The province's first parliament building was located close to the waterfront, at the foot of the road still known today as Parliament Street. But the territories to the north and east, along the lower reaches of the river, were not originally designated for settlement. The marshy riverside was deemed "miasmic" and generally unhealthy, and the lands along the west side of the Don became a "Government Park" or reserve. The first parliament building was burned in the war of 1812, and a few years later the seat of government was moved to a site at Front and John Streets, about a mile west of its previous location. The town grew mainly in this direction, to the north and west of Simcoe's original settlement. When the City of Toronto was incorporated in 1834 the lands east of Parliament Street were treated differently from the rest of the settlement—an administrative designation known as "city liberties." The few inhabitants of this region paid lower taxes and had fewer rights than city-dwellers: "From 1834 until the abolition of the Liberties in 1859, the Lower Don occupied an urban margin, both within the everyday experience of the city's residents and

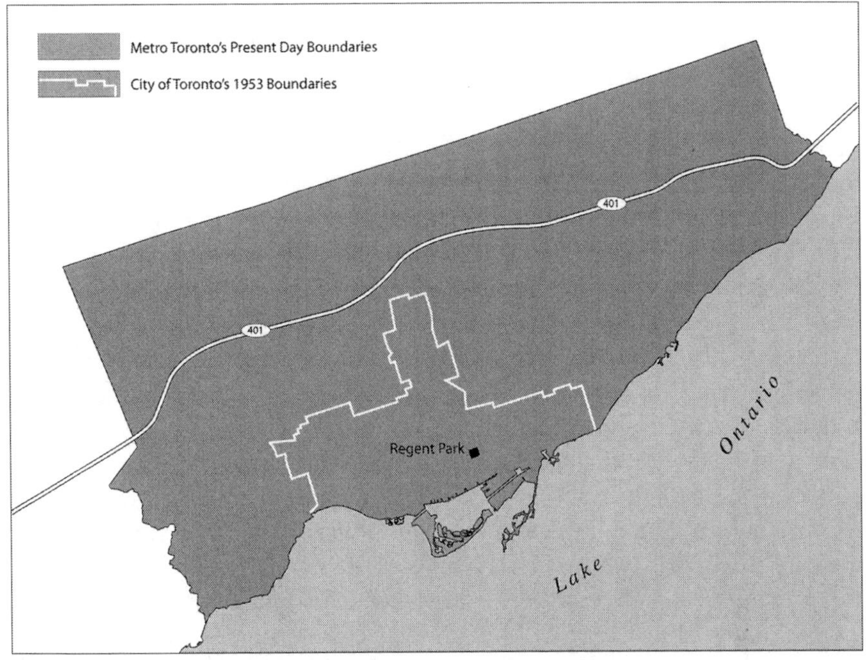

Figure 1.1 Map 1: Regent Park within the boundaries of Toronto.
Source: B. Levely

in the official sphere of city maps and jurisdictional boundaries" (Bonnell 2014, 26).

By the middle of the nineteenth century, however, industrialization made the banks of the Don a locus of factory production, including profoundly polluting forms of manufacturing such as paper-making, tanning and soap-making. All of these required large quantities of water for their operations and discharged their effluent back into the river. Those factories also required labour, and industrial growth was accompanied by residential settlement. The area between Parliament Street and the Don became a low-rent district populated mainly by working-class immigrants from the British Isles. The city atlas of 1858 shows some streets in the neighbourhood fully settled, though others—mainly in the northern section—still had much vacant land. In 1859 the future Regent Park neighbourhood became part of St. David's Ward in which, a decade later, the national census recorded a population of 11,000.

Cabbagetown

Irish settlers fleeing the potato famine of 1847 were especially numerous in this part of the city. Irish Catholics settled mainly close to Queen Street, where St.

Paul's, the city's first Roman Catholic church, had been built in the 1820s. This neighbourhood was sometimes known as Corktown, a designation that has been revived in recent years. Irish Protestants were concentrated further to the north, toward present day Dundas and Gerrard Streets. According to tradition, the immigrants' habit of growing vegetables in their small yards gave the neighbourhood the derogatory name "Cabbagetown". This term was applied at different times to various parts of the district, but most often to the very quadrant—bounded by Parliament, Gerrard, River, and Sydenham (later Shuter) Streets—in which Regent Park was later built (Rust-D'Eye 1984). From the 1970s onwards, the name Cabbagetown has been extended or transferred—first by realtors and then by residents—to describe neighbourhoods immediately north and west of Regent Park, in which extensive renovation and resettlement has been taking place.[1]

Introducing his semi-autobiographical novel, *Cabbagetown*, Hugh Garner described the neighbourhood where he grew up in the 1920s and 1930s as North America's largest Anglo-Saxon slum (Garner 1968, 7). Dwellings on the site included two-storey Victorian brick or brick-façade structures comparable to those that have been renovated in today's fashionable Cabbagetown. But the district's housing stock also encompassed single-storey cottages on narrow laneways, built—sometimes by the inhabitants themselves—in an era when housing codes were unknown. By Garner's day many of Cabbagetown's homes—of all types—were overcrowded and deteriorating. Critics saw these buildings as fire hazards and breeding-places for disease, and public health statistics seemed to bear out this assessment. Even the larger and sturdier houses did not conform to the health and safety standards of a later age. Some had outdoor toilets, and many lacked hot water. Heating was often by wood- or coal-stove rather than from furnaces. Houses, even small ones, were often subdivided among two or more families, sometimes with parents and children sleeping in a single room. Families that were fortunate enough to own their own homes—a not-insignificant minority among the residents[2]—often tried to make ends meet by taking in lodgers or subdividing the premises to accommodate multiple families.

Squalor and overcrowding increased during the Great Depression of the 1930s as incomes plummeted and families sought smaller and cheaper accommodation. Conditions in Cabbagetown and the adjacent Moss Park district were assessed in the Bruce Report—*Report of the Lieutenant-Governor's Committee on Housing Conditions in Toronto*—of 1934. It described the wider neighbourhood that included Cabbagetown as follows: 73 percent of dwellings below the minimum standard of amenities; 40 percent below minimum health standard; 9 percent with only outside toilets; 27 percent with no bath; 45 percent with no method of central heating; 55 percent verminous. Excluding rooming houses, 374 dwellings out of 3,047 surveyed housed two or more families, and 57 percent of dwellings were rated as overcrowded, i.e., housing more than one person per room (Bruce 1934, 18, 129–130).

Urban reformers of the era portrayed this area as a slum or derelict district in need of fundamental change. Cabbagetown's failings were measured in rates of specific diseases (e.g., tuberculosis, with a 63.6 cases per 100,000 incidence in Cabbagetown compared to 31.5 per 100,000 in more prosperous neighbourhoods) or overall mortality/morbidity (infant mortality in 1943–1945 was 5.52 percent, compared to 3.74 percent elsewhere in Toronto).[3] The district experienced 140 fires per 100 acres, compared to 23 per acre in "sound" districts. Arrests of adults and juveniles, almost unheard of in some other parts of the city, were counted in the hundreds in Cabbagetown. The overall cost to the city of providing municipal services was estimated at $95,000 per annum, a sum far greater than the net taxes the neighbourhood provided—just under $32,000 (Rose 1958, 67).

This picture, though it more or less matches Hugh Garner's fictional depiction of the district, must be understood in the context of the general economic distress of that era. At the turn of the twentieth century Cabbagetown had been a more diverse community, with a population that included skilled and semi-skilled workers and some middle-class professionals. By the 1930s business failures and long-term unemployment had reduced the living standards of many if not most Torontonians, with Cabbagetown and other low-income neighbourhoods experiencing the greatest difficulty. Even so, not all houses were in poor condition, and not all residents were in desperate poverty. The authors of the Bruce Report underscored that squalid conditions were not the whole story:

> If by a slum we mean a large area in which all or nearly all the houses are disreputable, decayed and dirty, in which numerous families are herded together, overcrowded, shiftless, perhaps criminal or semi-criminal, in which the decencies of life are neglected and the amenities of life are non-existent; then we can say that Toronto is free of slums.
>
> (Bruce 1934, 13)

Rather, in the eyes of the authors, the problem was "small and scattered groups of dwellings" where slum conditions could flourish.

Garner's irascible memoir of his own childhood acknowledged the unhealthy and disagreeable side of Cabbagetown, but still portrayed a diverse and vibrant neighbourhood. Deprivation, he argued, did not necessarily lead to squalor and misery. He was dismissive of social workers and liberal reformers who, in his view, misunderstood the people and communities they were trying to help:

> In my childhood years in Cabbagetown… we kids had everything going for us except money for clothes, fruit juices, and a stomach full of food, and

> what we didn't have we didn't particularly miss... Send a middle-class newspaper reporter down to a slum... and invariably they'll write a heart-rending and totally unrealistic piece of tearful crap about the worst, ugliest, sloppiest professional slum-dweller on the street... the clean decent poor families are seldom written about at all.
>
> (Garner 1973, 8)

Despite the Depression, Cabbagetown remained a zone of mixed industrial, commercial and residential uses. The Bruce Report found that more than 10 percent of residences had a business—usually a retail shop or workshop—on the premises. Small "mom and pop" grocery stores and other similar establishments were scattered through the residential streets, but so were larger factories or plants, including a foundry, a window-fabricating plant and several other industrial establishments. The future Regent Park neighbourhood also included several churches, taverns, and a hotel.

Creating Regent Park North

Toronto's leaders did not begin seriously planning the future Regent Park until the end of World War II, when Regent Park became the city's—and Canada's—first large-scale effort at slum clearance or urban renewal. Critics pointed out that by this time Birmingham, England—a city of comparable size—had already built 55,000 units of public housing, while Toronto was only now planning its first (Carver 1948, 18). The reasons for this difference were both economic and ideological. Local governments in Canada, especially in the 1930s, lacked the resources to undertake a massive program of demolition and reconstruction. Following the Bruce Report of 1934, Toronto reformers and activists called for demolition and replacement of Cabbagetown and other deteriorated "slum" neighbourhoods, but their efforts came to naught. In 1937 Toronto's voters rejected by a margin of almost 3:1 a referendum to take first steps in this direction. It would have authorized the beginning of a demolition-and-building program, which would have sought support from the higher levels of government (George 2011, 109–111). Such support did not materialize for another decade, and even then its scale was minimal.

In the US, the United Kingdom, and quite a few European countries in the 1930s, national governments took the initiative in establishing a legal and financial framework for demolishing slum housing and creating affordable alternatives. Construction of public housing was initiated in the US under the New Deal's Public Works Administration's program of job creation, and President Franklin Roosevelt presided in person at the dedication of the first such project, Techwood, in Atlanta, Georgia (Vale 2013, 66). But Canada's government was unwilling or unable to follow these examples. The National Housing Act of 1938 did introduce the principle of "direct lending by the government to municipal housing authorities and limited dividend corporations wishing to construct low rental housing," but the Act's direct-lending provisions were suspended after the outbreak of World War II. The Wartime Housing Corporation (1941) helped to produce more than 30,000 units of housing nationwide for workers in defence-related jobs and locations, plus another 15,000 for veterans in the years 1945–1949 (Wade 1984, 94), but public housing proposals such as Toronto's Regent Park did not figure in the federal government's plans.

By 1945 Canada was facing a serious deficit of housing, which was expected to intensify as war veterans returned home and began forming families. The shortage of housing was especially severe in Toronto and the surrounding municipalities, where construction costs soared. The price of renting or purchasing a home rose significantly, putting home ownership—at least temporarily—beyond the reach of many working families. Prime Minister Mackenzie King's Liberal government tried to address this issue through its Housing Acts of 1944 and especially 1945, under which federal funds were provided to assist construction of housing. Effective January 1, 1946 a federal corporation, the Central Mortgage and Housing Corporation (re-named the Canada Mortgage and Housing Corporation in 1979), was created. Its powers included the right to issue loans to "a limited dividend housing company" to support construction of low-rental housing; under another provision of the Act, grants were to be made available to municipalities for clearance of slums for this purpose. The terms and levels of support were, however, less than generous.[4] The government was not eager to get into the housing business, believing that this should be left to local and private initiative. One senior member of Cabinet, Louis St.-Laurent, declared in October 1947 that "no government of which I am a part will ever pass legislation for subsidized housing."[5] (Rose 1958, 85)

In the absence of federal and provincial support, Toronto's municipal leaders decided to go ahead on their own. A coalition of civic organizations persuaded the Mayor and Council to put the following question to voters in the municipal election of January 1, 1947: "Are you in favour of the City proceeding with the Regent Park slum clearance and rehousing project as a municipal improvement at an estimated cost of $5,900,000?" With Mayor Robert Saunders's strong endorsement, the referendum was approved by 62 percent of votes, allowing the city to raise the necessary funds through a bond issue. Planning began at once for the first, northern phase of Regent Park, which would house almost 1,300 families on a site of 43 acres. Regent Park North occupied the quadrant bounded by Parliament, Gerrard, River and Dundas Streets. According to a 1946 survey, 811 families were living on this site before redevelopment (Carver and Hopwood 1948, 34).

Through subsequent negotiations, the city arranged for CMHC to pay one-half of the cost of land acquisition, a sum that eventually reached $1.36 million. In addition, the provincial government provided a grant of $1,000 per new dwelling unit. Construction began in 1948 and was completed in 1956, with the final price tag (covering acquisition, demolition and construction) estimated at $16 million. About 15 percent of this sum came from federal and provincial contributions, while the balance was the city's responsibility—more than twice the sum approved in the 1947 referendum. The city was obliged to hold a second referendum in 1952 to authorize an additional $5 million in debentures; this time there was more opposition, but in the end the proposal won 54 percent of the vote (Rose 1958, 100–102,192).

The Regent Park development was touted as a product of citizen initiative, but it should be noted that the citizens who promoted it were not, in the main, residents of the area that was redeveloped. A central role was played by the Citizens' Housing and Planning Association, formed in 1944 as a coalition of civic activists, reformers and philanthropists (Rose 1958, 46–47). The CHPA seems to have drawn its membership from citywide organizations focused on municipal issues. At just this time, grass-roots organizations in other parts of the city were campaigning for publicly-funded, affordable housing. (Brushett 1999). But we find no evidence of such demands emanating from the residents of Cabbagetown, or of the relevant city agencies soliciting Cabbagetowners' views.[6] Kevin Brushett, who has closely studied grassroots housing campaigns of the era, observes that

> Regent Park residents themselves... silently watched the death of their neighbourhood, mere spectators to an event which for better or worse would transform... their lives... Ever since the first groups of town planners, architects, clergymen, and publicly spirited people roamed the streets of Cabbagetown in the 1930s, area residents remained skeptical, if not hostile, to plans to clear their area of so-called slums.
>
> (Brushett 1999, 54–55)

Community workers, in this author's view, approached their task in a spirit of paternalism rather than participatory planning.

Those who planned and promoted Regent Park did take a generally patronizing tone toward the residents. The negative features of the former neighbourhood were often exaggerated and presented in monochrome, while the benighted inhabitants were portrayed as desperate to improve their lives through better housing. This attitude was exemplified by a widely-shown 1953 dramatization, *Farewell Oak Street*, produced by Grant McLean of the Canadian National Film Board. The NFB was, of course, a body fully independent of the Housing Authority, but the views expressed echoed those of the planners and politicians who created Regent Park. *Farewell* was advertised as "The frank, dramatic story of what one Canadian city is doing to eliminate … the disease, broken homes and broken hearts which these housing jungles produce." The sixteen-minute film was shot on-site, and included footage of old and new housing. Neighbourhood residents were used as extras, but the principal roles were played by actors, and the script, narrated in stentorian tones by actor Lorne Greene, provided a moralistic commentary on the corrupting effects of slum living: "Down came … the verminous walls … the fire hazards, the juvenile delinquency, the drunkenness, the broken marriages … And up rose something new" (NFB 1953).

Another noteworthy feature of the film, and of much of the public discussion of Regent Park during its development and first years of operation, was "environmental determinism." The negative qualities of the old Cabbagetown neighbourhood were, in this view, the result of overcrowded and squalid living conditions. Once these were eliminated, the residents would also be transformed into exemplary citizens. This was a main theme of Albert Rose's 1958 study of Regent Park, which credited the new development with rehabilitating family life, improving physical and mental health, and reducing juvenile delinquency (Rose 1958, 103–170).

Inspired in part by the ideas of English social reformer Ebenezer Howard, Regent Park North was conceived as a "garden city." All existing structures on the site were to be demolished, regardless of how well or poorly they had been maintained. They would be replaced by a combination of two-storey town houses and small apartment buildings three storeys in height, each containing 48 to 52 dwelling units. The result would be a park-like setting featuring much open space[7] with no through streets transecting it. Children would be safe from traffic, and households and trees and gardens would flourish. With the exception of one school and one church, all non-residential land uses would be excluded from the site. In place of old Cabbagetown's mix of residential, retail and industrial uses, Regent Park became exclusively residential. Not even Dundas Street, the arterial road that divided Regent Park North from the later-built Regent Park South, had a single grocery store, coffee shop or tavern where residents might congregate.

In 1952 the Housing Authority modified the original plan to include several six-storey buildings, thereby increasing the number of dwelling units in Regent Park North from 1,062 to 1,284. Most of the units faced inward, away from the surrounding arterial streets. Although much of the open space was treated as parkland or commons, provision was also made for tenants to plant gardens close to their homes. Judging from available records, the open spaces seem to have been widely used and well maintained during the first years of occupancy. City archives include photos of sports events and community gatherings. But in later decades they fell into neglect. Critics then faulted the original design for creating a no-man's land closed off from the surrounding city, with open spaces conducive to criminal activity.

Figure 1.2 Regent Park North, community garden, 2013 (now demolished).

Figure 1.3 Regent Park North (650 Dundas Street East), 2015: This was the first building opened for occupancy in 1949; the building was demolished in October 2015.

Construction of Regent Park North lasted almost a decade. The work was carried out in stages, with the intention—not always achieved—of allowing each wave of displaced residents to move directly into new units when their old housing was ready for demolition. In March 1949 the Bluett family, formerly of Oak Street, moved into a row house at 650 Dundas Street East (Figure 1.3), becoming the poster family for the new development. They posed gamely for a series of before-and-after photos showing the contrast between their previous home—cramped and poorly serviced—and their bright, spacious new quarters. Toronto newspapers and politicians hailed the new housing as a model social initiative, even "heaven" (*Globe and Mail* May 11, 1950). Another seven years would pass before Regent Park North was completed and fully occupied.

The Housing Authority was committed to re-housing all displaced residents who wished to move into the new units. Families that were living in Cabbagetown when the formal planning of Regent Park commenced (i.e., those that were listed on city assessment roles as of July 15, 1947) were given first priority, even if their incomes were significantly above the neighbourhood mean (see below). Among those who qualified,

> first consideration should be given to families with small children or to families living in quarters more or less unfit for human habitation, while secondary consideration should be accorded to those families which are living in those buildings which must be cleared from the land to provide… the sites for future buildings.
>
> (Housing Authority 1949)

In the first stages of relocation, the Housing Authority chose not to set a strict ceiling for eligibility. Instead a rent-geared-to-income formula was devised on a sliding scale, starting from the premise that rent should be approximately 20 percent of income. Families whose incomes were significantly higher or lower than average would pay a slightly greater or lesser proportion of their income as rent. For example, a four-person family with an income between $75 and $99 per month would pay 17.6 percent, while one with income between $300 and $324 paid 21.9 percent. Rent for this latter group was approximately the same as market rent; the authors of the rental scheme suggested that this "soft ceiling" would encourage higher income families to move out without directly excluding them (Carver and Hopwood 1948, 41).[8]

Regent Park's target population, at this stage in its history, was not just the poorest members of the urban population, but rather a broader demographic range that included low-to-middle-income families.[9] Just over 250 of the first 1,250 tenants were recipients of various forms of public assistance; the remaining 80 percent were self-supporting, mainly blue-collar workers (Rose 1958, 188). The afore-mentioned Bluett family exemplified this profile; father-breadwinner Alfred Bluett was an employee of the Canadian National Railroad. Income eligibility was based on the earnings of the primary wage-earner; if additional members of a household were also earning income, their contribution to the family's income was calculated at a flat $10 per month.[10] Wages and property values were low enough at this time that some Cabbagetown home-owners—possibly as many as 20 percent of all rehoused families—qualified for housing in the new units.[11] The Housing Authority's board reviewed individual cases and seems to have taken a rather lenient approach (Housing Authority 1949). This became a source of contention at the time of the 1952 referendum, when the project's critics lambasted the Housing Authority's policies: "Can you afford to pay someone else's rent whose income may be greater than your own?" (Rose 1958, 99).[12]

Almost half of the first occupants of Regent Park North were former residents of Cabbagetown (Rose 1958, 224).[13] If we take this figure as 550 families and compare it to the old neighbourhood's population of 820 families eligible for resettlement, the proportion rehoused may have been as high as 66 percent. Moving into Regent Park was, however, far from automatic. The Housing Authority went to considerable lengths to ensure that the families who were admitted would make suitable tenants. Families in the very lowest economic bracket, most of whom were receiving public assistance, were not automatically excluded, but their rent was subject to negotiation between Housing Authority and the Department of Public Welfare. Beyond simple economic criteria, Authority officials conducted home visits and extensive interviews, including with employers, with the aim of excluding "poor risks" and "incorrigibles." Albert Rose, who personally carried out some of the interviews, defended this approach as necessary to the health of the future community:

> As Regent Park was being considered and constructed many persons were worried lest the project become entirely populated by persons or families in the very poorest economic circumstances... While there is some criticism in the wider community that some of the most needy families in the city cannot be accommodated, there is much appreciation of the spirit and morale among those who have been housed... an important factor in the current *esprit de corps* among young and old people alike has been the healthy diversity within the project.
>
> (Rose 1958, 189)

C. J. Woolsey, Chair of the Housing Authority, put it more bluntly in 1952: "We cannot allow Regent Park to become the dumping ground of city reliefees" (*Toronto Star* 1952). Woolsey, supported by Mayor Allan Lamport, insisted that the Authority's first responsibility was prudent fiscal management rather than reduced-rent subsidy to welfare recipients.

Regent Park South

In December 1953 Toronto City Council passed a resolution proposing negotiations with provincial and federal authorities to construct an additional

960 units of housing as Regent Park South. This second phase of construction was a direct continuation of the first, and would cover the adjacent tract of land bounded by Dundas, River, Sydenham (later Shuter) and Regent Streets. Although these blocks had been part of the Regent Park plan from the very outset, the urban political environment had now changed in two significant ways.

First, Canada's federal government had altered its approach to affordable housing. Under the National Housing Act of 1949 the CMHC was empowered to offer mortgages to cover 75 percent of the cost of constructing public housing, provided that the remaining 25 percent was covered by a provincial government.[14] Regent Park South was one of the very few cases in which the public-housing provisions of the Act were deployed (Oberlander and Fallick 1992, 54). Federal funding brought with it new regulations that significantly altered the managerial structure of public housing. Decision-making shifted upward to the provincial and (on planning matters) the federal level. The Housing Authority of Toronto, an appointed body that answered to Toronto City Council, was deemed unsuitable for the job of running the new development. Instead this responsibility was entrusted to a newly-created Metropolitan Toronto Housing Authority, the members of which were appointed in line with new provincial guidelines.[15] The new administration soon tightened the THA's loose and sometimes generous criteria of eligibility for occupants of subsidized housing.

Second, Toronto's municipal structure was reorganized through the creation of a broader Metropolitan tier of government in 1953. This was a federation that joined the City of Toronto with twelve surrounding municipalities. Each of the affiliated units retained its own elected council, with responsibility for some local services, but certain important functions such as police, water supply, roads and transit, and social services were entrusted to the Metropolitan level.

Plans for Regent Park South followed the broad principles of Regent Park North. All existing structures would be levelled. The replacement housing units would be designed mainly for families with children. The interior streets would all be dead-ended to prevent through traffic, and the principle of single-use zoning continued: According to architectural historian Christopher Armstrong, the principal designer of Regent Park South (Peter Dickinson) "was not allowed to be quite as radical as Le Corbusier [the internationally-renowned Swiss-French architect whose work Dickinson emulated] in incorporating shops and social services into the buildings (though he did design a separate recreation centre and a day care that were never built)" (Armstrong 2014, 246). Like their neighbours to the north, the residents of Regent South would have to go off-site to find shops and social amenities.

Unlike its predecessor, however, the new development would abandon the garden city approach in favour of taller buildings. Some planners objected in principle to high-rise towers, and the first architectural plan called for 20 units just six storeys tall (Housing Authority 1953). But in the plan's final iteration a smaller number of much taller buildings was substituted, with total occupancy approximately the same: five apartment towers, up to 14 storeys in height, alongside 250 row-houses. This style of construction—termed "towers in the park"—was inspired by the work of Le Corbusier.

Regent Park's towers were aligned to face away from the nearby arterial roads:

> In Regent Park South the towers seem to be placed randomly, with reference neither to Dundas Street nor to the boundaries of the newly created square. However, they were carefully arranged to run with the hands of the compass, either directly north/south or east/west. It is a good example of planning with regard to factors that have little relationship to the actual environment.
> (Sewell 1993, 110)

At a later point some critics began to see this design as a source of social dysfunction.

Another conspicuous feature of both halves of Regent Park was an emphasis on housing large families. We already noted that singles and two-person families found little provision in the plans for Regent North. The total number of bachelor apartments was 31; and of one-bedroom apartments, 190. In Regent South, there were no bachelor units, and just 35 one-bedrooms. By contrast, Regent North included over 100 units with four or more bedrooms (making 8 percent of total occupancies), and Regent South had over 200 (27 percent of occupancies.) The size of units and families became a subject of controversy in later decades.

About 1,000 additional housing units were built in Regent Park South, making a combined total of 2,083 occupancies in Regent Park North and South, with an overall population of about 10,000. Construction was completed in 1960, just six years from the date of final approval and four years from the start of demolition.

Regent Park, in common with many public housing projects in other jurisdictions, experienced a "honeymoon" period during its first years of operation. It was, for a brief time, treated as a model development: Planners and officials from other places traveled to Toronto to witness first-hand how well it was operating. Tenants were generally pleased with their new accommodations. In the first years of operation the rents received by the Housing Authority turned out to be higher than had been forecast. The city's expenditures on fire and crime control in the neighbourhood went down. Measures of physical and mental health in the community all showed apparent improvement.

By international comparison, Toronto and Canada were late-comers to the field of public housing. By the mid-1950s in Britain and much of northern Europe a large proportion of the urban population was already living in state-subsidized housing. In the United States, large-scale public housing projects were a familiar part of the landscape in New York, Chicago and other major cities. Regent Park, as Canada's first major foray into this field, started out with significant advantages. It was a local initiative, funded with the explicit support of taxpayers. In contrast to some other jurisdictions, construction seems to have been of high quality, without cutting corners through favouritism or corruption. It was designed to serve a rather broad spectrum of low- to low-middle-income residents rather than just the neediest. In principle, Regent Park's planners and managers should have been able to follow best international practice, and also to learn from mistakes that were made in other jurisdictions. Instead, the positive indicators of the first decade were soon reversed. The neighbourhood became a widely stigmatized space, regarded by many as a symbol of failure of public housing. Today, in a different international context, Regent Park is once again attracting international attention. A new generation of planners (and developers), having assessed the achievements and shortcomings of the old Regent Park, is offering a new vision of how the community can be rebuilt, including: densification, redesign of the built environment, a combination of market and subsidized housing, and a broad array of measures to address the economic and social needs of the population. The Toronto Community Housing Corporation (TCHC) has embarked upon a twenty-year experiment that is now almost halfway complete. The chapters that follow will evaluate what went wrong in the first Regent Park, what is now being attempted, and what, to the present point, has been achieved.

Notes

1 James Lorimer, who lived in present-day "Cabbagetown" in the late 1960s, discovered that his neighbours found the name offensive: "Respectable residents object on the grounds that Cabbagetown is a name which refers to the area to the south of Gerrard Street... most of which was demolished to make way for the Regent Park–Moss Park public housing projects. In fact, however, most city residents use this name to refer to Toronto's Anglo-Saxon, working-class 'slum' areas... Protests from local people have deterred many outsiders, including politicians and newspaper writers, from referring to the area as Cabbagetown. Everyone recognizes this as an abusive name" (Lorimer and Philips 1971).

2 According to a 1946 survey, approximately 20 percent of householders in the Regent Park North area (i.e., north of Dundas Street) owned their homes. The value of these properties and the incomes of their owners were low enough that some proportion of displaced homeowners would qualify for rental in the future Regent Park (Carver and Hopwood 1948, 44).

3 These are almost identical to the numbers put forth by proponents of slum removal in Atlanta, Georgia, in the 1930s (Vale 2013, 71–74).
4 John Bacher (1993, 177) cites archival correspondence among senior officials of the Department of Finance, preparing to draft the legislation to create CMHC. The new corporation was to measure its success "by the amount of activity not undertaken… in the public housing field." Its primary duty would be "finding ways and means for private enterprise to look after needs in the economic field."
5 Two years later, as Prime Minister, Mr. St.-Laurent toured Regent Park and described it as a "milestone" in slum clearance. "It must be obvious," he observed, "that low-rental housing cannot be provided without some kind of financial assistance [from Ottawa]." In the same year, despite the PM's pronouncement, Minister of Reconstruction and Supply R. H. Winters warned Toronto not to expect much help: "…whereas rental housing of this kind may be desirable, now is not the time to proceed on a large scale." [City Archive of Toronto, Fonds 200, Series 1183, Subseries 1, file 6: "Regent Park Housing Redevelopment 1947–1954; minutes of Toronto Housing Authority."
6 The minutes of the Housing Authority, July 4, 1949, refer to a brief submitted by a Regent Park Ratepayers Association. Rose (1958, 85) indicates that a delegation of 26 members presented a petition claiming that 80 percent of Regent Park residents were opposed to the housing scheme. The group also complained that projected rents were excessive, and that compensation for expropriated homes was insufficient. More broadly, the petitioners objected to "the failure of the Housing Authority… to consult residents or allow any tenant participation in policy making."
7 According to Rose (1958, 181) out of 42.5 acres that comprised the Regent Park North site, only 20 percent was covered by buildings. The remainder was open space, including roadways, paths, and parking lots as well as grass and recreational space.
8 A ceiling and floor were adopted in 1950 ($72 maximum rent, $29 minimum), but the minimum limit was not applied to Regent Park North (Rose 1958, 96, 103).
9 Albert Rose, Professor of Social Work at the University of Toronto and an executive member of the Toronto Citizen's Housing and Planning Association, argued against setting the poorest families apart from the wider community. He proposed instead that 40 percent of tenants should be from the lowest third of the income range, along with 40 percent from the middle third and 20 percent from the upper. This, in his view, would promote the twin goals of diversification and balance (Rose 1952, 5).
10 In this regard the Housing Authority departed from the standards set by CMHC, which counted all family members' earnings as part of the household budget. The Authority could set its own rules in Regent Park North because the City was the main funder; in Regent Park South, federal/provincial definitions were applied (Rose 1958, 97).
11 Home ownership in this neighbourhood was, of course, not necessarily a sign of affluence. A property might be heavily mortgaged, and a resident-owner might take in roomers or other tenants in order to cover the costs of ownership.
12 Rose (1958) reproduces, opposite page 99, a full-page advertisement in the *Globe and Mail*, November 29, 1952, signed by the Property Owners Association of Toronto.
13 According to Rose's (1958) figures, 822 households resident in Cabbagetown in 1947 were eligible for resettlement into Regent Park. Of these, "between 450 and 500" were living there in 1958, and another hundred had lived there for a while but moved away. Note that the number of household units displaced was considerably greater than 822, because several categories of residents were ineligible for resettlement. The latter group included individuals who moved into Cabbagetown after January 1, 1947. As well,

Regent Park provided little accommodation for single persons living alone or for two-person households.

14 These provisions of the Act were not being vigorously promoted at this time, as CMHC and the federal Cabinet put most of their housing dollars into promoting construction and purchase of new single-family homes. Critics complained that most CMHC programs were benefitting a prosperous minority of citizens who could qualify for home mortgages.

15 Albert Rose, who served as Vice-Chair of the Metropolitan Toronto Housing Authority from 1956 to 1964, summed up the change: "… all the planning and architectural design in urban renewal in Canada was undertaken by the federal agency, Central Mortgage and Housing Corporation, in conjunction with some agency of the appropriate provincial government. The local housing authorities are not consulted. They have not been considered appropriate participants in the urban renewal process. Instead their role has been seen as that of a management authority to operate the public housing or other aspects of the urban renewal programs when they are completed… The Metro Toronto Housing Authority [was] perhaps the most important organization of its kind in the entire nation… Nevertheless, this apparently powerful group began its work with no authority to develop a program of public housing and urban renewal throughout Metro Toronto." (Rose 1972, 68)

References

Armstrong, Christopher. 2014. *Making Toronto Modern: Architecture and Design 1895–1975*. Montreal: McGill-Queens University Press.

Bacher, John C. 1993. *Keeping to the Marketplace: The Evolution of Canadian Housing Policy*. Montreal: McGill-Queens University Press.

Bonnell, Jennifer L. 2014. *Reclaiming the Don: An environmental history of Toronto's Don River Valley*. Toronto: University of Toronto Press.

Bruce, Herbert A. 1934. *Report of the Lieutenant-Governor's Committee on Housing Conditions in Toronto, 1934*.

Brushett, Kevin. 1999. "'People and Government Traveling Together': Community Organization, Urban Planning, and the Politics of Post-War Reconstruction in Toronto, 1943–1953." *Urban History Review/Revue d'histoire urbaine* 27(2): 44–59.

Carver, Humphrey. 1948. *Houses for Canadians; a study of housing problems in the Toronto area*. Toronto: University of Toronto Press.

Carver, Humphrey and Alison L. Hopwood. 1948. "Rents for Regent Park." Civic Advisory Council of Toronto.

Housing Authority of Toronto. 1949. City Archive of Toronto, Fonds 200, Series 1183, Subseries 1, file 36: "Regent Park Housing Redevelopment 1947–1954; minutes of Toronto Housing Authority."

Housing Authority of Toronto. 1953. City Archive of Toronto, Fonds 200, Series 723, File 215: "Regent Park South."

Garner, Hugh. 1968. *Cabbagetown: A novel*. Toronto: Ryerson Press.

Garner, Hugh. 1973. *One Damn Thing After Another*. Toronto: McGraw Hill Ryerson Ltd.

George, Ryan. 2011. "The Bruce Report and Social Welfare Leadership in the Politics of Toronto's "Slums", 1934–1939." *Histoire sociale/Social History* 44(1): 83–114.

Lorimer, James and Myfanwy Phillips. 1971. *Working people; life in a downtown city neighbourhood*. Toronto: J. Lewis & Samuel.

NFB (National Film Board of Canada). 1953. *Farewell to Oak Street*. Grant McLean, Director. www.nfb.ca/film/farewell_oak_street. (Accessed January 10, 2017).

Oberlander, H. Peter and Arthur L. Fallick. 1992. *Housing a Nation: The Evolution of Canadian Housing Policy*. Canada Mortgage and Housing Corporation.

Rose, Albert. 1952. "Housing administration in Canada, 1952." *Canadian Welfare* December 15.

Rose, Albert. 1958. *Regent Park: A Study in Slum Clearance*. Toronto: University of Toronto Press.

Rose, Albert. 1972. *Governing Metropolitan Toronto: a Social and Political Analysis, 1953–1971*. Berkeley: University of California Press.

Rust-D'Eye, George H. 1984. *Cabbagetown Remembered*. Boston Mills Press.

Sewell, John. 1993. *The Shape of the City: Toronto Struggles with Modern Planning*. Toronto, Buffalo and London: University of Toronto Press.

Toronto Star. 1952. "Can't Dump Reliefees in Regent Park—Housing Board." November 18, 11.

Vale, Lawrence J. 2013. *Purging the Poorest: Public Housing and the Design Politics of Twice-cleared Communities*. Chicago and London: University of Chicago Press.

Wade, Jill. 1984. "Wartime Housing Limited, 1941–1947: An overview and evaluation of Canada's first national housing corporation." Master's thesis, History, University of British Columbia.

2

Regent Park, 1960–2000

What Went Wrong (or Right)?

The history of public housing in North America in the second half of the twentieth century has been turbulent and contradictory. Developers, planners and other public officials pursued widely divergent goals, and battled over the purpose, the intended clientele, and the design principles that should underlie the housing they were building. Some were inspired by European, social-democratic models of affordable housing, publicly built and subsidized to serve a broad population of low-to-middle-income renters. Others argued for a minimal investment in housing that would meet the needs of only the poorest and most dependent citizens. Advocates of the first position argued for high-quality design and construction, while their critics often opposed any "frills" beyond a basic provision of shelter. Once built, public housing became a different kind of battlefield: "The projects" were widely scorned and stigmatized as squalid and crime-ridden, while tenants struggled—often in vain—to improve the quality of their environment and assert some degree of personal control over it.

A symbolic moment came in 1972 when officials in St. Louis, Missouri began razing the Pruitt-Igoe urban housing project. This high-rise development was less than twenty years old, but had already deteriorated to a point deemed to be beyond repair. Its 33 high-rise towers had a vacancy rate above 40 percent, due to high rates of crime and vandalism as well as poor maintenance. One by one, the 11-storey buildings were demolished with explosives—an image that, in the language of a later generation, quickly "went viral" around the world. Was there an ironic echo from the *Farewell to Oak Street* film's "down came the verminous walls…"?

Pruitt-Igoe was not an isolated example. In many other cities public housing projects came to be shunned as failures of urban planning. Chicago's Cabrini-Green, Atlanta's Techwood, and New Haven's Elm Haven, though not demolished until decades later, were all associated in the public mind with decay and lawlessness. By the late 1960s or early 1970s the same was true of Regent Park.

The planners and politicians who created Regent Park had good reason to expect a better outcome. In contrast to many public housing projects in the

United States, the two phases of Regent Park did not suffer from obviously shoddy construction or inadequate funding—two characteristics of much public housing in the United States (Goetz 2013, 32–35). On the contrary: Contemporaries described Regent Park North as unlovely but solidly built, to a generally high standard of construction.[1] Regent Park South was hailed for its architectural innovation, and in 1961 its architect, Peter Dickinson, was awarded a Massey Silver Medal for the originality of his design.[2]

Nor did Regent experience the extreme racial segregation and the accompanying tensions prevalent in so many cities south of the border. Toronto was no racial utopia, but Regent Park did evolve and flourish as a multi-racial, multi-ethnic community.

Nonetheless the development soon became stereotyped—rightly or wrongly—as a socially dysfunctional, physically deteriorated space. Complaints were heard even in the first years of operation, and came from some of the project's earliest supporters (Tumpane 1952). Jane Becker, a journalist with extensive experience with public housing, visited Regent South in December 1960 and observed that new buildings already looked twenty years old. Broken glass and litter as well as vandalism were ubiquitous throughout the common spaces of the project.[3] Public officials quoted in her article attributed the damage to overcrowding and an over-abundance of children in spaces not conducive to orderly behaviour:

> in large apartment buildings… children must be supervised from several storeys up, damage is greater and morale lower than where housing is provided on a more personal level… The [Metro] housing committee believes semi-detached and row houses produce happier living conditions, as well as being less expensive to maintain…
>
> (Becker 1960)

Before the decade ended, another reporter described the development as a "filthy, crime-infested human jungle" (Allen 1968a). Significantly, this particular article was based upon survey data collected from residents themselves. 127 tenants from Regent Park South completed questionnaires and another 48 were interviewed face-to-face. Two-thirds of respondents expressed dissatisfaction with their living quarters, and half reported that they had had to call police on at least one occasion. They objected to being stereotyped and stigmatized, but 20 percent said they were afraid or unwilling to invite friends or relatives to their home, and 85 percent expressed the hope of someday moving elsewhere. Half complained of vandalism and rowdyism. Their complaints were confirmed by the *Toronto Star* reporter's description of the premises, where

> oceans of disinfectant… can't hide the human waste in the elevators. If the elevators work at all, there's no telling which floor you'll arrive at because the buttons have been burned or chipped off… Blackened walls and burnt floor tiles are visible in each of the five high-rise buildings.
>
> (Allen 1968c)

Numerous theories were offered to account for Regent Park's shortcomings. Some critics blamed the physical design of the buildings and their surroundings. Others faulted the city and province for failing to provide sufficient financial and managerial support to the project. This was the argument of reporter David Allen, author of the above-quoted article. In a series of lengthy articles about Regent Park South in 1968, he approvingly quoted one resident's assessment of management as indifferent to tenants' well-being or concerns. The housing authorities' only interest, in this view, was in collecting rents and minimizing the costs of maintenance (Allen 1968c).

After describing widespread vandalism and property destruction by youths, Allen opined that

> The project itself corrupted many of the young people and set them on a systematic course of revenge. The campaign to wreck Regent Park South is a guerrilla action waged by warriors driven underground and fighting back in the only way they know how.
>
> (Allen 1968b)

Variations on these themes were heard again and again over the following decades. Critics argued that the problems were not just financial but administrative—a top-down organization that was unresponsive to residents' needs and concerns. But other commentators put the blame for the project's failings on the tenants themselves, for failing to care for the premises or uphold standards of civil behaviour.

This chapter reviews these criticisms, and the efforts to renew or improve Regent Park between 1960 and 2000. It also examines parallel developments in adjacent districts of the city, where the issues surrounding affordable housing were addressed in other ways.

A Failure of Design?

Peter Dickinson's design for the towers of Regent Park South was praised by architects for its modernist innovation. Inside the 14-storey buildings, housing units were mainly of two storeys, a style known as "skip level" or "maisonette." Some apartments extended across the entire width of a building, allowing

Figure 2.1 Back yard, 14 Blevins, 2014.

sunlight to penetrate from several sides, and promoting easy ventilation. Internal stairways connected the two floors of a unit, and elevators stopped only at alternate floors, making common hallways unnecessary on the floors in between. The buildings were oriented to the points of a compass in order to maximize exposure to sunlight. Units were provided with balconies, but these were removed after a few years, apparently because they allowed too easy access from one apartment to another. A small number of ground-floor units included private yards.

Dickinson's plan was inspired in part by Le Corbusier's *Unité d'habitation* project in Marseilles (built in the late 1940s, it is also known as *Cité radieuse*). The French original is still occupied today, as market-level rather than rent-subsidized housing. It is widely admired, and has been designated an architectural landmark by the French government. As of 2014 it was expected to receive UNESCO designation as a World Heritage site. But Dickinson's project met a different fate. As early as 1966 it was being blamed for crowding too many people together, in spaces that discouraged civility. In 2013 the last of its five towers fell under the wrecker's ball.

Regent Park South differed from the Marseilles *Cité* in several important respects. For example, the French project incorporated, along with residential apartments, a range of facilities and services, among them a hotel, shops and a recreational centre. In contrast, the Toronto site was built around the idea of single-use zoning, which meant that all non-residential land uses were excluded. Residents had to walk a minimum of several blocks to reach the shops and services of Parliament Street. At several moments during and after construction, Toronto planners debated including a few retail establishments within the project, and eventually one small strip of three or four shops was added, but these hardly addressed the needs of 2,000 families. The only concession to residents' everyday convenience was the provision of laundry facilities in several of the tower buildings. Tenants—especially those who had to bring their laundry from one building to another—complained that these were insufficient.[4]

The Marseilles project was built to serve a more well-to-do clientele, including a range of family sizes. Regent Park was distinctive not just for its low-income population but also for its concentration of large families with children. Statistics from 1961 show an average of 3.4 children per family in Regent South, compared to 2.6 in Regent North and 1.4 for the entire Central Metropolitan Area (Purdy 2003, 61). Planners decided at the beginning of the development to build very few apartments for one- or two-person households. Of the 1,280 units in Regent Park North, just 30 were single-bedroom. Regent South went even further: More than one-fourth of its living units were of four or more bedrooms. The result was that children accounted for a very large proportion of Regent Park's population, especially in the Dickinson towers, where approximately 65 percent of inhabitants were minors.

By the mid-1960s various observers were blaming the tower design for fostering unsocial and/or antisocial behaviours. In a policy memo written in December 1966, senior planning official R. W. McCabe questioned the entire rationale for building on the scale of Regent South. While he acknowledged the apparent cost-efficiency of building to higher density, he argued that the initial savings were more than offset by the additional costs of operating these—in his view—socially dysfunctional structures:

> There is incontrovertible evidence that high-rise buildings in public housing projects are bound to create physical and social difficulties and high costs of maintenance… [In high towers] there are many more opportunities for the tenants to come into contact with each other in the communal areas of laundry, elevators, lobby, etc. The problems of friction and bickering are enlarged, as well, by the large number of children who are forced to play in halls, corridors, stairways, and the elevator cab... It is impossible to overcome the social and physical disturbance and friction caused by 600 people using a common lobby and other facilities, particularly when 65 percent of the users are children… Once a project gets beyond 300 families, it is necessary to provide a community centre, a day nursery, extensive playgrounds and generous amounts of landscaped open space. It also becomes necessary to install a resident manager and to introduce an element of "Big Brother".
>
> (Housing Authority 1960)

McCabe believed that these problems—budgetary, in his view, as well as social—were peculiar to the high-rise buildings, and that row housing was a better alternative, offering "excellent family accommodation, with adequate play space at ground level, little social friction, a minimum of communal facilities, less administrative interference, much lower maintenance costs, and higher rentals than the towers." Such accommodation would, he suggested, foster more of a sense of responsibility among the residents.

McCabe's comments reflected the attitudes of many municipal, provincial and federal policy-makers of the era. Architectural critics countered that the Dickinson buildings' problems were caused not by design but by use: either the tenants were abusing the premises or the city and province were neglecting their upkeep, or some combination of both. This disagreement continued for more than four decades, into the first years of Regent Park's second redevelopment. A particularly dramatic incident occurred in 2013, when a fifteen-year-old boy, wounded by gunshot, had to be carried down stairs from the top floor of one of the towers because the elevators were not working. Alex Bozikovic, an architectural journalist, argued that the boy's death should not be blamed on faulty planning: "the building did not kill anyone" (Bozikovic 2013).

When, in the course of redevelopment, TCHC applied to demolish the Dickinson towers, architects and preservationists campaigned to save at least one of the buildings as a historic landmark of Modernism. Discussion focused on 14 Blevins Place, and John Bentley Mays, writing in the Toronto *Globe and Mail*, described Dickinson's design as

> a fine, honest expression of what mattered to the humane modern architects of mass housing: excellent cross-ventilation, copious natural lighting, density without a sacrifice of privacy, and a strong sense of the social and communal… the architecture embodies a style of serious social conscience that should never be forgotten.
>
> (Mays 2013)

Christopher Hume, architectural critic for the rival *Toronto Star*, took an opposing position, describing the Dickinson building as a monument to failure:

> 14 Blevins is the sort of nondescript slab one sees throughout this city and countless others. Talk of the significance of its "pattern of fenestration" sounds fatuous, even ridiculous… its real importance has more to do with how 20th-century architecture failed miserably in its attempts to house the poor…
>
> (Hume 2013)

When the issue of demolition was put to public discussion, in the context of broader redevelopment of the entire Regent Park site, residents of the tower were adamant in opposing renovation and rejecting the possibility of moving back. City Council spent some time exploring possible alternate uses ("repurposing"), but in the end decided to issue a demolition permit. 14 Blevins Place joined Pruitt-Igoe among the ghosts of urban renewal.

Although some critics such as R. W. McCabe (above) focused on specific problems in the high-rise buildings, the wider Regent Park environment, including the North as well as South sections, was also faulted on other grounds for poor design and planning. One group of critics—including civic activist and former Toronto mayor John Sewell—argued that by going "off the grid" planners had isolated the community from its surroundings, with numerous negative effects.

In other cities, especially in the United States, public housing was often sited alongside expressways or other barriers, with the specific aim of setting it apart from middle-class communities. By contrast, Regent Park was situated in the midst of a thriving metropolis. And yet its physical design and administration established less visible barriers that were not easily crossed.

The critics' argument focused on the absence of through streets, along with a series of other design decisions that served to isolate Regent Park from the wider metropolis. With no shops or services along its narrow culs-de-sac, the neighbourhood offered outsiders little reason or opportunity to pass through. Instead, the rest of the city saw "the Park" from the outside, from the perspective of the arterial streets that flowed around it.

Figure 2.2 14 Blevins, demolition, 2015.

Regent Park's residents, meanwhile, found themselves living in a sterile, inward-focused and largely closed community. Dwelling units were set back from the surrounding arterial streets, and were laid out at angles to the internal streets. The result, in the view of numerous critics, was to discourage community members from informally watching out for one another—a concept summarized by urban theorist Jane Jacobs as "eyes on the street":

> the public peace—the sidewalk and street peace—of cities is not kept primarily by the police, necessary as police are. It is kept primarily by an intricate, almost unconscious, network of voluntary controls and standards among the people themselves, and enforced by the people themselves. In some city areas—older public housing projects... are often conspicuous examples—the keeping of public sidewalk law and order is left almost entirely to the police and special guards. Such places are jungles.
>
> (Jacobs 1961, 32)[5]

The large open areas between dwellings, instead of promoting a "garden community," sometimes became dead spaces, a venue for youth gangs and drug dealing. Nancy Smith, ex-Chair of the Ontario Housing Corporation, summarizes the Jacobs argument:

> People around a community during the day, such as seniors out walking, homebound mothers, and storekeepers, must be able to see what is going on so that they can keep an eye on things. And designers did not provide for mixed use or higher concentrations of people, both of which would lead to use of space during day and evening hours. The key ideas are that what makes space livable is people, and that people, in an effectively arranged environment, will keep an eye on things and take an interest.
>
> (Smith 1995, 917)

Single-use zoning, a feature of many if not most large-scale public housing projects of the era, was another negative factor. The absence of shops, compounded by the dearth of recreational and other social facilities, was an impediment to lively street life.[6] This was noted in the 1969 report of the federal Task Force on Housing and Urban Development, which compared public housing projects to "huge human filing cabinets stamped 'residential only' and without any of those places of encounter that help make life more than existence..." (Hellyer 1969, 45).

The day-to-day administration of Regent Park reinforced the message that it was a world apart. The community had, for example, its own system for garbage removal, relying on incinerators as well as large outdoor collection bins that were located in the courtyards between buildings. The Housing

Authority also employed its own security staff, enhancing the residents' sense of separateness, of living in a regulated world different from surrounding neighbourhoods. In 1966 R. W. McCabe described what he called a "Big Brother" administration, but argued that the design of Regent South made this necessary. Sporadic efforts to include tenants in the day-to-day management of the premises did not, by most accounts, serve to overcome the "us versus them" feelings of many community members.

One more spatial feature of Regent Park that was noted in its first years of existence was the division between its North and South. Until 1968 the two operated under separate administrative systems, but even after they were formally united the physical layout—with arterial Dundas Street running between them with almost no traffic lights to facilitate pedestrian crossing—led many residents to feel that there were two communities rather than one (Regent Park Heritage Commemoration Strategy 2015, 3). This feeling seems to have been especially strong in boys and young men, among whom rival gangs flourished in Northside and Southside.

Taken together, these features of the built environment surely served—if inadvertently—to shape social interaction. It would be a great overstatement and oversimplification, however, to suggest that they prevented residents from coming together as a community or from collectively making creative use of the space they shared. On the contrary, long-time tenants describe Regent Park as a lively and robust community capable of taking care of its own members and—sometimes—mobilizing in support of shared goals. Residents complain that the neighbourhood has been misunderstood and misrepresented in the press. In the late 1990s David Zapparoli, a photographer who grew up in Regent Park, assembled a photo exhibit, later published in book form, addressing the question: "Why do they never report the good things that happen?" He admires "the grace and intricacies of the human interactions that are the foundation of the real community… [The residents'] lives *are* ordinary. The sensationalism that is played out by media is just that, out but hardly the reality" (Zapparoli 1999, 33).

To residents, the spaces that outsiders found threatening sometimes had a different meaning. As one elderly resident put it in an interview, "Well I go to Regent Park unaccompanied, at 2:00, 3:00, 4:00 in the morning. Nobody bothers me, I am not scared to be [there]. But I won't go on any streets [outside the Park], I am more scared of these people in the streets than in the Park."[7]

Teenagers spoke enthusiastically about "The Boardwalk," an unpaved lane that followed the course of the former Oak Street; here they would sometimes congregate, using the path as a kind of promenade, even though at other hours it was put to different uses by youth gangs.

Joint community action was also a recurring theme among residents. A relatively early example of neighbours coming together was a campaign in

1968, launched by a group calling itself BLAST (Blevins Place Association of Some Tenants), calling for construction of a swimming pool. The members raised almost $3,000 and picketed City Hall, but no pool was built at that time (Purdy 2004, 528). This organization grew into the Regent Park Community Improvement Association (RPCIA), which flourished through the 1970s and campaigned successfully for various improvements to the Park's environment and services, including creation of a swimming pool in Regent North and two ice rinks. Efforts were also launched to build a community centre in Regent South—Regent Park North had had such a centre since 1954—but city and provincial authorities were less responsive. Community members launched a fund-raising campaign based on a tithe of $2 per month per household, and over the course of a decade and a half a total of $17,000 was raised. Eventually the City and the OHC, perhaps shamed by the neighbourhood's efforts, came up with a further $160,000. Additional funding from federal and provincial agencies was then secured, with the result that the centre was built without using the monies that had previously been collected.[8] In 1986 the community centre was finally opened (TCHC 2007, 6). More than twenty years later, when the centre was scheduled for demolition, many residents lamented its passing, even though it would be replaced by larger and better-equipped facilities. The old centre was, in this view, "ours."

Still another example of joint community action was the Peace Garden, created at the turn of the millennium by a group of mothers who called themselves "The Dreamers." Some had lost children to gun violence, while others feared that all children in the community were at risk. In the words of one of the founders, "There was too much violence in the community and too much pain… As a mother, every time you hear another child dies due to violence or accident, you feel that pain." The garden was conceived both as a memorial (including a plaque listing the names of victims) and as an island of tranquillity. Originally located in a courtyard near 605 Whiteside Place, it was relocated in 2014 to a more prominent location near the Christian Resource Centre at 40 Oak Street (TCHC 2014).

A different group of critics, assessing the effects of Regent Park's separation from the wider community, has argued it has been in some ways beneficial to the residents' sense of community and ability to act together. Concentrated poverty, according to this argument, enhances individuals' "dense networks of friendship and support," which may be compromised in a more socially and economically integrated social community (August 2014). But the critics of isolation warn that this kind of solidarity comes at a high price. John Sewell, assessing the pros and cons of social isolation, offered the following comment:

> If [residents] attempt to use other neighbourhood recreation facilities [outside Regent Park], they are often told they have "their own" facilities

> that they should use. Recreation facilities do not help knit public housing communities together, but are another example—much like the private dead-end road systems found in many large projects—of how the project is different than what surrounds it... Experience in Toronto with a recreational facility built in Regent Park South in the early 1980s after countless demands by residents and local politicians teaches that it is used only by project residents. Worse, it has become a focus for criminal activity (drug dealing) rather than a means of alleviating social problems.
>
> (Sewell 1994, 152)

The design of buildings and the layout of the surrounding streets and open spaces seem to have exerted important influences—negative more often than positive—on the ways that people lived their lives. Planners and residents of the new Regent Park have every reason to pay close attention to their predecessors' choices and their effects. Indeed, many of the design decisions in the new Regent Park have been made as explicit reversals of the plans that were drawn up sixty years ago. But even though architecture, landscaping and urban design contributed in important ways to the community's development, their influence cannot be reduced to environmental determinism. Other forces affected Regent Park's evolution, for better and for worse.

Who Pays? Who's in Charge?

The building of Regent Park North began with a referendum in which City of Toronto voters approved a bond issue to support construction. A second referendum five years later faced stronger opposition but also passed. At this time Toronto, receiving only token support from the federal government and none from the province, was ready to "go it alone" to build affordable housing. The City Council also drew up a financial plan that recognized the fiscal implications of turning over a large tract of land to public housing, and forecast a long period in which the public housing site would be taxed at a lower rate than other residential properties. The Housing Authority of Toronto (HAT) also anticipated shortfalls in its operating budget, and was pleasantly surprised in the first years of Regent Park North's operation when rent revenues came in at a higher level than expected (Rose 1958, 98).

Administrative responsibility for Regent Park North was assigned to the HAT, an appointed body that operated in an arms-length relationship with City Council. Albert Rose, Professor of Social Work at the University of Toronto and one of the earliest and most enthusiastic promoters of the project, warned in 1952 that this top-down system of management could have detrimental effects:

> scant attention is being paid at this time to the role of the tenant of public housing as a person, as a citizen, and as a responsible participant in the administration of the project. ... [The tenant] is likely to be issued a handbook of rules and regulations dealing with such significant questions as animal pets, flower pots on window-sills, and television aerials. No mention will be made of the way in which he may stand for election to the Housing Authority because the tenants are represented only through the staff... Our preoccupation to date has been with planning, inter-governmental negotiation, and day-to-day problems of construction, and this is one reason why the tenants' role in administration has been neglected. Such neglect may easily prevent the growth of first class citizenship which participation and responsibility would foster.
>
> (Rose 1952, 5)

Rose's warnings seemed confirmed when tenants found themselves confronting a bureaucracy that tried to prevent them from erecting TV antennas (*Globe and Mail* September 11, 1951). The dispute began when Alfred Bluett, one of the first tenants to move into Regent North, tried to put up his own antenna and eventually did so in contravention of the THA rules. Two years later, as the THA was debating whether to erect a community antenna, the Regent Park Ratepayers' and Tenants' association argued that—contrary to rules put forward by THA member William Dies—reception should be available to all residents regardless of what level of rent they were paying (*Globe and Mail* December 22, 1953). Eventually the antenna was put up, at a cost estimated at $50,000; but the Authority's plan to charge each user $2.50 per month was met by bitter complaints from tenants (*Globe and Mail* March 16, 1954).

Regent Park South was differently financed, with CMHC providing 75 percent of the costs of obtaining the land and erecting buildings, and the Province of Ontario paying the remaining 25 percent. Again the receipts from rentals were expected to fall short of the sums needed to cover mortgage costs as well as on-going maintenance of the buildings. The change in financing brought changes in the managerial structure, with more authority shifting to the provincial level. A new Metropolitan Toronto Housing Authority (MTHA) was created, but its powers were narrowly circumscribed by provincial oversight. Top-down management became even more pronounced, and more remote from the lives of residents. Rose, who served as vice-chair of MTHA, described the frustrations its members felt at their "stunted" role; though they were responsible for the largest public housing complex in the country, their responsibilities were defined just as narrowly as those of the smallest municipality (Rose 1972, 56).

By the mid-1960s voters and politicians were less generously disposed, and the ongoing costs of administering this large public housing project began to be reconsidered. On one hand, the new Metropolitan Toronto Housing Agency imposed stricter eligibility criteria for Regent Park South, increasing the proportion of families from the very lowest income bracket and thereby reducing the amounts of rent taken in. Almost simultaneously, City Council members began to complain about the burden of carrying Regent Park on the tax rolls. By 1966 the City was petitioning the Province to "relieve the City of Toronto of its subsidization of the Regent Park (South) Housing Development by paying full taxes on such project..." (Housing Authority 1960). Overall administration of Regent Park South had already, in 1964, been shifted from the MTHA (which was abolished) to a newly-created provincial body, the Ontario Housing Corporation. Discussions were begun with the aim of transferring Regent North as well. Alderman June Marks, who represented Regent Park's ward on City Council, denied that she and her colleagues were planning a provincial "takeover" of Regent Park; she argued that "centralized management" could produce savings of $750,000 per year in administrative costs. "The taxpayers of Toronto," she maintained, "are already overtaxed and cannot afford to build or rehabilitate housing" (*Globe and Mail* 1966). Two years later the Housing Authority of Toronto was dissolved. Responsibility for Regent North was transferred to the Ontario Housing Corporation.

These discussions and changes took place in the context of a broader reconsideration of public housing. In the early 1960s the federal government had expanded CMHC's mandate to fund construction of new developments on the model of Regent Park South. The National Housing Act was amended in 1964 to provide CMHC funding for up to 90 percent of capital costs for creating public housing. Over the following decade the number of public housing units in Canada increased more than tenfold, to a total of around 115,000 (Sewell 1994, 134–135). But these efforts met strong resistance from the private housing sector, whose representatives insisted that the free market was the better way to house most Canadians. Public housing, according to this argument, should be limited to a very small minority of needy and dependent families and individuals who were in "core need." Implicitly or explicitly, proponents of this view often favoured keeping the amenities and comforts of public housing to a minimum.

The pros and cons of public housing were debated in 1968 when Paul Hellyer, Minister Responsible for Housing in the newly-elected Liberal government of Pierre Trudeau, headed a Task Force on Housing and Urban Development. Part of its mandate was to review the operations of CMHC with respect to public housing. Members of the task force visited all the provinces and territories of Canada, holding formal and informal meetings and visiting—sometimes unannounced—some of the sites that they were evaluating, Regent Park among them. They received about 250 briefs from individuals and organizations, and heard about 125 oral presentations.

The Hellyer Task Force report concluded that large-scale public housing in Canada was, in the main, not adequately fulfilling its mandate. Two lines of criticism were presented: First, measured in dollars and cents, it was not cost-efficient. Regent Park was singled out as an example where per-unit construction costs were said to have exceeded those in the private sector. The second line of criticism arose, according to the report, from the complaints of public housing residents, and from a general perception that big public housing projects had become "ghettos of the poor." Their concentration of social problems was conducive to alienation and fatalism. Residents felt stigmatized, but without being motivated to improve their lives: "Every sign indicates that public housing does nothing to reduce the root problems of poverty, while increasing many of them and adding new ones..." (Hellyer 1969, 54–55).

In response, the task force recommended a moratorium on federal funding of large public housing projects pending completion of "a thorough research program into the economic, psychological and social issues of public housing." (ibid., 55) The Report marked a watershed in Canadian housing policy. From 1969 onwards, no new Regent Parks would be created.

This left the question of what to do with Regent Park and the other projects that were already built or under way. The task force recommended that several options be explored, including building more recreational facilities, experimenting with mixed land use within the zones of housing projects, and adjusting the rental scales to create more incentives for tenants to raise their incomes. It also called for a "conscious effort to erase the kind of *lord-and-master relationship* that tends to exist between tenants and their public supervisors…" (ibid., 55; italics added).

Having frozen funding, at least temporarily, the federal cabinet responded coolly to the report's other recommendations, especially its proposal to encourage cities to establish land-banks for future development, which would have limited the opportunities of private developers (Bacher 1993, 235). Hellyer, who disagreed with the Prime Minister on other issues as well, resigned from the government. But over the following years, some of the task force's suggestions were pursued—at Regent Park and in other Ontario public housing communities. Recreational facilities were added, and residents were offered, on an experimental basis, a limited role in management. Social services and community organizations became solidly established in the community, including the Christian Resource Centre (1964), Regent Park Community Health Centre (1973), and Pathways to Education (2001), a project of the Regent Park Community Health Centre. By the 1990s more than two dozen social-service organizations were working in the community.

But difficulties in upkeep and smooth operation of the properties remained, and the lines of authority continued to run downward from the provincial level. Regent Park residents complained that the premises were left in a poor state of repair, but the budget never seemed to suffice. Over the course of the 1970s and 1980s additional levels of administration were created but it often seemed that public housing was a "white elephant" whose expensive upkeep was an unwanted burden. In 1980 a new, locally-based body—bearing the same name as the former Metropolitan Toronto Housing Authority—was created to oversee the operation of Toronto's 110 largest public housing projects. Its portfolio comprised 32,000 housing units, including Regent Park (*Globe and Mail* August 18, 1980), but provincial funding and oversight continued. John Sewell, who served as Chair of this body in the mid-1980s, described its operations in language similar to Rose's twenty years earlier:

> In essence, MTHA does not have the authority to control any of the matters that concern it. It must abide by province-wide policies set by ministry personnel and by an appointed OHC board, none of whom have any responsibility for running projects. MTHA has all the responsibility to run a very large housing portfolio, but none of the authority to do so. As any manager will note, the arrangement is a recipe for disaster… management action is often filled with a sense of powerlessness and resignation, limitations that underlie the many problems in public housing: the difficulty tenants have in transferring from one unit to another; the strange point-rating system used to select new residents; the Draconian and ineffective policy that prohibited MTHA residents from having pets; and so forth.
>
> (Sewell 1993, 145)

In the late 1990s the Conservative provincial government led by Mike Harris decided that the status quo was untenable, and took steps to transfer full responsibility for public housing to municipalities. Most provincial budgetary support was terminated. In Toronto in 1998, Metropolitan Toronto Housing Company Ltd. and the City of Toronto Non Profit Housing Corporation were removed from provincial jurisdiction and merged into the Toronto Housing Company. Four years later, that new body was amalgamated with the Metropolitan Toronto Housing Corporation to create the Toronto Community Housing Corporation. This entity was given responsibility for approximately 58,000 units of housing and 162,000 tenants across Metropolitan Toronto. The TCHC inherited a long waiting list of residents who met the economic criteria to live in subsidized housing. It also was assigned control of badly deteriorating housing stock, with a budget insufficient for renovation. Under the leadership of Derek Ballantyne, first Director of TCHC, the corporation began exploring new ways of addressing these problems.

A "Ghetto of Poverty"?

The planners who created Regent Park in the 1950s intended to build an economically diverse community. Albert Rose noted in 1958 that, using 20 percent of household income as a benchmark for the appropriate cost of housing, almost two-thirds of Canada's population could not afford to rent or purchase a home at market prices (Rose 1958, 18). Regent Park, as envisaged by Rose, Humphrey Carver, and other early advocates, was to address the needs of a wide swath of this constituency rather than be limited to the very poorest among them. The original eligibility criteria for residents of Regent Park North were fairly broad and flexible, with the result that the initial community resembled the low-to-low-middle-income Cabbagetown that it had displaced. Unlike many public housing projects in the United States, Regent Park resettled a substantial proportion of displaced residents into new housing.

The Housing Authority went to some lengths to accommodate displaced residents of the former Cabbagetown, who may have accounted for two-thirds of Regent Park North's original residents. The authority was, however, at pains to ensure that "immoral" and irresponsible tenants not set the tone for the new development. Donald Bellamy, a graduate student at the Faculty of Social Work, University of Toronto, carried out in 1953 a longitudinal study of families rehoused and not rehoused in Regent Park, and found many favourable social indicators of change in the neighbourhood. He pointed out, however, that these were likely the result of population changes resulting from the Housing Authority's policies:

> In view of the decreasing relief costs among persons rehoused, and the excessively higher costs for those not rehoused in the project, it is obvious that the net result of reconstructing Regent Park was the transfer of a significant number of relief recipients to other municipal areas, thereby increasing the case loads there. Thus, as regards economic status, a remodeled community was created in Regent Park at the expense of other neighbourhoods and communities.
>
> (Bellamy 1953, 111)

Eligibility criteria were significantly narrowed under the MTHA's administration of Regent Park South, and subsequently in Regent North. The proportion of former Cabbagetowners in Regent South was sharply lower, partly because of the speed with which demolition and construction were carried out. A few years later Albert Rose described the new regime in an interview with journalist Graham Fraser:

> So they went in—Boom! They knocked the whole [neighbourhood] down, and people vanished… they could only trace about one quarter of the people. The rest had vanished. That was the alternative to "custom-tailoring" [as practiced in Regent North]. And that was the beginning, in my view, of the terrible concern about "urban renewal".
>
> (Fraser 1974, 60)

Over the course of the 1960s the proportion of former Cabbagetown residents dropped significantly, while the number of welfare recipients, especially single mothers, rose. In the 1950s, single-parent households accounted for less than 10 percent of the population of Regent Park, but by 1970 they made up for 44 percent of families in Regent Park North and 27 percent in Regent South (Purdy 2003, 62). Rose, whose earlier, optimistic view of Regent Park has been noted, put this change into a broader context when he summed up, in 1964, the state of public housing in Canada:

> Not only do "the poor pay more"… for all elements of a standard of living including shelter but they are more vulnerable to social breakdown, they require a great variety of social services... We have constructed huge villages of the poor, disabled, and handicapped, vast collections of dependent and quasi-dependent families… who cannot provide or foster the indigenous leadership… required to build a strong neighbourhood. Moreover, the agencies charged with responsibility to meet the social needs of the new public-housing tenants have not yet developed satisfactory approaches and techniques required to build new viable communities.
>
> (Rose 1968, 320)[9]

In part, this change resulted from policy decisions, but it was also a consequence of wider social and economic trends in the city and region. Surely one relevant factor was turnover in Regent Park's population. It is noteworthy that in the first three decades of operation Regent Park's rates of turnover were approximately the same as among tenants in other rental accommodation in Toronto; only from the early 1980s did a different pattern start to emerge. What this meant in concrete terms was that the median length of occupancy in Regent was in the range of three to four years (Purdy 2003, 79). Turnover, could, of course, result from both negative and positive reasons—from eviction, for example, or from upward mobility. Some tenants were forced to move due to unsocial behaviour or rental arrears. According to Rose, about 100 families—almost 10 percent of the project's population—were asked to leave in the first seven years of Regent Park North's operation, some for misrepresenting their income, some for "unduly disturbing their neighbours," and still others for maintaining their units "below any acceptable standard" (Rose 1958, 177). But statistics from the mid-1960s show that an average of 175 households left Regent Park North *each year*. Comparing these numbers, one must conclude that that the great majority left of their own free will. It is notable that the market cost of housing, relative to average income was falling during the prosperous years of the later 1950s and 1960s. Undoubtedly this led some early Regent Park residents to move out into market rental or home ownership. Toronto Housing's Executive Director Robert Bradley reported in 1964 that 60 percent of departing tenants left to purchase homes, and another 35 percent to move into "superior apartments" (Steed 1964, 7). But if some residents used Regent Park as a stepping-stone to more attractive accommodation, those who took their places were more likely to come from lower-income groups with fewer prospects for leaving.

By Rose's account, in the early years of the Toronto Housing Administration tenants were closely screened before being housed in Regent Park, and their behaviour as tenants was also monitored. Evidence from later years suggests that the THA's successors were less successful in regulating antisocial behaviours. Tenants whose lifestyle was disruptive to their neighbours—for example, through substance abuse, family violence, or gang affiliation—were more likely to stay in the community while those with the wherewithal to move away continued to do so. "Problem" individuals or families were only a small minority of Regent Park's population, but they contributed disproportionately to the project's stigmatization.

To those who planned Regent Park in the 1940s, it was clear that substandard housing was closely associated with poverty. Planners may have imagined that, by improving housing, they could also overcome the other features of poverty that were manifest in old Cabbagetown. But poverty turned out to be many-sided and sometimes intractable. Unemployment, schooling and job training, family dysfunction and substance abuse were among the issues that remained to be addressed in parts of Regent Park's population. The persistence of these problems should be judged not just in terms of the housing that was provided, but in the context of the whole social "safety net" as it evolved in the latter half of the twentieth century.

A "Hotbed of Criminal Activity"?

In much press reportage, and in the minds of many Torontonians, Regent Park has been associated with high rates of crime since the 1960s. A review of newspaper stories over five decades turns up numerous accounts of murders, drug busts, and gang activity. As Sean Purdy has pointed out, "The media played a crucial role in constructing Regent Park as a dangerous problem area… as solely a site of poverty, behavioural problems and crime" (Purdy

2005, 531). But any careful researcher will recognize that there is a difference between anecdote—single events—and solid, consistent data. Have the actual rates and trends of crime in this neighbourhood really been higher, or has Regent Park been unjustly subjected to stereotyping and stigmatization?

Unfortunately year-by-year tabulations are not readily available for most of the years we are trying to study (Thompson *et al.* 2013, 929). Defenders of Regent Park have, at various times, tried to rebut the claim of excessive crime. In 1968 Stanley Randall, the Provincial Minister of Trade, responding to critical articles in the *Toronto Star*, asserted that the neighbourhood was no more unsafe than others: Police statistics showed crime rates no higher, and in some cases lower, than in surrounding districts (Randall 1968, 7).

To illustrate how, in his view, the daily press stigmatized the neighbourhood, Randall gave the example of newspaper coverage of a fight in which several Regent Park boys (along with others who were not from Regent Park) took part: one newspaper devoted a quarter of a page to the matter while, in the same issue, two youths from the suburbs charged with the much more serious crime of rape, rated only a few lines (ibid.).

Crime statistics from that era have not been available for the present study. Police data from the period 2004–2011 have, however, been tabulated by neighbourhood in order to compare 140 different sections of the city (Friesen *et al.* 2012). The series begins before the phased demolition of Regent Park was underway, and extends through the first two phases of relocation and demolition. In this compilation Regent Park is clearly demarcated within the exact boundaries of the public housing. The data indicate that in these years this district experienced relatively high rates for six categories of crime, but not significantly higher than other, less stigmatized downtown neighbourhoods. When tabulated on a per-10,000-population basis,[10] Regent Park's rate for assault was ranked 29 out of 140 city neighbourhoods; for sexual assault, 35/140; for break-and-enter, 21/140; for robbery, 27/140; for stolen vehicle, 27/140; for drug charges, 7/140; and for murder, 6/140 (note that this latter ranking was the result of a single murder—one out of 50 in the city—in the reference year of 2011). For theft above $5,000, the neighbourhood was ranked 122/140. For all categories except for murder and drug arrests, Regent Park's ranking was close to that of such middle-class Toronto districts as University or North Riverdale. And even in the categories of murder and drug charges the neighbourhood was not at the top of the list. Despite popular belief, Regent seems no more crime-ridden than many other sections of Toronto.

Interviews with residents, conducted by members of our research team and by various journalists and researchers, illuminate these numbers in several ways. Many members of the Regent Park community express fear and disapproval of criminal activity, especially the drug trade. One informant, for example, described how drug dealers would try ringing various apartment doorbells to get residents to let them into a building. Once, after she refused to buzz them in, she found that they had retaliated by draping a used condom over her apartment doorknob. Drug gangs have operated in Regent Park since the early 1980s, if not longer. In 1989, police officials were quoted as identifying Regent as the birthplace of the city-wide crack-cocaine epidemic of the 1980s (*Globe and Mail* 1989). The 1995 film *Return to Regent Park* gives extensive coverage to residents' complaints about drugs: One woman resident observes that "When I first come here the place was great and then when the crack came out it got really bad and we started having beatings, shootings, robberies." The film points out that, although drugs were widely sold in Regent Park, many of the sellers and purchasers came from other parts of the city—in one scene, a limousine is shown driving up to purchase drugs.

Neighbourhood activists have often cooperated with police in trying to bring these activities under control. A crackdown in July 1990, which brought 139 arrests, was described by Police Superintendent Keith Cowling as a "response to calls from neighbourhood residents anxious to rid their streets of drug dealers." Significantly, "more than half of those arrested were not residents of the Park" (*Globe and Mail* 1990). At other times, however, relations between community members and police have been less positive. In 1995 a riot broke out when police tried to make a drug arrest. In the aftermath, many residents complained that police from the local precinct (51 Division), who were mainly white, had a history of harassing black youths in Regent, and of using undue force against them. Determined to repair relations between the community and the police, the local commanding officer, Sgt. William Blair, launched a program of "community policing" that included foot patrols and more positive face-to-face interactions between officers and the local population. These steps were credited with improving police-community relations and reducing crime. Ten years later, largely on the strength of his reputation in Regent Park, Sgt. Blair was appointed Toronto's Chief of Police (Harding 2004).

Respondents in our interviews have complained that the problems of crime are overstated, and that the vast majority of residents have been unduly blamed for the activities of a few. As well, some researchers and critics argue that the Regent Park community has over time developed informal mechanisms for controlling crime; in this view, some of the more extreme outbursts of recent years have resulted from redevelopment, when established social networks were disrupted (Thompson *et al.* 2013). Other critics have noted that crime tends to be correlated with poverty, and that young people's involvement with drugs or other illegal behaviour must be understood in the context of widespread unemployment and lack of other opportunities. It remains to be seen whether the rates and patterns of crime will be altered by the further transformation of the Regent Park environment.

Issues of Self-Management

In the early 1970s the Ontario Housing Corporation, with encouragement from CMHC, began an experiment to enlist tenants in a program of self-management. Advocates of the plan hoped that grass-roots organization would improve day-to-day operations and address problems of vandalism and other disruptive behaviour. The results illuminate some of the problems that have continued to plague Regent Park over the subsequent decades, and the difficulties of addressing them within the OHC framework.

In 1973 the Regent Park Community Improvement Association, an independent group which had been demonstrating and lobbying for improvements to the Park's facilities, entered into an agreement with OHC. It included establishment of a Joint Tenant-OHC Management Board, composed of four tenant representatives and four from OHC. As well, a network of 24 "unit representatives" was created to maintain liaison between the Board and the tenant population. Sean Purdy, who studied this body's history, observes that for a period of several years the Board seemed to be achieving positive results, measured in lower rates of vandalism and higher community morale. By 1976 the OHC seemed ready to devolve more powers to the tenants, and was providing part-time salaries for 28 community agents. Purdy argues, however, that the Corporation's leaders were never whole-heartedly supportive of these arrangements. Tenants, moreover, were divided in their reactions to the Board's and reps' participation. Some viewed this as co-optation, accusing the reps of putting their own interests above those of the community. Issues around rent arrears and evictions seem to have been particularly acrimonious, and were likely compounded by the Board's ambiguous relationship to the OHC, which retained final decision-making authority in most matters. In 1978, after a dispute and strike over the pay scale for community workers, OHC abolished the Board (Purdy 2004, 537–540).

The 1980s and 1990s were a period in which governmental support for public housing generally declined. Construction of new housing was curtailed, and the budgets of existing developments such as Regent Park were stretched thinner and thinner. A backlog of deferred maintenance grew from year to year. In 1988 the Toronto press reported rumours that a portion of Regent Park might be sold to real estate developers, possibly to raise funds to renovate the rest (*Toronto Star* 1988). These same years saw a series of community initiatives aimed at improving conditions. The Regent Park Focus Community Coalition has been especially successful in its work with neighbourhood youth, and has operated continuously in the neighbourhood for almost thirty years.[11]

In 1996 a group chaired by former mayor John Sewell brought forward a proposal to raze and rebuild one quadrant of Regent Park North. The plan, supported by the Regent Park Northeast Redevelopment Working Committee, called for 163 houses to be demolished and replaced by 400 new units, of which almost one-third would be designated as market rental or purchase. In Sewell's description, the transformed community would get rid of many of the design features for which Regent Park had been criticized, such as the closed-off streets and single-use zoning. It would end up looking more like some of Toronto's older neighbourhoods such as Cabbagetown: "[the plan] would result in a very normal neighbourhood; you know, front yards, back yards, streets, laneways…" (Grange 1996). The proposal hinged on the City of Toronto, the owner of the land, essentially donating it to a private developer. One adviser to the committee, himself a developer, commented that "It would be really hard to figure out how to create quality housing for median-income people if we had to add in land costs" (ibid.). As well, the plan required cooperation from CMHC and the Ontario Housing Corporation. The Ontario Ministry of Housing gave provisional support to the idea, and in 1997 concluded a tentative agreement with a private developer (Phelp 1997). But the deal fell apart, and not long afterward the provincial government embarked on a more radical course, turning over all of its public housing stock to municipalities.

Clearly the faults that Regent Park displayed cannot be reduced to a single cause. At many points, a remote and indifferent administration allowed physical deterioration to occur—a problem compounded by chronic shortages of operating funds. At times community members stepped forward to propose—sometimes successfully—new ways of dealing with the shortcomings and the physical deterioration of the environment. Yet other members of the community, whether through antisocial behaviour or passive tolerance of same, reinforced its image of violence and squalor. Too often the positive accomplishments have been overshadowed or ignored due to the abundance of gangs and crime and the poor physical condition of the buildings and their surroundings. Regent Park's long history cannot be written off as an unmitigated failure, but its many failings pose a challenge for whomever and whatever comes next.

Urban Context

How does Regent Park's experience compare with that of the urban neighbourhoods that surround it? For the first decade or more of its existence, Regent Park was widely seen as a model of slum clearance and urban transformation. The downtown districts that surrounded it were, in this view, all promising candidates for similar treatment, designated by city planners as "deteriorated" or even uninhabitable, just as the original Cabbagetown had been. City officials expected that these areas would follow, more or less, the Regent Park pattern of wholesale demolition. The narrow streets and laneways with their one- and two-storey houses would be replaced by multi-storey dwellings in a modernist style. Variations on this plan were put forward through much of the 1960s, and some were fully implemented. But the city was changing in those years, in ways that altered the political and economic environment and encouraged new approaches to urban design and living. Eventually these changes would affect Regent Park itself, and shape its planned future.

Unlike many cities of the northeastern United States and some in eastern Canada, Toronto's downtown did not shrink or deteriorate in the second half of the twentieth century. Its suburbs grew rapidly, and its once-prominent manufacturing industries relocated elsewhere or closed their doors. But new downtown employment, mainly in the service and high-tech sectors, increased. Instead of draining population and resources to the suburbs, these changes stimulated a transformation and revitalization of many inner-city neighbourhoods, eventually including some adjacent to Regent Park. Few if any observers anticipated such a development at the moment when Regent Park opened its doors.

Over the next five decades the neighbourhoods surrounding Regent Park (see Figure 2.3) underwent a series of physical transformations, some following the expected model and others not. In some locations entire blocks or quadrants were bulldozed as Regent Park had been, in order to construct new "towers in the park." In others, old housing was renovated and the social composition of the neighbourhood changed from a population mainly of renters to one of owner-occupants. A third model synthesized elements of the first two, relying on smaller-scale selective demolition and renovation. Support for these various initiatives came from the provincial and federal governments—especially the CMHC mortgage program—but also from private-sector and non-profit bodies. Renovation of individual homes was accomplished mainly by private owners. By the turn of the millennium, the cumulative result was a new urban landscape that would help to define the choices planners faced when trying to re-imagine or re-design Regent Park. A brief review of these nearby developments is in order.

Moss Park Public Housing was built not long after Regent Park South. It is located south of Shuter Street between Parliament and Sherbourne Streets, on a site of approximately 18 acres (7.3 hectares). Like the Regent Park site, this tract of land had previously combined industrial and residential uses. As in Cabbagetown, many but not all of its buildings were in dilapidated condition. In 1960 a consortium of realtors proposed to develop the area under a CMHC mortgage and a long-term lease of land from the City (*Globe and Mail* May 31, 1960). Senior city officials, including Mayor Nathan Phillips and Senior Controller William Allen (who was also Chair of the Municipality of Metropolitan Toronto) initially spoke in favour of such a proposal. Private developers, Allen argued, could produce "a proper, healthy, full tax-paying

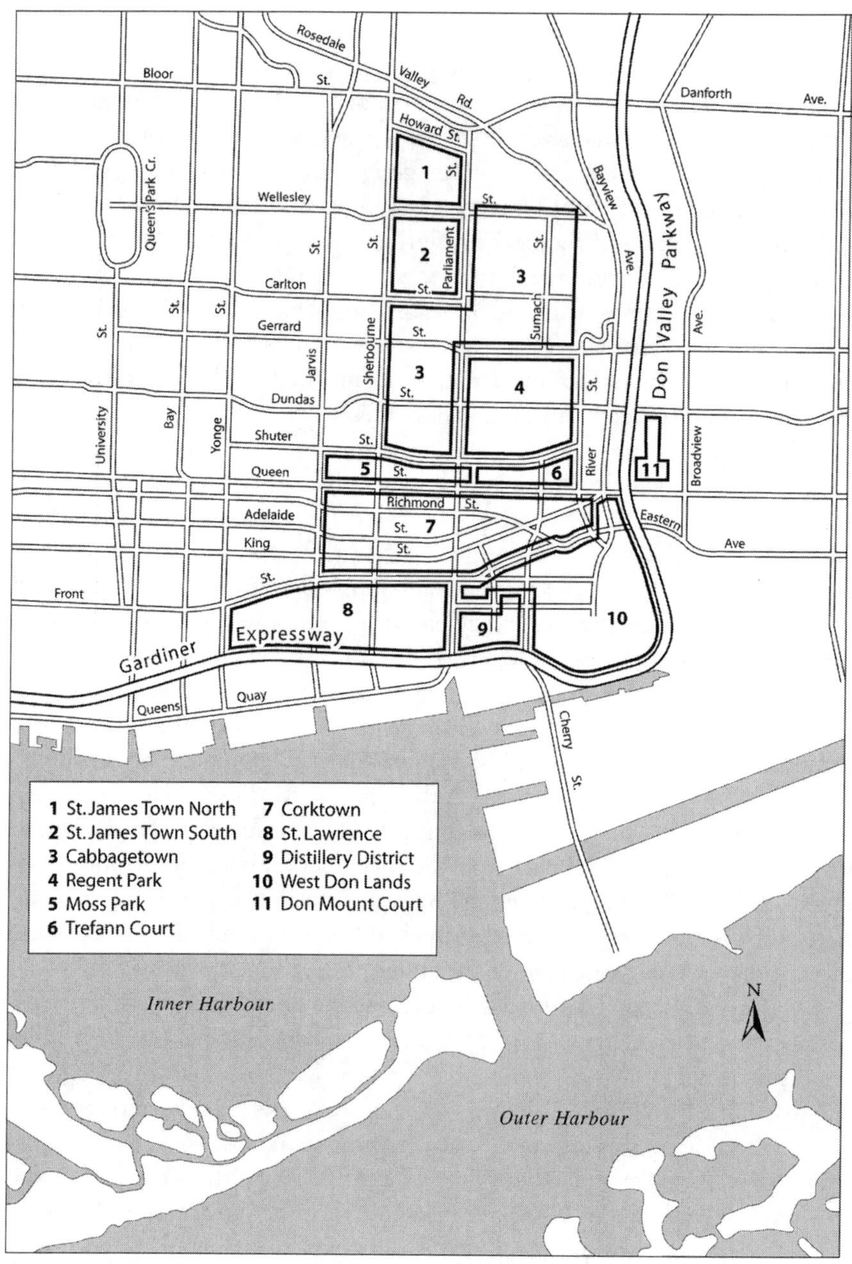

Figure 2.3 Map 2: Downtown Toronto neighbourhoods: Regent Park and surroundings.
Source: B. Levely

section of downtown Toronto" instead of homes for low-income families (*Globe and Mail* June 1, 1960). In the end, however, the city opted for public housing in the form of high-rise apartment towers, under a federal-provincial partnership similar to Regent South. Demolition began in 1962 and the first tenants began to move in in mid-1964. Rents were set at levels slightly higher than those of Regent Park North; nonetheless, by 1967 the project was running at a deficit of $150,000–195,000 (*Globe and Mail* March 23, 1967).

Architecturally, Moss Park Housing bears a strong resemblance to Regent Park South. It consists of three 16-storey structures, housing about 1,300 families. The surrounding neighbourhood includes the Moss Park Armory, a hockey arena, and several shelters for homeless people. It also includes, along Sherbourne Street, three tall apartment towers that are privately owned and managed, with rentals slightly below the average for downtown Toronto. Although the neighbourhood has been described as one of the poorest in the city, private homes along the side-streets immediately to the north have in recent decades undergone extensive renovation, and the district north of Shuter Street has been rechristened as Cabbagetown South (the name "Cabbagetown" had by this time lost its negative connotations). Like Regent Park and many other large-scale family-based public housing projects, the Moss Park housing project deteriorated significantly from the 1970s onward. In the early 1990s the Ontario Housing Corporation approved an upgrading of lobby and laundry facilities, but more ambitious plans for the surrounding site did not come to fruition (Smith 1995, 922; Sewell 1993, 232). Today Moss Park Housing, like much of the TCHC portfolio, is long overdue for major repairs or replacement.

St. James Town, located south of Bloor Street about one mile (1.6 km) to the north and west of Regent Park, also bears an outward resemblance to the modernist towers of Regent Park South or Moss Park. Unlike them, it came into being more through private than public initiative. Despite its proximity to the affluent Rosedale neighbourhood (located just to its north, but separated from St. James Town by a deep, wooded ravine) at mid-century this area had more in common with the lower-income streets of the original Cabbagetown. It was not quite a slum, but did contain a number of dilapidated properties, and was designated by planners in the 1950s as a zone for redevelopment. Private developers spent much of the 1950s and 1960s buying up lots and assembling land parcels. Anticipating demolition, the new owners had little incentive to maintain these houses, the more so since their deterioration drove down the price of adjacent properties. Despite widespread opposition from residents, in 1965 Toronto's City Council gave its approval for demolishing and rebuilding the quadrant bounded by Parliament, Wellesley, Sherbourne and Howard Streets. 18 apartment towers were constructed, ranging in height from 14 to 32 storeys. In common with Regent Park, St. James Town was built as a "superblock" enclave off the grid of city streets. As construction began, displaced tenants held mass demonstrations at City Hall to protest the condition of buildings that were scheduled for future demolition. The Toronto Housing Authority took possession of some 250 homes owned by absentee landlords, on grounds that they were unfit for habitation (*Globe and Mail* July 20, 1965).

St. James Town differed from Regent Park in several important respects. Only four of the 18 high-rise towers were built and managed as public housing. Perhaps significantly, these were erected after most of the other buildings were complete. The other 14 were built by private developers as market-rental housing. In contrast to Regent's single-use zoning, St. James Town included a supermarket and other shops and offices, and some of its buildings included such amenities as swimming pools and saunas. Its rental apartments were built in anticipation of a relatively well-to-do middle-class clientele—characterized at the time as "swinging singles." This group failed to materialize, and over time St. James Town came to house a lower-income population consisting mainly of families with children. Recent immigrants predominated to such an extent that the neighbourhood is sometimes described as a "landing pad" for new Canadians. The physical condition of many of the buildings began to deteriorate not long after construction, giving the area an exterior profile not unlike Regent Park or other poorly-maintained public housing. Indoor recreational facilities fell into disuse and were in many cases discontinued. A 1984 report of the Toronto planning department characterized it as having a long list of faults:

> poor access to buildings from public streets; a lack of safety at entrances and walkways; lack of outdoor recreation space… shabby appearance of the buildings because of poor construction, vandalism and inadequate maintenance… "pervasive apathy" among residents, a shortage of social services, and the ghetto image of the project.
>
> (York 1984, 5)

With a population estimated today to be between 15,000 and 25,000, this 32 acre (13 hectare) site is reputed to have the highest density of any neighbourhood in Canada. It has also been described, in the new millennium, as one of the 13 most economically deprived areas in Toronto.

To critics, Regent Park and St. James Town represented two sides of the same coin—a coin whose value they now began to question: Was this really "urban renewal"? Even though the first was built with public funds and management and the second by private enterprise, both were mega-projects that relied on demolition of entire neighbourhoods and communities. Both created a built environment that seemed impersonal and alienating. Both reflected the same planning assumptions—off-the-grid, high-rise buildings surrounded by poorly-designed open space that could easily be misused in ways threatening to residents. And both became enclaves of relative poverty—though to different degrees.

Although land assembly and large-scale development plans for adjacent districts continued through the 1960s, opposition began to coalesce. Distressed residents and home-owners found support in a cohort of reformist politicians that included two future mayors of Toronto, David Crombie and John Sewell, who supported challenges to the "bulldozer development" paradigm. Complaints about demolition and construction dovetailed with a bigger agenda of urban reform.

An early battleground was **Don Mount Court**, a neighbourhood on the east side of the Don River at Dundas Street, almost opposite Regent Park. Here as early as 1956 city planners proposed a public housing development that would expropriate 238 homes and displace some 1,200 residents. The affected homeowners objected to the whole idea of displacement, and to the planners' characterization of their neighbourhood as a slum, but they were especially angry at the low prices offered for their properties. Despite a series of public demonstrations and a good deal of publicity unfavourable to the City, the demolitions eventually went ahead. Don Mount Court became part of the city's portfolio of public housing, and soon displayed many of the negative features associated with Regent Park (Mair 2014). The public confrontation, however, had a galvanizing effect on anti-development groups in other neighbourhoods, among them **Trefann Court**. Some forty years later the Toronto Community Housing Corporation demolished Don Mount Court and replaced it with a mixed-income community now known as Rivertowne, a precursor to the much larger Regent Park redevelopment.

Located immediately south of Regent Park and directly east of Moss Park, the **Trefann Court** neighbourhood was a low-income district hardly different from old Cabbagetown. Its houses and small businesses were of similar vintage and in similar condition—some in poor repair, others less so. Trefann Court seemed an obvious candidate for some version of the wholesale demolition and redevelopment that Regent Park, St. James Town and Don Mount Court had experienced, and this was what city planners proposed. As early as the mid-1950s Trefann was identified as an urban renewal area;[12] landlords, expecting that their properties would soon be demolished, stopped making expensive repairs, with the result that many homes in the area became almost uninhabitable. But in 1966, when the City Council approved a redevelopment plan, many residents resisted. The opponents included property-owners, some of them resident and others absentee, who initially objected mainly to the prices that were being offered for their premises. But the campaign soon escalated to demand preservation of the neighbourhood from mega-development. Factions emerged among residents, property-owners and business-owners, and two rival organizations came forward claiming to speak for the community. Early meetings sometimes turned into shouting-matches. City aldermen and local politicians—among them David Crombie, a university lecturer on urban politics, and lawyers Karl Jaffrey and John Sewell—joined the debate and tried to mediate among residents, the Development Department and City Council. A Working Committee was struck, with representation from all interested parties, to produce an alternate scheme for redevelopment. In March 1972 City Council accepted the group's recommendations, which included preservation and restoration of many existing homes. Those that were demolished would be replaced, not by income-segregated public housing of the Regent Park model, but by small-scale units that would combine market-level and income-subsidized tenancies. Graham Fraser, who studied the dispute closely, concluded that

> The Working Committee managed to prove that "citizen participation"... not only can work in the planning process, but is able to produce complex solutions to difficult problems. The 1972 scheme was not only a more democratically produced plan that was more responsible to the people in the area than the 1966 scheme it replaced, but was obviously a more comprehensive, more sophisticated, better thought out piece of work.
>
> (Fraser 1974, 255)

Later commentators (Filion 1988) have generally agreed with this assessment, but historian Richard White offers some reservations:

> This new plan was something of a hodge-podge, reflecting perhaps that it was, quite literally, a product of planning by committee. It shows no comprehensive vision, unless that vision is a disregard of orthodox planning... Nor is there much sign of what might be called beauty... Planning had been transformed from what the planners wanted into what the affected public wanted...
>
> (White 2016, 286)

St. James Town South, a quadrant bounded by Wellesley, Sherbourne, Carlton and Parliament Streets also became a battlefield. This was another neighbourhood that the city's Official Plan had designated for slum clearance and high density development. In 1968 the Planning Board recommended that the city cooperate with a private developer to this end, and Meridian Property Management Corporation, developer of the St. James Town area to the immediate north, was more than ready to play that role. It had been acquiring properties over the preceding decade, and renting the existing homes—many in deteriorating condition—to short-term tenants. By 1968 the corporation owned roughly two-thirds of all properties in the district, but it had not applied for rezoning or filed plans for future development. At this point a Residents' Association, actively supported by John Sewell, began to campaign against Meridian's plans (Quigley 1974, 47ff.). In a presentation to the City's Executive Committee, they accused the company of using "block-busting" techniques: "They buy the house, fail to make any repairs, let it run down, move out the tenants... and pretty soon the neighbours want to sell their homes" (Came 1970). The association's larger concern was that at the end of this process the corporation would tear down all the existing homes and erect new housing that was beyond the means of present residents. Over the next several years Sewell and the association picketed and petitioned to force the developer to repair the existing properties. Their broader concern was to prevent further demolition or development on the site. In the end, Meridian abandoned its plans. Some houses on the site were renovated, some were purchased by the City for use as social housing. Two new non-profit housing cooperatives[13] were created, as well as some low-rise private housing. Only one middle-size tower building was erected, and its construction was delayed for more than two decades.

The experience of these latter two neighbourhoods was emblematic of broader changes in public opinion and public policy. These included a popular backlash against mega-planning, symbolized in Toronto by the successful campaign to stop construction of the Spadina Expressway. That proposed highway would have bisected—or, in critics' words, gutted—several residential neighbourhoods just west of downtown Toronto. For several years opponents petitioned, picketed and demonstrated against the plan. They were joined by US-born urban theorist and activist Jane Jacobs, who resettled to Toronto in 1969, having played a major role in defeating a similar highway plan in New York. In June 1971 provincial Premier William Davis announced that the plan would be abandoned: "Cities were built for people and not cars." In municipal elections a year later, reformist candidate David Crombie became mayor and the pro-development "Old Guard" that had previously predominated at City Council was reduced to a small handful of seats.

These events coincided with a growing wave of criticism directed against public housing, especially the Regent Park model. Critics from the left faulted large-scale public housing projects for their top-down bureaucratic administration, and for failing to provide many of the amenities of everyday life for tenants. Critics more to the right, among them Paul Hellyer, questioned the very premise of publicly-managed low-income housing, often citing Regent Park as an example of failure.

The Hellyer task force's recommendations on funding were followed, and after 1970 no new large-scale public housing projects were undertaken in Toronto or elsewhere in Canada. But in 1973 the Trudeau government, having lost its parliamentary majority in the election of 1972, struck a deal to secure the support of the New Democratic Party: Among other concessions, the Liberals agreed to amend the CMHC's mandate to support other forms of affordable housing (Dreier and Hulchanski 1993, 52; Bacher 1993, 227). Cooperative and non-profit housing developments were offered mortgage assistance. Unlike the large-scale public housing of the previous two decades, which imposed strict income limits on tenants, some of the new units were open to a much broader economic mix of residents, some rent-subsidized but many others paying close to market-level rent. These were projects on a smaller scale, mostly citizen-initiated and often resident-managed.

Housing of this type was actively promoted and successfully built in the 1970s in another district close to Regent Park—the **St. Lawrence Neighbourhood**. Located to the south and west of Regent, this was a "brownfield" industrial area that had fallen upon hard times. Factories from the Victorian era stood empty, and there were few residential structures. City planners, responding to criticism of Regent Park and other superblock housing efforts of the previous two decades, proposed a different pattern of development featuring through streets, mixed land use, and mixed-income housing. Some of the old factory buildings were renovated into public spaces such as theatres and restaurants. New housing—much of it in the form of non-profit cooperatives—was developed on a street-by-street basis that combined a variety of architectural forms and occupancies. Market-level towers and town houses were built side-by-side with co-ops and rent-subsidized housing units. Architectural critic Christopher Hume has described St. Lawrence as "a shining example of Toronto getting things right… a successful, fully functioning, mixed-use, mixed-income community" (Hume 2014).

The neighbourhood directly north of Regent Park, sometimes known as **Don Vale** but more often taking the name of **Cabbagetown**, followed a very different course. For much of the 1960s it appeared that this district would be leveled and turned into apartment towers on the model of St. James Town. In 1966–1967 city planners presented a comprehensive plan to redevelop the neighbourhood (Lorimer and Philips 1971; Quigley 1973). Would-be developers assembled properties toward this end, but their plans were interrupted by unexpected opposition. Over the next three years several different groups came forward claiming to speak for the community. One, led by civic activists Karl Jaffrey and Alan Samuel, emphasized affordable housing and the rights of tenants. A second group, speaking in the name of property owners, favoured rezoning and high-rise development. Eventually a separate Tenants' Association also formed. A revised set of planning proposals was presented to City Council in 1969 but was not implemented, due partly to the contentious claims of rival organizations, but mainly to the termination of financial support from the higher levels of government (White 2016, 277–279).

Behind these disagreements, a more subtle economic change was taking place. Middle-class buyers had begun purchasing and restoring the neighbourhood's old mainly-brick homes, seeing charm and potential where earlier generations had noticed only squalor and decay. Initially, the low price of properties in the area was a major attraction, and the first generation of renovators—sometimes termed "whitepainters"—were mainly do-it-yourselfers of relatively limited means.

Within a few years, however, a more upscale clientele was drawn to the neighbourhood, and the word "gentrification" began to be used to describe the change. According to geographer David Ley, gentrification entails two processes: middle class resettlement in the inner city, and residential displacement of lower income households from the inner city (Ley 1986, 521). Coined by Ruth Glass in the mid-1960s, the term came into general usage around the world sometime in the 1970s. Clearly the idea of renovating properties and neighbourhoods antedated the term by many years. Clearly, too, the idea of gentrification is as broad and imprecise as the term "middle class." In some localities, the middle-income families who buy and renovate homes are barely more prosperous than the tenants whom they are displacing; in others, builders and speculators are routinely purchasing and lavishly renovating houses for a much wealthier clientele. From the point of view of the displaced, these distinctions may not seem important. In principle, gentrification can occur in rural as well as urban areas, but in most of Europe and North America it has been concentrated in the core of cities—frequently in neighbourhoods that were earlier scorned for their poverty and dilapidation. The attraction to downtown—the positive assessment of inner-city living—is an attitude that contrasts sharply to the suburbanization that many countries experienced after the end of World War II. In the specific case of Toronto, urban planner David Hulchanski has identified a trend extending from 1970 to 2005, in which upper-income populations have become predominant in central downtown neighbourhoods while "poverty has moved from the centre to the edges of the city… The polarization of the city into wealthy neighbourhoods and greater numbers of disadvantaged neighbourhoods is continuing and middle-income neighbourhoods are disappearing" (Hulchanski 2010, 1).

In Don Vale/Cabbagetown, real estate values soared from the late 1970s onward, and investors began buying properties in order to gut and renovate them for immediate resale. New restaurants and shops appeared on nearby streets,[14] and boosters began describing the neighbourhood as "the largest continuous area of preserved Victorian housing in all of North America." Inevitably, the social profile of the area changed. The low-to-middle-income population that had previously predominated was largely, though not completely, displaced. The newcomers included a large proportion of what Richard Florida would later term "the creative class"—writers, artists, people from the news media, educators and other professional groups (Florida 2002). Perhaps ironically, and despite organized opposition from some property owners (Dineen 1974), some of the properties that had been assembled for demolition wound up being rehabilitated as mixed-income cooperatives. They became and have remained a major source of socio-economic diversity in the new Cabbagetown.

The broader district of which Regent Park was a part was transformed in different ways from the 1960s to the 1990s. Moss Park, Don Mount Court and (with some differences) St. James Town were rebuilt through demolition, more or less as Regent Park had been. Trefann Court and St. Lawrence took on a new character as mixed-income communities with a high proportion of affordable, nonprofit housing, while Don Vale/Cabbagetown experienced massive gentrification that drove up land values and transformed the social composition of the neighbourhood. The proximity of these latter areas would influence the future of Regent Park in at least two ways. On one hand, Trefann and St. Lawrence both provided examples of low-rent and subsidized housing that was not isolated or income-segregated in the ways that the old Regent Park had been. On the other, the emergence of Don Vale/Cabbagetown as a hip and fashionable neighbourhood helped create an upscale market for downtown living—something that would have been hard to imagine in the 1950s. As planners began exploring ways of refurbishing or replacing Regent Park, this market would strengthen the argument for mixed-income redevelopment.

The Area's Demography

At the middle of the twentieth century Toronto's east downtown—Cabbagetown by the broadest definition—was inhabited mainly by families of English, Scottish and Irish descent. Migrants from elsewhere—at that time mostly from eastern and southern Europe—were concentrated in other districts to the west of Yonge Street. Over the next five decades, and especially from 1970 onward, Canada's immigration profile changed, with the result that persons of non-European descent came to predominate. According to Statistics Canada, visible minorities made up 12.4 percent of immigrants who came to Canada before 1971; this figure rose to 67 percent in the 1980s, and by 2011 just 13 percent of new immigrants were born in Britain and Europe.

The greater Toronto area was by far most popular destination of immigrants, but within the metropolis migrants tended to cluster in specific areas, with Regent Park and St. James Town close to the top of the list. These changes redefined the Regent Park community, where by 2001 the proportion of immigrants[15] was 58 percent, as compared to 48 percent citywide. By ancestry, place of origin or ethnicity, Regent's population showed a very different profile from the city as a whole; 79 percent— more than twice Toronto's proportion of 37 percent— were counted as being of non-European descent. Among these, the most numerous identified themselves as Chinese, Vietnamese, Sri Lankan, Jamaican and East Indian. 16 percent of the district's population had arrived in Canada within the preceding five years, compared to 9 percent in Toronto as a whole. Interestingly, the percentage who were Canadian citizens showed a smaller difference—79 percent in Regent compared to 82 percent citywide.

Given the income restrictions on public housing, it is not surprising that low-income households predominated. More than 65 percent reported annual income below $30,000, compared to 29 percent in all of Toronto. These were households with far more children, on average, than in the rest of the city—29 percent of the population was below the age of fifteen, compared to 16 percent throughout the city (City of Toronto 2007).

In the new millennium these features of the population posed particular challenges for creating an inclusive plan for transforming Regent Park. Planners seeking community consultation had to conduct their discussions in six or more different languages. And their efforts to foster an inclusive community had to address not only socio-economic but also ethno-cultural diversity within the resident population.

Notes

1 Architectural critics were, however, not enthusiastic about the design of Regent North. Anthony Jackson, writing in 1959, observed that "The northern half took the brunt of vested interests' antagonism, and is a depressingly ugly argument for slum clearance" (Jackson 1959, 63). Jackson was much more positive about the design of Regent South.

2 Two years earlier, an article in *Canadian Architect* enthused that the towers' façade expressed "a vivacity that fills the court below with the joy of rhythm" (Jackson 1959, 71).

3 Compare this to the description provided by architectural critic Anthony Jackson just a year earlier: "…the court reverberates to the noise of children, digging up the grass, bathing under the improvised hose, climbing over the tree-stumps (and stripping the bark off trees)… gregariously shouting the joys of community living—over 2000 children (from apartments and houses) marking out the ground pattern of their activities… [T]he corridor problem was quickly solved: the children were simply kicked outside. But once outside the apartment and outside the range of their parents' hands, children will be children. Elevators are left open, linoleum corridors are cut by ice-skates, entrance hall and door glazing is quickly cracked…With only one corner set aside as a playground and crèche, the children act as locusts turning grass to dust and trees to deadwood. The playground is delightful… but hopelessly inadequate… Outside, the ground lies spoiled, waiting for the Authority to pave or replant. But the framework for success exists" (Jackson 1959, 68–72).

4 Anthony Jackson, evaluating Regent South in 1959, observed that balconies "provide forbidden drying space for illicit washing. Laundry space is in the basement, too small,

too far from the apartments, too unpleasant to have the children along. With basement washing rationed to twice a week, the housewife launders in her kitchen and defies authority" (Jackson 1959, 71–72).

5 Related arguments have been made by Newman (1973) and Coleman (1985).

6 The sole exception was a small strip mall built in Regent South in the mid-1960s. It included a laundromat, a mini-mart, and a hamburger restaurant, Root 'n Burger (sometimes Root Burger), once described as "the social and cultural centre of Regent Park (Regent Park Heritage Commemoration Strategy 2015, 3). According to a 1965 study, teens who hung out in this location were "targeted by police, who maintained a close surveillance of the juveniles, many of whom had minor brushes with the law and youth courts" (Palmer 2009, 193). Nostalgic residents recall the shop with affection. After its demolition, its sign was preserved and is now displayed in the café of the new Daniels Spectrum building.

7 This and all subsequent unreferenced quotations from residents and key informants are taken from confidential interviews conducted by Laura Johnson and/or members of the research team.

8 Those original contributions were kept in trust for almost three decades, and in 2014 their value had grown to more than $700,000. At that time the City and TCHC agreed to create a Regent Park Legacy Fund Trust that would pay out an annual grant "in support of community development, capacity building in the community and/or sponsor special events… A community panel comprised of members of the [Regent Park Community Reference Group— a group of Regent Park residents who contributed to the initial vision of a resident run community centre in Regent Park'], [TCHC] representatives, and other interested members of the Regent Park community will review and assess the ideas submitted and select the grant recipients on an annual basis" (TCHC 2014a, 3).

9 Although Rose's remarks were published in 1968, he first delivered them at a conference in 1964—an indication of how early he began to re-evaluate Regent Park's success.

10 Because population figures were available only for the census year of 2011, the compilers restricted their neighbourhood calculations to that one year; their interactive map does, however, show for each district of the city the number of incidents in each year from 2004 to 2011.

11 www.regentparkfocus.com/content/aboutus.html

12 The Planning Board's 1956 *Study on Urban Renewal* was described by journalist Graham Fraser as "terrifying in its simplicity, its sterility and its enormity. The whole area bounded by Queen, Dundas, River and Church Streets was to be bulldozed… [and replaced by] row upon row of barrack-like public-housing units, lined up in what planners call 'super-blocks'…" (Fraser 1974, 60).

13 Cooperative housing was a novelty in Toronto at this time—the result of changes in federal housing legislation and CMHC funding programs. See further discussion below, in relation to St. Lawrence neighbourhood, and in Chapter 3.

14 Nonetheless, many businesses serving a less affluent clientele continued and continue to flourish, especially along Parliament, Gerard and River Streets. Quite a few of these are oriented to particular sub-groups in the Regent Park community. In 1998 Penina Coopersmith observed that on Parliament Street "thrift and junk stores are located cheek by jowl with trendy restaurants, bakeries and boutiques. More often, they represent two solitudes—not of ethnicity, but of class" (Coopersmith 1998, 72). More than fifteen years later, the juxtaposition and the solitudes remain.

15 The relevant census tract included a larger territory than Regent Park, extending east to the Don River valley and south to Queen Street. As of 2001, these tracts were in

many ways similar to Regent; they also consisted mainly of low-income families, with a high proportion of immigrants, though not necessarily from the same countries.

References

Allen, David. 1968a. "Regent Park South: Noble experiment now called a failure." *Toronto Star* December 7, 1.

Allen, David. 1968b. "To most of its youth Regent Park South is just a place to wreck." *Toronto Star* December 9, 1.

Allen David. 1968c. "Regent Park South: Living here is like getting kicked in the teeth." *Toronto Star* December 10, 9.

August, Martine. 2014. "Challenging the rhetoric of stigmatization: The benefits of concentrated poverty in Toronto's Regent Park." *Environment and Planning* A 46: 1317–1333.

Bacher, John C. 1993. *Keeping to the Marketplace: The Evolution of Canadian Housing Policy*. Montreal: McGill-Queens University Press.

Becker, Jane. "Regent Park South 'Wrong as Housing Model.'" *Toronto Star* June 6.

Bellamy, Donald F. 1953. "A Study of the Impact of Public Housing on the Unemployment Relief Case Loads and Costs, the Causes of Indigency, and Family Sizes of Recipients in the Regent Park (North) Project of Toronto, 1950–52 Compared with 1945–47." Master's thesis, University of Toronto.

Bozikovic, Alex. 2013. "NO MEAN CITY: A killing, 'the projects,' and the new Regent Park. January 23. spacing.ca/toronto/2013/01/23/3a-killing-the-projects-and-the-new-regent-park. (Accessed January 10, 2017).

Came, Barry. 1970. "Pickets City Hall with residents: Sewell says Meridian attempting to create a slum south of St. James Town." *Globe and Mail* July 9: 5.

City of Toronto. 2007. "Regent Park Social Profile, 2006." Prepared by the Social Policy Analysis & Research section in the Social Development, Finance and Administration Division. Data from Statistics Canada, Censuses 2001 and 2006. www1.toronto.ca/wps/portal/contentonly?vgnextoid=80ccb3d0122c1410VgnVCM10000071d60f89RCRD&vgnextchannel=1e68f40f9aae0410VgnVCM10000071d60f89RCRD. (Accessed January 10, 2017).

Coleman, Alice. 1985. *Utopia on Trial: Vision and Reality in Planned Housing*. London: Hillary Shipman.

Coopersmith, Penina. 1998. *Cabbagetown: The Story of a Victorian Neighbourhood*. Toronto: James Lorimer and Company.

Dineen, Janice. 1974. *The Trouble with Co-ops*. Toronto: Green Tree Publishing Co.

Dreier, Peter and David Hulchanski. 1993. "The Role of Nonprofit Housing in Canada and the United States: Some Comparisons." *Housing Policy Debate* 4(1): 43–80.

Filion, Pierre. 1988. "The Neighbourhood Improvement Plan: Montreal and Toronto: Contrasts between a participatory and a centralized approach to urban policy making." *Urban History Review/Revue d'histoire urbaine* 17(1): 16–28.

Florida, Richard. 2002. *The Rise of the Creative Class*. NY: Basic Books.

Fraser, Graham. 1974. *Fighting Back: Urban Renewal in Trefann Court*. Toronto: Hakkert.

Friesen, Dwight, Pras Rajagopalan and Jamie Strashin. 2012. "Toronto Crime by Neighbourhood." CBC News, October 24. www.cbc.ca/toronto/features/crimemap. (Accessed January 10, 2017).

Globe and Mail. 1951."Housing Authority Orders Removal of Television Aerial in Regent Park." September 11: 13.

Globe and Mail. 1953. "Regent Park's Aerial Problem." December 22.

Globe and Mail. 1954. "Antenna Cost Seen Topping Price of Set." March 16: 5.

Globe and Mail. 1960. "Realtors to Propose Plan for Moss Park." May 31: 5.

Globe and Mail. 1960. "Favor Studying Change For Moss Park Project." June 1: 5.

Globe and Mail. 1965. "St. James Town Tenants Draft City Hall Protest." July 20: 5.

Globe and Mail. 1966. "Regent Park North Letter to the Editor." Alderman June Marks, July 29.

Globe and Mail. 1967."Investigation ordered into Moss Park costs." March 23: 8.

Globe and Mail. 1980. "Head of new OHC body seeks image change." August 18: 5.

Globe and Mail. 1989. "Regent Park Residents Say No to Drugs at Rally." August 21.

Globe and Mail. 1990. "Regent Park Drug Sweep Nets Charges." July 6.

Goetz, Edward G. 2013. *New Deal Ruins: Race, Economic Justice, & Public Housing Policy*. Ithaca, NY: Cornell University Press.

Grange, Michael. 1996. "Regent Park plan sign of new direction: Private funds sought for public housing." *Globe and Mail* February 2: A1.

Harding, Katherine. 2004. "Regent Park Hero Pegged as Next Top Cop." *Globe and Mail* July 10.

Hellyer, Paul T. 1969. *Report of the Federal Task Force on Housing and Urban Development*. Ministry of Transport. (January).

Housing Authority of Toronto. 1960. City Archive of Toronto, Fonds 200, Series 1353, File 216: "Regent Park South."

Hulchanski, J. David. 2010. "The Three Cities Within Toronto: Income Polarization Among Toronto's Neighbourhoods, 1970–2005." Toronto: Creative Commons.

Hume, Christopher. 2013. "14 Blevins a monument to our pattern of failure." *Toronto Star* November 11.

Hume, Christopher. 2014. "Big Ideas: Learning the lessons of St. Lawrence Neighbourhood." *Toronto Star* May 3.

Jackson, Anthony. 1959. "Apartments, Regent Park South, Toronto." *Canadian Architect* 4(9): 62–73.

Jacobs, Jane. 1961. *The Death and Life of Great American Cities*. New York: Vintage Books.

Ley, David. 1986. "Alternative Explanations for Inner-City Gentrification: A Canadian Assessment." *Annals of the Association of American Geographers* 76(4): 521–535.

Lorimer, James and Myfanwy Philips. 1971. *Working People*. Toronto: J. Lewis & Samuel.

Mair, David. 2014. *Boundaries, narrative frames, and the politics of place in public housing redevelopment: Exploring Toronto's Don Mount Court/Rivertowne*. Toronto, York University. yorkspace.library.yorku.ca/xmlui/handle/10315/27645. (Accessed January 10, 2017).

Mays, John Bentley. 2013. "As Regent Park rebuilds, a pause to consider what came before." *Globe and Mail* February 28.

Newman, Oscar.1973. *Defensible Spaces*. New York: Macmillan.

Palmer, Bryan D. 2009. *Canada's 1960s: The ironies of identity in a rebellious era*. Toronto: University of Toronto Press.

Phelp, Margaret.1997. "Ghetto's remake builds optimism: Toronto's Regent Park hopes new public-housing project will dramatically change neighbourhood." *Globe and Mail* November 28: A10.

Purdy, Sean. 2003. "'Ripped off' by the System': Housing Policy, Poverty, and Territorial Stigmatization in Regent Park Housing Project, 1951–1991." *Labour/Le Travail* 52: 45–108.

Purdy, Sean. 2004. "By the People, For the People: Tenant Organizing in Toronto's Regent Park Housing Project in the 1960s and 1970s." *Journal of Urban History* 30(4): 519–548.

Purdy, Sean. 2005. "Framing Regent Park: the National Film Board of Canada and the construction of 'outcast spaces' in the inner city, 1953 and 1994." *Media, Culture & Society* 27(4): 523–549.

Quigley, Maureen. 1973. *Citizen Participation in Development in the City of Toronto*. Ontario Department of Municipal Affairs.

Randall, Stanley. 1968. "Randall Charges Star One-Sided on Regent Park." *Toronto Star* December 13: 7.

Regent Park Heritage Commemoration Strategy. 2015. "Community Meeting 1 Summary." www.regentparkstories.ca.

Rose, Albert. 1952. "Housing Administration in Canada, 1952." *Canadian Welfare* December 15.

Rose, Albert. 1958. *Regent Park: A Study in Slum Clearance*. Toronto: University of Toronto Press.

Rose, Albert. 1968. "The Individual, the Family and the Community in the Process of Urban Renewal." *University of Toronto Law Journal* 18: 3.

Rose, Albert. 1972. *Governing Metropolitan Toronto: a Social and Political Analysis, 1953–1971*. Berkeley: University of California Press.

Sewell, John. 1993. *The Shape of the City: Toronto Struggles with Modern Planning*. Toronto, Buffalo and London: University of Toronto Press.

Sewell, John. 1994. *Houses and Homes: Housing for Canadians*. Toronto: James Lorimer and Co.

Smith, Nancy. 1995. "Challenges of Public Housing in the 1990s: The Case of Ontario, Canada." *Housing Policy Debate* 6(4): 905–931.

Steed, Nicholas. 1964. "Public Housing Ends Family's Slum Life", *Toronto Star* September 25, 7.

TCHC (Toronto Community Housing Corporation). 2007. *Regent Park Social Development Plan*.

TCHC (Toronto Community Housing Corporation). 2014. "New Street Names—Dreamers' Way." *Community Update Newsletter*. (September).

TCHC (Toronto Community Housing Corporation). 2014a. "Regent Park Legacy Funds: Staff Report, Action Required." Ref. AFS # 18369, April 3.

Thompson, Sara K., Sandra M. Bucerius and Mark Luguya. 2013. "Unintended Consequences of Neighbourhood Restructuring: Uncertainty, Disrupted Social Networks and Increased Fear of Victimization among Young Adults." *British Journal of Criminology* 53: 924–941.

Toronto Star. 1988. "Is Ontario set to privatize public housing?" September 23: A27.

Tumpane, Frank. 1952. "Problem at Regent Park," *Globe and Mail* December 11.

White, Richard. 2016. *Planning Toronto: The Planners, the Plans, their Legacies, 1940–1980*. Toronto and Vancouver: UBC Press.

York, Geoffrey. 1984. "Planners tackle St. James Town faults." *Globe and Mail* December 7: M5.

Zapparoli, David. 1999. *Regent Park: The Public Experiment in Housing*. Toronto: D. Zapparoli.

3

Public Housing Policy in an International Context

> Fifty years ago, public housing was considered the most significant answer to accommodating families with low incomes. Today, it is reviled.
>
> (Sewell 1994, 132)

> Public housing is not... a single program, proceeding with an internal logic from one stage to another... Rather, it is a set of responses, pushed by varying interests, resisted by other again varying interests, in widely varying circumstances.
>
> (Marcuse 1995, 249 ff.)

The terms "public housing" and "social housing" have often been used interchangeably, to denote a wide array of programs and facilities. What those programs have in common is an attempt to subsidize affordable shelter for individuals and families who would otherwise have difficulty meeting their own housing needs. But the definition of "difficulty," and hence of eligibility for housing, has varied widely from place to place and from decade to decade. Over the past century public- or social-housing initiatives have been supported to differing degrees by public funding, sometimes assisted by, and/or channelled through, private, non-profit agencies or organizations. But the forms that aid took, and the organizational framework through which it was provided, were also diverse.

Regent Park itself has gone through numerous changes over time. It began in the late 1940s as a municipal effort, with very little support from higher levels of government. As originally conceived and administered, it housed a spectrum of families whose economic needs ranged from moderate to extreme. Over the first two decades of operation, the pattern of funding shifted, with Canada's federal government providing the greatest support for construction of public housing and the Province of Ontario taking over the main responsibility for ongoing operations. Meanwhile the profile of Regent Park's target population narrowed significantly until only Toronto's neediest residents were eligible to live there.

Varying definitions and systems of planning and support for the development of social housing and public housing have been deployed in other settings.

Despite differences in timing, the long arc of Canadian housing policy and practice shares many characteristics with public housing as it evolved in other jurisdictions.

Origins of Public/Social Housing

In most industrialized countries, a demand for affordable housing can be traced to the latter decades of the nineteenth century, when urban growth and squalor reached levels hitherto unseen. In earlier times, the meagre shelter that charitable bodies and local governments provided in almshouses and poorhouses was generally restricted to the "impotent poor"—individuals whose age, health or physical condition prevented them from working. But the booming cities and industrial centres of Britain, Europe and North America created poverty of a different kind, on an unprecedented scale. Millions of new settlers were housed in tenements or makeshift slums. This was a population whose needs—and complaints and demands—made the older social safety nets obsolete. In a few locations, better-quality housing was built by philanthropists or progressively-minded employers; a classic example was Scotland's New Lanarck factory community, built by Robert Owen early in the nineteenth century. Such facilities were, however, rare exceptions. Most city-dwellers and industrial workers lived in overcrowded and unhealthy conditions. By the end of the nineteenth century, reformers and critics of various orientations—humanitarian, conservative, liberal, socialist—were addressing the problems of urban poverty and housing. By the turn of the twentieth century, Belgium, Britain and France had all passed legislation to promote the creation of social housing, and most European countries followed within the next two decades. But only after World War I were their concerns translated into large-scale housing reforms. (Lévy-Vroelant *et al.* 2014a, 280 ff.)

The war stimulated new initiatives for several reasons. All the belligerent countries faced the problem of housing large numbers of veterans. Perhaps even more importantly, the war had a radicalizing effect on the working population of many nations. After three years of unimaginable carnage and economic privation, citizens of many nations began to question not only the political leadership but also the socio-political order that had made the war possible. The Russian Revolution of 1917 challenged the whole international system, and was followed by unsuccessful uprisings by left-wing groups in such countries as Hungary, Finland and Germany. Taken together, these factors made many different governments willing to experiment with new forms of housing that might, if they succeeded, defuse unrest and improve the health—and perhaps even the moral well-being—of working populations.

Vienna was a social housing pioneer. Under a social-democratic government from 1918 to 1934, "Red Vienna" created more than 350 housing estates with a population of more than 60,000. In combination with a rent-control system for private dwellings, these well-designed and well-serviced homes ensured that affordable housing was available to a large proportion of the working population. They became a symbol of the city's welfare-state achievements, which were widely mistrusted and opposed in Austria's conservative hinterland. During the short-lived civil war of 1934, the socialist paramilitary militia, the *Schutzbund*, barricaded itself in the housing complexes, which were extensively bombarded by right-wing forces.

In Britain the Town Housing and Planning Act of 1919 offered subsidies to local councils to create up to 500,000 units of social housing in three years under the slogan "Homes for Heroes" (Wilding 1973). Although its results came nowhere near that ambitious target, it marked the beginning of a new trend in housing production. Over the following decade some 75,000 new units of social housing were produced in Scotland alone, marking the beginning of an era in which social ("council") housing became the dominant form of tenure. Local (council) authorities built 70 percent of all housing in Scotland between 1919 and 1940; in England and Wales, the comparable figure was just under 30 percent, but this translated into more than a million dwellings (Robertson and Serpa 2014, 44; Holmans 2005, 47).

The municipal government of Berlin, with an orientation similar to Vienna's, confronted greater economic problems in the immediate postwar years, and was slower to begin building social housing. Nonetheless, between 1924 and 1932 some 160,000 new units were created, some of them designed by members of the Bauhaus school of architectural modernism. In the Netherlands—a non-belligerent in World War I—a different configuration of political and economic forces led to construction of some 30,000 units of social housing in the 1920s. These were located not just in major cities but also in towns. Here, as in Vienna and Berlin, the intended clientele was not unskilled labourers or the unemployed, but rather artisans, clerks, union members and better-off members of the working population, who were carefully screened before being admitted.[1] New housing was intended not just to provide shelter but also to inculcate "proper" or "respectable" behaviour. This mission was often enforced by inspectors or health workers: "The municipal authorities tried to use social housing to consolidate the formation of an active, healthy and skilled working class and its municipal supporters… the purpose was 'to give the proletarians dignity and turn workers into citizens…' " (Malpass 2014, 282–283).

Canada too experienced a housing shortage at the end of World War I, accompanied by a wave of social unrest, but here the response was different. Instead of promoting social housing, the federal government offered grants to municipalities for the construction of new private homes. These were meant to be sold to veterans and working people at lower-than-market prices and with reduced-rate mortgages. The scheme did not produce the desired results, and was soon abandoned:

> In 1919 the threat of social upheaval was real enough to silence opposition to the principle of assistance for low-income housing. But by 1921 the political climate had changed so dramatically that housing had vanished from the political agenda altogether.
>
> (Bacher 1993, 62)

The Great Depression of the 1930s influenced social housing in two ways. In many countries the economic crash initially produced a sharp drop in housing starts, thereby increasing the problems of overcrowding and poor living conditions. Deepening economic problems, however, also brought pressure for job creation and economic stimulus, leading some national governments to undertake new programs of housing construction. Statistics from England and Wales show a precipitous drop in municipal housing starts from over 100,000 in 1928 to an annual average just above 50,000 over the next eight years, followed by a sharp up-tick from 1937 to 1939, when the threshold of 100,000 was once again surpassed.

In the United States ideas of slum clearance and housing reform had been urgently discussed since the end of the nineteenth century. Muck-raking reformers such as Jacob Riis had exposed the squalor of tenement life and campaigned—with some success—for improved zoning laws and housing codes. But with a few isolated exceptions, construction of below-market social housing—much less the idea of using government funding to create such housing—was dismissed as utopian or socialistic until the advent of Franklin D. Roosevelt's "New Deal." In 1933 advocates of housing reform persuaded the President to include "low-rent housing and slum clearance projects" in the National Industrial Recovery Act that was then being drafted (von Hoffman 2005, 229). Local governments and private corporations were unenthusiastic, and only a handful of projects were launched before the Act—parts of which were declared unconstitutional by the US Supreme Court—expired. Advocates for public housing ("the housers") then began lobbying the President and Congress for a more permanent and effective law. After extensive hearings and negotiations, a bill was passed—the Wagner-Steagall Act of 1937. Falling far short of the hopes and expectations of housing advocates, it illustrated many of the cross-currents and contradictions of the era (Radford 1996). In Alexander von Hoffman's summation, "To the dismay of the housers, Congress created not a broad-based program to house a majority of the population in small planned communities, but rather a narrow program aimed at sheltering the very poor and eliminating slums" (von Hoffman 2005, 243).

Even though the target population was narrower than reformers had hoped, it was not, in this era, the "poorest of the poor" who were rehoused. Until the mid-1950s, US public housing would accommodate mainly what one official termed "those who need *some* help," while excluding most families from the lowest income levels (Vale 2013, 15).

Peter Marcuse has argued that in the US "neither the forces for nor the forces against public housing at its origins were united or homogeneous in their positions or attitudes" (Marcuse 1995, 247). Some advocates of slum clearance opposed the creation of public housing, and some "housers" opposed slum clearance, arguing that public housing should instead be built on vacant land. Labour unions in the construction trades, and some representatives of the building industries, were enthusiastic because of job creation. Other labour groups were divided in their responses to the idea of social housing. Owners of real estate and managers of rental properties were suspicious of any program that might compromise the value of their holdings or compete with them for tenants. And throughout the United States, north as well as south, most politicians were committed to maintaining a racially segregated pattern of housing. The result of these conflicting demands and hopes was a program that built relatively little social housing, and did so on terms that would minimize opposition from entrenched interests. When, after World War II, the US federal government embarked on a much larger program of demolition and construction, it stayed mainly within the narrow definitions and parameters that were set in the 1930s legislation—or narrowed them further.

The government of Canada began very tentatively to explore the idea of public housing in the latter 1930s, but the outbreak of war in 1939 put an end to such initiatives. During the war years a newly-created crown corporation, Wartime Housing Limited, created and managed low-rental housing for munitions workers and the families of military personnel. This unprecedented intervention into the housing market was met with approval by provinces and municipalities. At the end of the war some reformers proposed to extend the corporation's mandate into the field of civilian public housing, but the idea was opposed by C.D. Howe, then-Minister of Reconstruction, and senior officials of the Finance Department (Wade 1984, 145). The Liberal government preferred to promote housing through private-sector channels, and created the Central Mortgage and Housing Administration to this end.

Growth of Public/Social Housing after 1945

World War II damaged or destroyed whole cities across much of Europe, with the result that (for example) France and the Netherlands both lost in the range of 20 percent of all housing stock (Lévy-Vroelant *et al.* 2014a, 284).

Even in countries that did not experience wartime devastation, veterans returning from war and starting new families produced a "baby boom." The demand for new housing was enormous, and yet postwar recovery was in many cases slow, putting market-priced accommodation out of reach for much of the citizenry. The governments that confronted these challenges were, in many European states as well as the United Kingdom, favourably disposed to welfare-state or social-democratic solutions. They undertook massive programs to produce affordable housing, using various forms of subsidy and administration to supplement or bypass the private housing market. Over three decades from 1945 to the mid-1970s, social housing accounted for a large proportion—sometimes even a majority—of new housing starts. An extreme example was Scotland, where by the 1970s two-thirds of all households lived in council housing (Robertson and Serpa 2014, 44). In the Netherlands social housing's share of new construction rose steadily through the 1950s, 1960s and 1970s, levelling off above 40 percent thereafter (Elsinga and Wassenberg 2014, 26); but in those same decades in the city of Amsterdam the figure was 90 percent (Fainstein 2010, 150). In England the social-rental sector reached a peak of 5.5 million housing units in 1979—just over 30 percent of all dwellings in the country (Whitehead 2014, 106). Statistics from France, Sweden and Austria give a similar picture. But in Ireland, where social housing was built mainly for various categories of people in need, the proportion has rarely been higher than 15 percent (Redmond and Norris 2014, 146).

Apart from Ireland, the afore-named countries also aimed to produce housing that was socially inclusive. Elsinga and Wassenberg's characterization of the Dutch system could describe many others: "… the social rental sector [was] regarded as a service for a broad cross-section of the population, aimed at providing decent and affordable housing for all, following ideas of social equality and uniformity" (Elsinga and Wassenberg 2014, 28).

Yet the forms of tenure varied widely from country to country. In the case of Scotland and England, until the 1970s almost all social-housing occupants were tenants on council estates, under municipal administration; since that time, a growing proportion of social housing has been shifted to non-profit housing associations and registered social landlords (Robertson and Serpa 2014, 43; Whitehead 2014, 107). In the Netherlands social housing is organized through local housing associations, some of them municipally owned. Denmark and Austria also rely upon limited-profit housing associations. In contrast, France's social housing is organized in three tiers, corresponding to different economic strata in the population (Lévy-Vroelant *et al.* 2014b, 124).

Two other features of public housing were common to most European states in the postwar decades and especially after 1960. One was an emphasis on tall modernist towers as the preferred mode of social housing. An extreme example was the Red Rose housing estate, built on the outskirts of Glasgow in 1962.

This was an ensemble of eight towers ranging from 28 to 31 storeys—the tallest structure of its kind in Europe at the time of construction. Like the Dickinson towers of Regent Park, the project was promoted as an inexpensive and socially progressive way of addressing housing needs. But it began encountering problems as soon as tenants moved in:

> On letting of Blocks 1 and 2… the high proportion of children, in 31 storey towers with only two lifts, created a reputation for juvenile delinquency which blighted the entire scheme even before its completion. Block 2 was stigmatised as the "worst" on the scheme by residents, management and the police; for example, a tenant complained to the Corporation that an old lady's hat had been "pulled from her head because she had the temerity to check boys who were stoning the watchman"…
>
> (Glendenning and Muthesius 1994, 321)

The Aylesbury Estate in London, built less than a decade later, had a similar design and encountered similar problems, as did many tower projects in various European states (Lees 2014, 922).

During these same decades, most European states, in common with Canada and the United States, were experiencing demographic changes that ultimately affected the clientele base for social housing. On one hand, birth rates declined steadily from the 1950s onward, and by the mid-1970s the Total Fertility Rate in most countries was approaching or had crossed the level of 2.1—the threshold below which, over time, population growth will become negative. For providers of social housing, this meant that some families were having fewer or no children, and would seek different accommodation than previous generations had required. Offsetting these changes, however, was a large influx of migrants from outside Europe. As the proportion of immigrant families grew, they created a new demand for social housing. Migrants also showed, on average, a greater propensity to live in multi-generational families, including greater numbers of children than their European-born counterparts; this made them natural candidates for the larger, multi-bedroom units in existing public housing.

In some locations such as the outskirts of Paris, these two trends dovetailed, with the result that new migrants became concentrated in tower blocks of social housing, effectively isolated from mainstream society. The social consequences of this isolation are to this day being debated. Parallel conditions could be found in Regent Park from the 1970s onwards, but with one important difference. Migrants in northern Europe tended to concentrate by country or region of origin, with the result that French banlieues housed mainly North Africans, Amsterdam's equivalent settlements were inhabited predominantly by Surinamese or Moroccans, and so forth. Regent Park, by contrast, was home to large groups of immigrants from many different corners of the world, with no single group predominating.

In post-war development of public housing, both the United States and Canada followed different paths from Europe and the United Kingdom. The number of public housing units increased, but the scale of growth was much smaller than in most European states. In the United States in 1945 the number of federally subsidized public housing occupancies was around 200,000; the total grew steadily until the mid-1980s, when it levelled off just below 1.5 million (Vale 2013, 28). During those years federal funding waxed and waned, supplemented in some jurisdictions by support from state and municipal government and philanthropic agencies (Marcuse 1995, 251). Criteria for eligibility were redefined, with the result that the proportion of tenants in extreme need—e.g., single-parent households—increased sharply. In Nicholas Bloom's summation, "many city officials outside New York allowed public housing to become a welfare program, a racial program, a slum clearance program, a dumping ground for urban renewal, and only secondarily a long-term housing program. They rarely got it right" (Bloom 2008, 266).

The American Housing Act of 1949 was denounced by Congressional opponents as a fatal step toward socialism. Its supporters overcame powerful opposition from such lobbying groups as the National Association of Real Estate Boards, the National Association of Home Builders, and the US Savings and Loan League. But the legislation was modified to address at least some critics' concerns; public housing was defined in terms that would limit its scope and effectiveness in a number of ways. Jennifer A. Stoloff, reviewing the history of public housing in the US, observes that the 1949 Act

> benefited business interests by limiting the program to the very poor and leaving the working class to be housed by private builders. Limiting the program in this way ensured non-competitiveness with the private sector and was not motivated by a desire to serve the most needy in society.
>
> (Stoloff 2004, 3–4)

Later federal housing programs in the 1960s provided further tax incentives and subsidies to private developers in order to promote low-cost housing. But as Stoloff reports, these efforts were often undermined by corrupt practices and scandals in the 1970s (ibid., 4).

The net result of these federal initiatives was a public-housing system that, as Edward Goetz summarizes, operated within strict and confining limits: *Decentralized administration and local control over siting* allowed (mainly white) middle class officials and communities to veto public housing proposals, as a result of which most projects were confined to central-city areas of concentrated poverty. *Cost-containment* "led to short-cuts, the use of inferior materials, and regrettable design decisions." *Tenant selection* initially favoured the "working poor," but over time the criteria were narrowed to "emphasize families with severe need living on public assistance" (Goetz 2013, 29–38). These problems were compounded by *mismanagement:*

> Public housing was the backwater of local public administration in many cities, reserved for patronage appointments of politically connected individuals with little expertise in running a large and complicated social service and welfare program of the type that public housing had become.
> (ibid., 38)

Public housing in the United States was, in this era, presented in the context of a wider array of social-welfare benefits. In many jurisdictions these programs were the subject of political contestation. Notions of the "deserving" and "undeserving" poor figured prominently, along with the idea that public housing should be temporary accommodation, to be used only until the residents could become self-sufficient. Proponents of this line of reasoning were often casual about the shabby and minimal quality of much public housing: If it was more comfortable, people would have less incentive to leave. Conservative critics also tried, often successfully, to impose narrow and punitive restrictions on recipients of housing or other welfare supports. A notable example was the "man in the house rule" by which a single mother could lose her eligibility for public housing if she was found to be "cohabiting" or having sexual relations with a man, even as an occasional visitor. Social workers or housing authority staff were permitted to conduct night visits to determine whether tenants were breaking this rule. Only in 1968 did the US Supreme Court rule (King versus Smith) that this practice was unconstitutional.

These practices and conditions were not universal. Goetz acknowledges that they have, often unfairly, overshadowed the "quiet successes" that were achieved in many localities, including (sometimes) New York City. But the fate of public housing in such cities as Chicago and St. Louis led many American policy-makers to regard the system as a failed experiment. By the 1980s construction of large-scale family housing projects had ended, and efforts were under way to radically transform or demolish many existing complexes, and to shift federal support to different channels.

The Canadian government was slow to support public housing. The National Housing Act of 1946 created the Central Mortgage and Housing Corporation to address the nation's need for affordable housing. But the corporation's energies and resources were directed mainly into programs to promote construction and ownership of private homes. It provided loans and mortgage insurance and offered, at different times, various programs to reduce interest rates to home-buyers and support home ownership (e.g., the Assisted

Home Ownership Program introduced in 1971). In the period from 1946 to 1971, when approximately three million new housing units were built in Canada, CMHC financed or assisted approximately one-third of that total (Miron 1988, 245). Support for slum clearance and rental public housing was also part of the organization's mandate, but the scale of support was significantly lower: By 1964 only 12,000 housing units of this type had been built. Amendments to the Housing Act in that year created new funding possibilities, and over the course of the next fifteen years some 165,000 units of public housing were added—about 5 percent of all new housing in that period (ibid., 252). Public housing in Canada displayed some of the same faults—and attracted some of the same criticism—as its US counterpart.

After the Hellyer Task Force report of 1969, CMHC support was directed away from large-scale family housing projects of the Regent Park type, and more toward independent housing associations—cooperatives, or non-profit housing providers (see next section). Housing of this type was generally acknowledged to function more smoothly and economically than the older, governmentally-administered public housing entities such as Regent Park.

Changes after 1970

It was no coincidence that the "golden years" of public housing construction coincided with a protracted period of general prosperity in most of Europe and North America. The following years brought slower economic growth and heightened uncertainty, and with it a turn toward a neoliberal political economy, epitomised by Thatcherism or Reaganism but echoed in many other countries. Taken together, these changes inevitably affected housing policies. In Michael Harloe's summation,

> Full employment gave way to persistent structural unemployment, which never reverted to the low levels of the previous era, even when the economies recovered from recession. Faltering growth, high unemployment, ageing populations and other factors placed new demands on state welfare expenditures, while the scope for financing these expenditures was curtailed. (Harloe 1995, 366)

> Even in Denmark and the Netherlands [which had the highest levels of social housing] there was an increasing concentration of lower-income households in the [social] sector and the loss of middle-income tenants or sources of new demand. In every case, too, this result had been brought about

> largely as a result of deliberate state action which had aimed to channel housing demand away from the social sector towards the private market.
> (ibid., 507)

Despite diversity in the scale of public housing and the modes of delivery, all of the countries discussed here experienced major changes to their programs in the last decades of the twentieth century. All today are facing further challenges. Enthusiasm for such housing has waned in most jurisdictions, and budgetary limits have been imposed, even though waiting lists for admission to social housing continue to grow. Construction of new public housing stock has slowed or stopped, and repair and upkeep of existing units has, in many cases, declined. Prominent examples of public housing—among them Glasgow's massive Red Road and London's Aylesbury—have been demolished. To differing degrees, a neoliberal social agenda has supplanted the welfare-state orientation of earlier times.

A further commonality has been the narrowing of public housing's mandate—the tightening of criteria of eligibility. Countries that had aspired to a universalistic system of housing as part of a comprehensive welfare regime have scaled back their support. Those that began with restrictive definitions narrowed them further. Increasingly, public/social housing has been directed to, or limited to, recipients in "true need"—e.g., single-parent families, the elderly, disabled persons. In some countries, notably Britain, this change has been accompanied by increased incentives for the least-poor residents to purchase their units and become independent home-owners. In other cases, the institutional framework for delivering social housing has been transformed. The result has often been a process described as "residualization," in which the main groups remaining in public housing are those who have no other alternatives.[2] Often, though not always, this process has had a racial dimension, which further widens the gap between social-housing residents and the surrounding society.

Gentrification is the other side of this coin. In jurisdictions where former social-housing tenants have been enabled and encouraged to purchase their homes, the purchasers have generally been from the most secure or least impoverished strata of the tenant population. And the units that have been purchased have been the most desirable. Renovation and resale of such properties increases their prices, though the greatest beneficiaries may not be the original purchasers. The net result has often been a widening gap between the "improving" owner-occupants and the "residual" tenants who could not afford to move out of social housing. And the units which remain under public administration tend to be the least desirable.

Some of the most dramatic changes occurred in **England**, where the 1980 Housing Act established the "Right to Buy": Tenants in council housing or in housing associations could purchase, on very favourable terms, the homes where they had been living. This right had existed prior to the legislation, and as early as 1972 some 45,000 tenants had bought their units. But Margaret Thatcher's Conservative government reduced the obstacles and increased the incentives, with the result that an estimated 1.2 million homes were sold to occupants in the following decade (Harloe 1995, 429). The proportion of owner-occupied dwellings, which had hovered around 50 percent in the 1960s and 1970s, rose to 70% percent in 2001, but has since declined. Private rentals, accounting for barely 10 percent of all occupancies in England in 1980, rose to 18 percent in 2011 (Whitehead 2014, 106).

Proponents of the law saw it as fostering a spirit of ownership and independence. Critics complained that it undermined communities, encouraged speculation (through resale), and left the poorest residents of public housing in a worsened condition. The pace of purchases slowed after 1990, and in 2014 the cumulative total number of buy-outs was estimated around two million (Whitehead 2014, 107). This left approximately four million units of social rental housing still in operation—roughly 18 percent of total housing stock. Over the past three decades ownership of these shifted away from local (council) authorities toward non-profit housing associations, which in 2011 accounted for over 40 percent of all social rentals and 23 percent of new housing completions. The social sector's overall share of *new* housing fell from around 50 percent in the post-war years to just over 10 percent in 2001, but has since risen (ibid., 106–108). Similar trends can be seen in Scotland, where the drop in the proportion of social housing was more precipitous (Robertson and Serpa 2014).

The Netherlands, with the highest proportion of social rental housing of any European state, also experienced a decrease in total occupancies and a trend toward marketization. In 1985, 40 percent of all housing units in the country were in social rental, but by 2009 that figure had fallen to 33 percent. The change was due mainly to growth in the number of owner-occupied dwellings, with private unsubsidized rentals playing an insignificant role. Concurrently, the economic criteria for living in subsidized housing were narrowed; legislation in 2011 established €33,000 as the maximum annual income for resident families. This still left about 40 percent of the country's population eligible for social housing (Houard 2013, 49–51, 67). Social housing in the Netherlands has always been organized through non-profit local associations (*woning corporaties*). Legislation of the 1990s gave these bodies more independence from the state, but also narrowed their mandate to a smaller section of the population. More recently (2015) the associations' powers have been further curtailed.

Amsterdam has been the site of an especially ambitious series of initiatives in social housing. Its Bijlmermeer district was built on the southern outskirts of the city in the 1960s and 1970s, a massive development intended to house

100,000 people. It was planned according to the same modernist principles that defined Regent Park: single-use zoning, massive and uniform high-rise apartment towers, and an insular separation from the rest of the city. By the 1980s, with just half of its residential structures in place, the project was experiencing high vacancy rates. Its population consisted largely of new immigrants. Unemployment, criminal behaviour and social alienation were widespread and municipal authorities began to redefine their objectives and create a new Biljmermeer. It would be economically and spatially diverse, constructed through public-private partnership. Some of the tower blocks were demolished, replaced by a dense network of lower-rise buildings that combined residential units with small workplaces and retail establishments (Wassenberg 2011). Residents of the district took a prominent role in planning its transformation. Middle-income households were attracted to the neighbourhood as purchasers of new market-priced homes (Fainstein 2010, 153–159). A few years later the Slotervaart district of Amsterdam embarked upon a similar program of reconstruction (Saunders 2010, 292–295). In both places diversity, spontaneity and community engagement seem to have produced positive results, but neither project has been in place long enough to support generalized conclusions.

Although public housing in **France** (*habitation à loyer modéré*, or HLM) has encountered many of the problems that other European states have experienced, new construction since 2005 has made this country one of just two in Europe (along with Denmark) where social housing has increased, in both relative and absolute terms, in the new millennium. In 2011 almost 100,000 new social-housing units were constructed, as against 50,000 units demolished or sold to tenants. (Lévy-Vroelant *et al.* 2014b, 124). With 4.2 million occupancies, the sector houses about ten million people, roughly one-sixth of the country's population. Private, occupant-owned housing accounts for about 15 million; that sector's share of total housing has been growing and continues to grow, but at a slightly slower pace than social housing. In recent years the private rental sector has been declining. Much of the older construction "consists of large mono-functional estates, and they concentrate different kinds of problems: rapid dilapidation of the buildings, bad maintenance, social difficulties, and geographical marginalization" (Lévy-Vroelant 2014, 491).

French housing policy encourages social mix and integration, but also divides social housing into three different strata according to income. As well, the great majority of HLM stock is concentrated in a relatively small number of municipalities, especially the largest ones. The largest and most problematic estates are found on the outskirts of Paris. Beginning in the 1970s, neoliberal reforms changed the funding system, shifting some state support away from construction (the "supply side") and into directed subsidies toward families (the "demand side") that were considered vulnerable. As well, the norms for living space were reduced. Since that time social housing has been characterized by greater concentrations of poverty, with immigrant and racial-minority populations being further concentrated in some of the least desirable facilities—tower apartments in suburban districts (*banlieue*) that have been the scene of large-scale rioting on several occasions since the early 1980s (Lévy-Vroelant *et al.* 2014b, 128 ff.). Despite the many shortcomings of HLM housing, in 2014 about 1.5 million households were on waiting-lists to obtain a place (Lévy-Vroelant 2014, 491).

Despite or because of these changes, public housing redevelopment in many Western European cities has simultaneously attempted in various ways to avoid economic and cultural segregation and promote social mix. While social housing policies in France, for example, require tenure mix (Blanc 2010), recent research in three cities by Lelévrier (2013) finds that spatial closeness across income and social groups fails to promote social closeness between newcomer and established population groups. Similarly, while Italian housing policy mandates socially mixed social housing communities, Mugnano and Palvarini (2013) find no evidence that this policy promoted social interaction. The Netherlands also boasts policies supporting mixed tenure housing to foster socially cohesive, mixed income communities. But research in that country by Bolt and van Kempen (2008) found evidence that social mix is beneficial to middle class residents without benefitting low-income ones. Some observers (Fainstein 2010) have drawn cautiously optimistic conclusions about Amsterdam's efforts in Bijlmemeer and Slotervart, but other researchers are more critical (Uitermark and Bosker 2014). If the two Amsterdam projects *are* making headway, they seem to be isolated exceptions to a generally negative picture.

US Experience Post-1980

In the United States, as in Canada, the scale of public housing and the role of the national government in supporting it have never come near the levels of Britain, France or the Netherlands. But for this very reason, the American experience may be more directly relevant to Canada's choices and policies, and warrants closer attention.

As in Canada, enthusiasm and support for public housing, especially large-scale family-oriented "projects," declined from already-low levels in the last decades of the twentieth century. As early as 1973 President Richard Nixon put a temporary freeze on new federal funding for public housing under the Department of Housing and Urban Development (HUD); it was lifted a year or two later, but planners and legislators became more and more reluctant to continue past practice which had, in many jurisdictions, produced disappointing results. From the late 1970s to 2002, HUD's authorized budget (expressed in constant dollars) fell by 59 percent. Expressed as a percentage of the total federal budget, HUD's share fell from 5–8 percent in the 1970s to less than 2 percent thereafter (Dolbeare and Crowley 2002, 5, 16).

In 1974 the Congress passed a Housing and Community Development Act, Section 8 of which introduced the idea of channelling HUD funding directly to low-income citizens, in the form of portable or semi-portable vouchers that could (sometimes) be used to subsidize rental of private-sector housing. Tenants were allowed find their own housing, with or without the assistance of local housing authorities, thereby avoiding the concentrated poverty found in large public housing facilities. They would be obliged to pay 30 percent of their income for rent, while the voucher would—subject to review and approval—cover the difference between that sum and market rent. In the following years HUD continued to support housing construction on a limited scale, along with repair and rehabilitation of older projects, but the voucher program became a central part of the HUB mandate.

Ever since the Wagner-Steagall Act, federal support for low-income housing had been channelled through local agencies, with mixed results. Now, in the face of abundant evidence of persistent poverty and housing need, many of these began to look for new ways of dealing with these issues, including demolishing "the projects" and dispersing their inhabitants. Their concern was not only that the older, large-scale projects such as Chicago's Cabrini-Green were badly serving their tenants' needs, but that they were often an obstacle to redevelopment/gentrification of surrounding areas. Developers and investors were reluctant to build new (market-level) housing or retail facilities close to places where more prosperous citizens feared to tread. If public-housing neighbourhoods could be made more attractive and less intimidating, this could promote a larger urban transformation. Properly organized, such a change might also improve the lives of public-housing tenants. But because most of the older social housing was built with federal funding, and because further federal funding—albeit on a smaller scale than in the 1960s—was still an essential ingredient in redevelopment, HUD continued to play a major role in most cities' plans.

Until the 1980s HUD would not approve demolition of public housing unless a one-for-one replacement plan was prepared. This policy began to change during the administration of President Ronald Reagan, when the one-for-one rule was first breached. By this time local public housing administrations in many cities were seeking permission to tear down older units, especially of the tower variety, and to develop mixed-income housing in their place. They argued that the older housing stock had deteriorated to a point beyond repair: The cost of refurbishing buildings would exceed the price of demolishing and replacing them. Tenants in a number of cities including Washington D.C., Bridgeport, Kansas City and El Paso complained that this was a strategy to drive them out, and that the poor state of the units was caused by deliberate neglect: The housing authorities were failing to carry out necessary repairs, and were leaving large numbers of units vacant, in order to create conditions in which demolition would appear inevitable. This argument of "de facto demolition" or "demolition by design" was presented in a series of lawsuits in the later 1980s and early 1990s, in some of which the tenants as plaintiffs won their case—either through a court decision or an out-of-court settlement (Goetz 2013, 53–60).

In 1995, as a result of negotiations between HUD and the Congress, the replacement rule was conclusively laid to rest. This was part of an overall transformation of HUD's mandate (Cisneros 1996, 9). Three years earlier that agency had launched the HOPE VI (Homeownership and Opportunity for People Everywhere)[3] initiative, intended to redevelop the most severely distressed public housing projects. HOPE VI provided grants to support demolition, rehabilitation, reconfiguration, or replacement of obsolete or severely distressed public housing projects. HUD would now channel funding to cities on a competitive basis, using four criteria: there must be a need for redevelopment, there must be the capacity of the local housing authority to see the project through to completion, there must be a quality plan, and the project must have the potential to leverage other capital (Goetz 2010, 139). But instead of guaranteeing displaced tenants a right to return, HOPE VI offered them a range of other choices, with particular emphasis on Section 8 vouchers. In 2010 HOPE VI was replaced by a program called Choice Neighbourhoods, with a similar mandate.

Over two decades these programs have produced an impressive scale of transformation. Lauded in some quarters as an antidote to "the awful, corrosive impact of intensely concentrated poverty and [its] dehumanizing low standards and expectations"[4] (Goetz 2013, 103–104), HOPE VI's accomplishments have also been seen as a "full-scale attack on public housing… employed as a means of eliminating entire communities of poor black residents" (ibid., 110). Arguments pro and con have focused on two fundamental issues: the Right of Return and how it was (or wasn't) exercised by displaced public-housing tenants; and the effects of social mix in the communities that replaced former public housing.

Right of Return

In the US, the Right of Return was promised to public housing tenants who were displaced in the US HOPE VI program redevelopment's public housing redevelopment initiatives. A panel study evaluating eight HOPE VI sites across the US conducted by Abt Associates and the Urban Institute on various aspects of that program concluded that by 2002 displaced tenants' rate of return—while quite variable from project to project—was overall quite low, at 14 percent (Buron *et al.* 2002). Addressing that variability in rates of return more recently in projects across the country, Popkin (2010) reported a range from less than 10 percent to 75 percent, but observed that the higher percentages of return were more likely to have been reported for sites that had been rehabilitated rather than razed and rebuilt (ibid., 58). In those rehabilitated sites, presumably, the burden on tenants to relocate would have been less than in the sites of demolition and rebuilding.

Much of the research on Right of Return has focused on two cities—Chicago and Atlanta—that were at the forefront of the changes that HOPE VI promoted. Both have been extensively studied by planners, sociologists and economists, but the conclusions these experts reached have been widely divergent.

Chicago's *Plan for Transformation* (CHA 2000) has been one of the US's largest redevelopment initiatives. It was drawn up after many years of controversy, including tenant lawsuits, abortive attempts at redevelopment, and a four-year interval (1995–1999) during which HUD exercised stewardship over the "dysfunctional" local housing authority (Goetz 2013, 81). The new plan proposed to renovate or demolish more than 25,000 housing units, replacing income-segregated tower projects with low-and mixed-rise, mixed-income communities of a New Urbanist design. The targeted neighbourhoods were, without question, sites of what William Julius Wilson has termed concentrated racialized poverty (Wilson 1987). The goal was to re-house residents in more diverse neighbourhoods and, on the old sites, create new communities on a different basis. Original residents were supposed to have a Right of Return to their rebuilt communities, but critics questioned whether this stated objective was really a smoke-screen for a different agenda: to gentrify these neighbourhoods and disperse the racially segregated African American low-income populations living there.[5]

The Chicago plan included four housing components. In addition to the new mixed-income units that replaced some aging public housing projects, a second group of older occupancies was renovated and continued as public housing. As well, the Housing Authority continued to offer subsidized units in small-scale housing scattered through the city. Fourth, a significant number of tenants whose previous homes were demolished were offered vouchers that would subsidize their rent in private rental accommodations. Along with these arrangements, the plan proposed to expand the social supports available to tenants, with the aim of building self-sufficiency. This was coupled with stricter occupancy requirements, designed to weed out criminal and anti-social behaviour (CHA).[6] With regard to these limitations, it could be argued that Chicago's system ends up housing less "residual" elements of the population, by excluding the most marginal or difficult cases.

Writing in 2004, Venkatesh and Celimli indicated that although some 75 percent of CHA households displaced in the *Chicago Plan for Transformation* had indicated a desire to return to their rebuilt neighbourhood, an estimated fewer than 20 percent would likely have that option (Venkatesh and Celimli 2004). As evaluated more recently by Graves and Vale, a comprehensive review of the extensive research on that project indicated that while the original project buildings have been demolished, the *Plan for Transformation* has failed to deliver on the social objective of returning original residents to rebuilt neighbourhoods. By their report, between 1999 and 2007 just 2,100 of 27,000 eligible households were able to exercise their Right of Return to the redeveloped neighbourhoods where they formerly resided (Graves and Vale 2012, 264). According to other sources, an additional 7,500—about 40 percent of them senior citizens—were relocated to other CHA developments, and about 2,500 to CHA scattered-site housing. A further 3,000 received vouchers to subsidize rental elsewhere. In sum, slightly more than 50 percent of the households living under CHA jurisdiction in 1999 were still in some form of CHA- or HOPE VI-supported housing in 2007. Almost half of the original households had left.[7] In a more recent publication, summarizing Chicago's new approach to managing its public housing, Edward Goetz wrote acerbically: "If public housing is dead, it is Chicago that killed it" (2013, 75).

A few years earlier, the Atlanta (GA) Housing Authority (AHA) embarked upon a similar initiative, aiming to replace 6,418 rental public housing units with 5,837 mixed-income occupancies, of which 2,256 would be for public-housing-eligible families (Boston 2005, 395). As in Chicago, the new units were part of a large-scale urban transformation that included massive investment in surrounding areas (Vale 2013, 90–154). Displaced families that were unable to return to their original neighbourhoods would receive vouchers for rental housing elsewhere. Thomas Boston (2005) used AHA data to trace the experiences of one cohort ("the treatment group") of displaced households from 1995 to 2001 and compare it to a control group of households that were not displaced. Attrition in both groups over the period was around 50 percent. Among those who remained within the AHA system, Boston found that just 17 percent of the displaced were able to return to the new mixed-income developments, while 60 percent used vouchers to obtain other housing. In the control group, 63 percent remained in their original housing at the end of the seven-year period, and 24 percent took vouchers to move away. Boston found that, for both groups, socioeconomic status—by several measures including employment and mean income—improved for households who moved with vouchers, and for those who moved into mixed-income communities. But for those who stayed in conventional public housing, and for households from the treatment group who moved into other public housing instead of taking vouchers, there was little improvement. Boston concluded that "households relocated out of public housing experienced more positive outcomes than households who continued to live in conventional housing projects" (ibid., 405).

Edward Goetz offered a rebuttal to Boston's findings, pointing out that, for Atlanta's HOPE VI program of demolition and reconstruction to be judged a success, the overall differences between the treatment group and the control group should have been greater. He also argued that families who moved with vouchers achieved only moderate improvement in their living circumstances:

> most do not escape low-income neighbourhoods altogether. Many do not even escape high-poverty neighbourhoods… The neighbourhoods that can provide the most benefits to poor households are off-limits… either because those communities will not accept replacement affordable units or because the market will not allow for the use of vouchers.
>
> (Goetz 2005, 409)

Boston, replying to this criticism, reiterated that any movement out of the concentrated poverty of public housing had been shown to have beneficial effects. This discussion leads to the related issue of social mix, and of the advantages to low-income families of living close to, or together with, more well-to-do neighbours.

Social Mix

One of the premises of HOPE VI and related programs is that socio-economic integration will be beneficial to poor people who previously lived in concentrated poverty in public housing. The Chicago Housing Authority defines its mission as "to build and strengthen communities by integrating public housing and its leaseholders into the larger social, economic and physical fabric of Chicago" (Chaskin and Joseph 2015, 4). Such integration, if successful, would provide low-income residents with social models, social networks and social capital that would enable/encourage them to improve their own lives through, for example, education and employment; the proximity of higher-income residents would "lead to higher levels of accountability to norms and rules through increased informal social control," and "generate new market demand and political pressure to which external political and economic actors are more likely to respond, leading to higher quality goods and services available to all residents" (Joseph, Chaskin and Webber 2007, 373). Concretely, this demand might affect policing or the quality of schools, or municipal services such as street-cleaning and garbage collection.

Research in a number of different socially-mixed US housing projects redeveloped under the HOPE VI program, finds little positive social interaction between the residents from various income groups.

Many US projects have attempted to bring together middle- and low-income residents in newly-built neighbourhoods where large-scale public housing previously stood. Researchers have evaluated the extent to which social mix, in the form of social interaction among those income groups, has occurred. Evidence from studies in various localities suggests that interaction among mixed housing populations occurs only on a very limited scale. Graves's recent study in Boston (Graves 2011), for instance, revealed how bureaucratic requirements—such as segregating parking areas by tenure, and enforcing restrictions on "loitering"—served as impediments to cross-class social interaction. Also in Boston, Tach's (2009) ethnographic research examined community involvement by residents at various income levels, finding that the original lower income residents were more active in such community work than previous researchers had posited, while middle-class neighbours showed less interest. Research by Joseph and Chaskin (Joseph and Chaskin 2010) in a number of different socially-mixed US housing projects redeveloped under the HOPE VI program, finds little positive social interaction between the residents from various income groups. In a more recent and comprehensive study of three Chicago communities, these two authors have reached a similar conclusion: Although moving from public housing into mixed neighbourhoods has brought some improvement to the lives of low-income residents, they still experience "incorporated exclusion" from the wider communities in which they are now located:

> While relocated public housing residents often express familiarity and general connection to the overall neighbourhood… for the most part they have not become engaged in its activities. Nor, besides enjoying relatively safer and better-designed surroundings, have they been able to benefit from the changes in these neighbourhoods to improve their economic conditions. We also find little evidence of inclusionary democracy.
>
> (Chaskin and Joseph 2015, 216)

The HOPE VI housing strategy results in temporary displacement for many low-income households, significantly affecting the lives of residents. Much research centres on tracking residents as they move, instead of understanding their lives at the original site. Manzo, Kleit, and Couch (2008) who did look at residents' sense of community at the original public housing site, found that residents had very strong bonds of support with neighbours, contrary to the popular negative stereotypes about public housing projects. Manzo *et al.* recommend a re-visioning of how public housing projects are to be redeveloped, acknowledging the place attachment of residents whose communities must go through redevelopment. They further recommend that evaluations of HOPE VI redevelopments include staff perspectives on residents' experiences handling relocation. Gibson (2007) provided an example, looking at a public housing project in Portland, Oregon called Columbia Villa, which was set to be redeveloped. She found that although it was labelled as one of the worst public housing projects, residents had formed strong bonds, felt safe, and forged an inclusive community. Compared with many other HOPE VI projects, this one had a high rate of return after redevelopment, with only some 33 percent of original residents deciding not to return, either because they were satisfied with their new housing accommodation or not willing to move again.

Consistent with Gibson's findings, Goetz also argued that while relocation away from dilapidated public housing projects can aid in the reduction of residents' stress and fear related to crime and disorder, it also disrupts social support systems that are particularly important to low-income families. He reported that

> The HOPE VI record for most of the original residents is of limited and inconsistent benefits. Their moves to marginally better neighbourhoods leave them feeling safer on average, but do not consistently generate other material benefits.
>
> (Goetz 2010, 152)

The HOPE VI strategy is intended to redevelop public housing, but Hanlon (2012) argues that the demolition/disposition activities have resulted in luxury condominiums replacing public housing, and ultimately the loss of over 210,000 units of public housing stock. Demolition and disposition procedures are not programs. In some jurisdictions they have exceeded the mandate of HOPE VI and avoided the requirement of replacing at least some units of public housing. Hanlon concludes that more capital funds must be made available to maintain the current housing stock, as well as funding to redevelop and increase the housing stock. While this need is apparent, municipalities are faced with this dilemma worldwide as securing funding is a significant challenge almost everywhere.

The evolution of New York City's public housing system since 1990, described by Nicholas Bloom (2010) as "public housing that works," offers an instructive contrast to the policies followed in Chicago and Atlanta. The New York City Housing Authority (NYCHA), with direct responsibility for about 420,000 tenants, is by far the largest body of its kind in North America. Faced with many of the problems that have been described in other localities, including crime, vandalism, and deterioration of physical plant, the NYCHA has chosen to renovate existing tower buildings and redefine the target population. In Bloom's account, the Authority has put more emphasis upon community revitalization than demolition, with only a minuscule number of apartments being lost to the system. Instead, "renovated apartments are now indistinguishable from private market rentals in every way except cost" (Bloom 2008, 267). The renovation program has emphasized improvement of community amenities and landscaping, as well as improved repair services to tenants. Bloom puts particular emphasis on efficient management, under rigorous supervision; he contrasts New York City's long experience and expertise in this area with the performance of housing authorities in most other American cities. The physical environment has been reshaped to promote safety and community use, and thereby reduce crime.[8] This has been done in the context of a transition from what Bloom terms "welfare-state public housing"—a model that had prevailed from the late 1960s to the early 1990s—to "affordable housing" that

> serves the working poor rather than the poorest or welfare tenants. Not only are these working-poor tenants able to cover a more reasonable proportion of the cost, but also their behavior is, with some justification, considered to be superior to the welfare underclass.
>
> (ibid., 246)

Bloom describes this change as a return to the mission of public housing as first conceived in the city in the 1930s. Attracting "working poor" families to public housing does not mean excluding poorer tenants, who still account for a majority of occupancies. But it does mean applying stricter standards of admissibility and conduct, excluding any tenants who engage in criminal or antisocial behaviour. Crime has not been eliminated from NYCHC's buildings, but rates of criminality seem to be declining. Bloom describes the Authority's emphasis on control as "a sufficient, if regrettable, substitute for the multiple sources of authority one finds in a typical urban neighbourhood" (ibid., 266)—preferable to the lawlessness that has often disrupted public housing communities.

Canadian Public Housing Policy Since the 1980s

During the last decades of the twentieth century and the first years of the new millennium, governmental support for public housing has shown an overall decline, but without including dramatic new initiatives comparable to Britain's "Right to Buy" or the US's HOPE VI. In the early 1970s the Liberal federal government of Pierre Elliott Trudeau phased out CMHC funding for construction of new public housing of the Regent Park type, but in 1974 created new funding directed at "third sector"—non-profit and cooperative—providers of affordable housing (Bacher 1993, 227). Mixed-income cooperatives in particular operated as independent self-governing entities in which some proportion of units was reserved for subsidized low-income tenants, while the rest were occupied by better-off households paying close to market rent.[9] From the early 1970s to the 1990s, CMHC subsidized non-profit cooperatives by providing start-up grants and mortgages well below market interest rates. The 1973 federal legislation on co-ops included the following among their purposes: "to house mainly families whose incomes may be too high for public housing; and to encourage the integration of families and individuals of varying incomes" (CMHC 1990a, 3). In neighbourhoods such as Toronto's St. Lawrence, such co-ops provided an impressive record of stability and community integration (Hayes 2009). Nonetheless CMHC support for this sector was cut and ultimately terminated.

The Progressive Conservative government of Brian Mulroney, which came to power in 1984, steadily lowered the scale of support for new social housing construction. The number of units funded dropped from 31,200 in 1980 to 15,000 in 1990 and 8,200 in 1993. The ongoing costs of public housing were a major concern. A CMHC report published in 1990 surveyed the state of public housing across the country, and concluded that most of it was in a satisfactory state of repair; only 4 percent of units did not meet Minimum Property Standards. The system would, however, require approximately $350 million for repair and replacement, plus $133 million for additions and upgrades. Total expenditures in the program in 1986 had been approximately $1.1 billion, and revenues were around $500 million, resulting in a deficit of $600 million. CMHC's share of this sum amounted to $329 million or $1,698 per unit (CMHC 1990b, 274–287). Besides giving capital construction grants, CMHC was empowered to undertake long-term contractual commitments to subsidize existing public and social housing, with the result that future federal governments inherited unbreakable budgetary obligations that reached $1.9 billion by the mid-1990s and will continue well into the twenty-first century (Pomeroy and Falvo 2013, 3).

In 1992 support for co-operative housing was eliminated from the federal budget (Dreier and Hulchanski 1993, 46). The Liberal Party, which in opposition had criticized this and related cuts, did not reinstate the housing program when it became the governing party in 1993. Instead, in the context of an across-the-board program of deficit reduction, Jean Chrétien's Liberal government moved to transfer all housing responsibilities to provincial governments (Pomeroy and Falvo 2013, 4). Some additional federal funding for housing was added between 2001 and 2006. The successor Conservative government of Stephen Harper showed little interest in supporting social or public housing.

Support for public or social housing from the Province of Ontario followed an up-and-down course. As early at 1988 the *Toronto Star* described a confidential federal-provincial report that was said to be under consideration, proposing an overhaul of the social-housing portfolio. It used the phrase "locational obsolescence" to describe older downtown public housing sites such as Regent Park, on land that was attractive to private developers: "Land values may have risen to the point that public housing is no longer 'the highest and best use,' for the site and it may be advantageous to sell part or all of the project site…" (*Toronto Star* 1988).

The report seems never to have been released, and the (Liberal) government of the day took no action in the proposed direction.

The next provincial government—of the left-leaning New Democratic Party, led by Bob Rae—took steps to support cooperative and non-profit social housing when federal aid stopped. But that government's range of action was constrained by economic recession. And meanwhile the cost of maintaining existing projects such as Regent Park continued to weigh on the provincial and municipal budgets. In 1995, financial consultant KPMG reported that the Metropolitan Toronto Housing Authority, which administered 110 Toronto public housing properties on behalf of the Ontario Housing Corporation, needed $223 million to overcome a backlog of necessary maintenance. Without new expenditures, aging buildings would soon become uninhabitable. Yet the agency's annual revenue was just $90 million. The consultant recommended selling off some of the MTHA's properties, including at least part of Regent Park (Wright 1995).

The Rae government that commissioned the report was defeated in a general election before it could respond. But the successor Conservative government of Mike Harris soon took more drastic steps to remove public housing from the provincial budget. As part of its "common sense revolution" program of cutting taxes and reducing expenditures, the Harris government withdrew from the field of public/social housing and devolved all responsibility to 47 local agencies, among them the Toronto Community Housing Corporation, an amalgam the MTHA with two other agencies that operated social housing in the municipality of Toronto. This set the stage for a reconsideration of the place of public housing in Toronto, and of the future of Regent Park.

Notes

1 By way of comparison, Scottish authorities early developed two tiers of council housing and social housing, with the latter intended for lower-income groups—a distinction that has had long-term consequences (Malpass 2014, 283).

2 "… as higher income households advance into ownership, the residual group is becoming more marginalized from both the labour and housing market. That is, renters are becoming less able to find and retain employment and housing without some level of government support." (CMHC 2001, 1).
3 This acronym was first used for a program called HOPE I during the Reagan administration.
4 Goetz is quoting Renee Glover, former head of the Atlanta Housing Authority.
5 This controversy is the subject of a 2015 feature documentary film, *70 Acres in Chicago*, by Ronit Bezalel and Catherine Crouch, documenting the Cabrini-Green redevelopment on the Near North Side of the city.
6 Criteria in the CHA's Minimum Tenant Selection Plan (MTSP) included the following: requirements relating to tenants' status as working (a minimum of 120 hours per month by household head) or equivalent activity including job-training or other education; limitations on the amount of household debt and past history of bankruptcy or rent default; no criminal record over past three years; no, drug or alcohol abuse (CHA MTSP). Additionally, many management functions were turned over to private contractors, who could apply additional criteria (Berg 2004, 2).
7 Vale and Graves, citing unpublished research by Thomas D. Boston, report the following reasons for departure from CHA-supported housing: 3,008 illness or death (mainly from elder housing); 3,256 moved to other jurisdictions; 2,425 skipped or moved without giving notice; 1,399 evicted (Vale and Graves 2010, 9).
8 Significantly, the changes listed by Bloom include the closing of through streets and replanting of formerly paved areas (ibid., 258)—a strategy precisely opposite to that adopted in the redevelopment of Regent Park.
9 Non-profit co-ops operate under legislation similar to that which governs condominiums. In co-ops, however, the individual members (share-owners) do not have ownership of their units or equity in the overall cooperative. Managerial supervision is entrusted to an elected board, which sets the rental rates and is responsible for arranging an annual audit and holding periodic meetings of the full membership. When members leave, their shares revert to the co-op, with no monetary gain. The board of the cooperative can then advertise the unit and bring in a new member. Unlike condominiums, cooperatives typically rely on committees of members to perform many management and maintenance tasks, including member selection and sometimes repairs.

References

Bacher, John C. 1993. *Keeping to the Marketplace: The Evolution of Canadian Housing Policy*. Montreal: McGill-Queens University Press.

Berg, Kristine. 2004. "Implementing Chicago's Plan to Transform Public Housing." Paper presented to The Changing Face of Metropolitan Chicago, Conference on Chicago Research and Public Policy. citeseerx.ist.psu.edu/viewdoc/download?doi=10.1.1.511.1556&rep=rep1&type=pdf. (Accessed December 21, 2015).

Blanc, Maurice. 2010. "The Impact of Social Mix Policies in France." *Housing Studies* 25(2): 257–272.

Bloom, Nicholas Dagen. 2008. *Public Housing that Worked: New York in the Twentieth Century*. Philadelphia: University of Pennsylvania Press.

Bolt, Gideon, Ronald van Kempen and Maarten van Ham. 2008. "Minority ethnic groups in the Dutch housing market: Spatial segregation, relocation dynamics and housing policy." *Urban Studies* 45(7): 1359–1384.

Boston, Thomas D. 2005. "The Effects of Revitalization on Public Housing Residents: A Case Study of the Atlanta Housing Authority." *Journal of the American Planning Association* 71(4): 393–407.

Buron, Larry, Susan J. Popkin, Diane Levy, Laura E. Harris and Jill Khadduri. 2002. "The HOPE VI Resident Tracking Study: A Snapshot of the Current Living Situation of Original Residents in Eight Sites." The Urban Institute. (November). www.urban.org/UploadedPDF/410591_HOPEVI_ResTrack.pdf. (Accessed March 15, 2015).

Chaskin, Robert J. and Mark L. Joseph. 2015. *Integrating the Inner City: The Promise and Perils of Mixed-Income Public Housing Transformation*. Chicago and London: University of Chicago Press.

Chicago Housing Authority (CHA). ND. "Minimum Tenant Selection Plan." www.thecha.org/file.aspx?DocumentId=1209. (Accessed June 23, 2016).

Chicago Housing Authority (CHA). ND. "Plan for Transformation." www.thecha.org/about/plan-for-transformation. (Accessed June 23, 2016).

Cisneros, Henry G. 1996. *Renewing America's Communities from the Ground Up: The Plan to Complete the Transformation of HUD*. Collingdale, PA: Diane Publishing.

CMHC (Canada Mortgage and Housing Corporation). 1990a. *Consultation Paper on the Federal Cooperative Housing Program*.

CMHC (Canada Mortgage and Housing Corporation). 1990b. *Public Housing Program: Program Evaluation Report*.

CMHC (Canada Mortgage and Housing Corporation). 2001. "Residualization of Rental Tenure: Attitudes of Private Landlords Toward Low-Income Households." Research Highlight. Socio-economic Series 93.

Dolbeare, Cushing N. and Sheila Crowley. 2002. "Changing Priorities: The Federal Budget and Housing Assistance, 1976–2007." Washington, DC: National Low-Income Housing Coalition.

Dreier, Peter and David Hulchanski. 1993. "The Role of Nonprofit Housing in Canada and the United States: Some Comparisons." *Housing Policy Debate* 4(1): 43–80.

Elsinga, Marja and Frank Wassenberg. 2014. "Social Housing in the Netherlands." In *Social Housing in Europe*, Ed. Kathleen Scanlon, Christine Whitehead and Melissa Fernández Arrigoitia. Chichester: John Wiley & Sons.

Fainstein, Susan. 2010. *The Just City*. Ithaca: Cornell University Press.

Gibson, Karen J. 2007. "The relocation of the Columbia Villa community: Views from residents." *Journal of Planning, Education, and Research* 27(1): 5–19.

Glendenning, Miles and Stefan Muthesius. 1994. *Tower Block: Modern Public Housing in England, Scotland, Wales and Northern Ireland*. New Haven: Yale University Press.

Goetz, Edward G. 2005. "Comment: Public housing demolition and the benefits to low-income families." *Journal of the American Planning Association* 71(4): 407–410.

Goetz, Edward G. 2010. "Desegregation in 3D: Displacement, dispersal and development in American public housing." *Housing Studies* 25(2): 137–158.

Goetz, Edward G. 2013. *New Deal Ruins: Race, Economic Justice, and Public Housing Policy*. Ithaca, NY: Cornell University Press.

Graves, Erin M. 2011. "Mixed outcome developments: Comparing policy goals to resident outcomes in mixed-income housing." *Journal of the American Planning Association* 77(2): 143–153.

Graves, Erin M. and Lawrence J. Vale. 2012. "The Chicago Housing Authority's plan for transformation: assessing the first ten years." *Journal of the American Planning Association* 78(4): 464–465.

Hanlon, James. 2012. "Beyond HOPE VI: Demolition/Disposition and the uncertain future of public housing in the U.S." *Journal of Housing and the Built Environment* 27: 373–388.

Harloe, Michael. 1995. *The People's Home? Social Rented Housing in Europe and America*. Oxford: Blackwell.

Hayes, David. 2009. "Housing coop still thriving 30 years later." *Toronto Star* November 24.

Holmans, Alan E. 2005. *Historical Statistics of Housing in Great Britain*. Cambridge: Cambridge Centre for Housing and Planning Research.

Houard, Noemie. 2013. "Le Logement Social aux Pays Bas." *OFCE* 2(128): 49–72.

Joseph, Mark L., Robert J. Chaskin and Henry S. Webber. 2007. "The theoretical basis for addressing poverty through mixed-income development." *Urban Affairs Review* 42(3): 369–409.

Joseph, Mark L. and Robert J. Chaskin. 2010. "Living in a mixed-income development: Resident perceptions of the benefits and disadvantages of two developments in Chicago." *Urban Studies* 47(11): 2347–2366.

Lees, Loretta. 2014. "The Urban Injustices of New Labour's 'New Urban Renewal': The Case of the Aylesbury Estate in London." *Antipode* 46(4): 921–947.

Lelévrier, Christine. 2013. "Forced relocation in France: how residential trajectories affect individual experiences." *Housing Studies* 28(2): 253–271.

Lévy-Vroelant, Claire. 2014. "Contradictory Narratives on French Social Housing: Looking Back and Looking Forward." *Housing Studies* 29(4): 485–500.

Lévy-Vroelant, Claire, Christoph Reinprecht, Douglas Robertson and Frank Wassenberg. 2014a. "Learning from History: Path Dependency and Change in the Social Housing Sectors of Austria, France, the Netherlands and Scotland, 1889–2013." In *Social Housing in Europe*, Ed. Kathleen Scanlon, Christine Whitehead and Melissa Fernández Arrigoitia. Chichester: John Wiley & Sons.

Lévy-Vroelant, Claire, Jean-Pierre Schaefer and Christian Tutin. 2014b. "Social Housing in France." In *Social Housing in Europe*, Ed. Kathleen Scanlon, Christine Whitehead and Melissa Fernández Arrigoitia. Chichester: John Wiley & Sons.

Malpass, Peter. 2014. "Histories of Social Housing: A Comparative Approach." In *Social Housing in Europe*, Ed. Kathleen Scanlon, Christine Whitehead and Melissa Fernández Arrigoitia. Chichester: John Wiley & Sons.

Manzo, Lynne C., Rachel Garshick Kleit and Dawn Couch. 2008. "'Moving three times is like having your house on fire once': The experience of place and impending displacement among public housing residents of a public housing site". *Urban Studies* 45(9): 1855–1878.

Marcuse, Peter. 1995. "Interpreting 'Public Housing' History." *Journal of Architectural and Planning Research* 12(3): 240–258.

Miron, John. 1988. *Housing in Postwar Canada: Demographic Change, Household Formation and Housing Demand*. Kingston and Montreal: McGill-Queens University Press.

Mugnano, Silvia and Pietro Palvarini. 2013. "Sharing space without hanging together: A case study of social mix policy in Milan". *Cities* 35(1): 417–422.

Pomeroy, Steve and Nick Falvo. 2013. "Housing Policy in Canada Under the Harper Regime." Presented to the European Network for Housing Research, June 2013. www.google.ca/search?q=pomeroy+falco+2013&ie=utf-8&oe=utf-8&gws_rd=cr&ei=nfGbV4-iAcnEjwTJ7LDYBQ#q=european+network+for+housing+research+2013+pomeroy. (Accessed July 29, 2016).

Popkin, Susan J. 2010. "A glass half empty? New evidence from the HOPE VI panel study." *Housing Policy Debate* 20(1): 43–63.
Radford, Gail. 1996. *Modern Housing for America: Policy Struggles in the New Deal Era*. Chicago: University of Chicago Press.
Redmond, Declan and Michelle Norris. 2014. "Social Housing in the Republic of Ireland." In *Social Housing in Europe*, Ed. Kathleen Scanlon, Christine Whitehead and Melissa Fernández Arrigoitia. Chichester: John Wiley & Sons.
Robertson, Douglas and Regina Serpa. 2014. "Social Housing in Scotland." In *Social Housing in Europe*, Ed. Kathleen Scanlon, Christine Whitehead and Melissa Fernández Arrigoitia. Chichester: John Wiley & Sons.
Sewell, John. 1994. *Houses and Homes: Housing for Canadians*. Toronto: James Lorimer and Co.
Stoloff, Jennifer A. 2004. "A Brief History of Public Housing." Washington, D.C.: US Department of Housing and Urban Development. Paper presented at the annual meeting of the American Sociological Association, San Francisco, CA. reengageinc.org/research/brief_history_public_housing.pdf.
Tach, Laura. 2009. "More than bricks and mortar: Neighbourhood frames, social processes, and the mixed-income redevelopment of a public housing project." *City and Community* 8(3): 269–299.
Toronto Star. 1988. "Is Ontario set to privatize public housing?" September 23: A27.
Uitermark, Justus and Tjerk Bosker. 2014. "Wither the 'Undivided City'? An Assessment of State-Sponsored Gentrification in Amsterdam." *Tijdschrift voor Ekonomische en Sociale Geografie* 105(2): 221–230.
US Supreme Court. *King v. Smith, 392 US 309 (1968)*. supreme.justia.com/cases/federal/us/392/309/case.html. (Accessed April 11, 2016).
Vale, Lawrence J. 2013. *Purging the Poorest: Public Housing and the Design Politics of Twice-cleared Communities*. Chicago and London: University of Chicago Press.
Vale, Lawrence J. and Erin M. Graves. 2010. "The Chicago Housing Authority's Plan for Transformation: What Does the Research Show So Far?" Final Report, June 8, 2010. John D. and Catherine T. MacArthur Foundation. Department of Urban Studies and Planning, Massachusetts Institute of Technology.
Venkatesh, Sudhir A. and Isil Celimli. 2004. "Tearing down the community." National Housing Institute (NHI). *Shelterforce*. www.nhi.org/online/issues/138/chicago.html. (Accessed January 10, 2017).
von Hoffman, Alexander. 2005. "The End of the Dream: The Political Struggle of America's Public Housers." *Journal of Planning History* 4(3): 222–253.
Wade, Jill. 1984. "Wartime Housing Limited, 1941–1947: an overview and evaluation of Canada's first national housing corporation." Master's thesis, History, University of British Columbia.
Wassenberg, Frank. 2011. "Demolition in the Bijlmermeer: Lessons from Transforming a Large Housing Estate." *Building Research & Information* 39(4): 363–79.
Whitehead, Christine. 2014. "Social Housing in England." In *Social Housing in Europe*, Ed. Kathleen Scanlon, Christine Whitehead and Melissa Fernández Arrigoitia. Chichester: John Wiley & Sons.
Wilding, Paul. 1973. "The Housing and Town Planning Act 1919 – A Study in the Making of Social Policy." *Journal of Social Policy* 2(4): 317–334.
Wilson, William J. 1987. *The Truly Disadvantaged: The Inner City, The Underclass, and Public Policy*. Chicago: University of Chicago Press.
Wright, Lisa. 1995. "Regent Park selloff plan eyed: Agency can't pay massive repair bill." *Toronto Star* March 12: A1.

4
A New Regent Park
The Planning Process

At the turn of the millennium, the City of Toronto faced many of the housing problems that other cities have confronted. The need or demand for public housing was at least as great as it had ever been, but the supply had long since stopped growing. Much of the existing stock of public housing was forty or more years old and in deteriorating condition. Existing models of large-scale public housing for families were blamed for ghettoizing poverty and creating new slums in which crime and dysfunctional behaviour flourished. But any attempt to address these problems would be constrained by budget: A succession of governments, both federal and provincial, had made it clear that they would not be providing much—if any—new financial support in this area. Even basic upkeep was in question, since the Ontario government had passed responsibility for social services and housing down to the municipal level.

It was in this context that Derek Ballantyne became the Chief Executive Officer, first of the newly amalgamated Metro Toronto Housing Corporation (1998) and then, with a further merger, of the newly formed Toronto Community Housing Corporation (2002). Responsible for 58,000 public housing occupancies, the organization faced an enormous backlog of overdue repairs and a long waiting list of applicants seeking admission to social housing. Ballantyne and his staff began exploring new ways of coping with these problems:

> I think there was a unique moment, because nobody knew what to do… so there was no hard culture being set or outcomes being asked for other than make this better, generally, see what we can do with this, and make it run. So we were given a lot of latitude in that respect and there was nobody sort of hovering over us.
>
> (Ballantyne, personal communication, April 1, 2015)

Ballantyne describes being surprised by several features of his new portfolio. On one side were the negative attitudes his team encountered from residents of public housing:

> the degree of alienation from community and the degree of separateness from the rest of the city, particularly… [in] the neighbourhoods where public housing was very present, was striking to me… [There was a] kind of binary dependency and dislike for the housing corporation's intermediation in most people's lives. I found it a bit shocking—[that] there wasn't more engagement within those communities with civil society in a broader sense, with communities, with neighbours, with institutions.
>
> (ibid.)

And yet this was only half the story. Those same neighbourhoods—and Regent Park in particular—had resources and experience that could make them receptive to new ideas or new ways of organizing their environment:

> there is a richness of community and a wealth of intelligence in those places… we also think of these communities as communities of deficient social capital and so on but, it isn't really true. Some of the places are very vibrant and interesting and people are looking for ways to engage. So in some ways the response that we had was: How do we capture that energy and intelligence, how do we bring it in as a more constructive force?
>
> (ibid.)

At the same time, having almost no budget to support innovative programs, TCHC officials began exploring various forms of public-private partnership, in order to bring private capital into a system that would, if successful, replace or renovate social housing and put it on a new footing. The lands on which public housing was located were potentially of great interest to investors. Regent Park in particular was situated within walking distance of Toronto's downtown, cheek-by-jowl with neighbourhoods where house prices were soaring. As in Atlanta's Techwood or Chicago's Cabrini-Green areas, private developers were ready to step in. But prior to making any redevelopment plans, the Toronto Community Housing Corporation undertook to assess the Regent Park community's readiness for such an initiative.

Stage 1: Community Consultation

Beginning in 2002 the TCHC employed a consultant team to explore the community's openness to change, its priorities, and its goals in the longer and shorter terms. Ballantyne recalls the reasons for starting by consulting the community, the approach that was taken, and the key message that was conveyed:

> we started it in a series of small conversations and we got to the point where we felt comfortable to go forward and say that we would like to do something here. We did I think a relatively good job with inclusive planning. We brought community voices into the process particularly around framing principles, around framing what the outcome should look like, and we did that by trying to aggregate the community voices, engaging a team of planners whose number one piece in their mandate was: You cannot do what you typically do, which is go back to your office, draw up a pretty picture, and come back and tell us all about it and call that consultation. You can't… You are going to have to talk to the community.
>
> (ibid.)

The researchers who led the consultation acknowledged that the residents of Regent Park had little reason to trust the TCHC's representatives as they set about their work. The neighbourhood had been through several previous rounds of plans and discussions, notably in 1996–1997, which had ultimately come to naught. Tenants were also suspicious that, having surveyed the community, planners and developers would ignore community advice and build to their own preferences. Many residents feared that, once displaced, they would be unable to return. For a consultation exercise to produce meaningful results, it would have to be an iterative process that could win the confidence of residents. Survey questionnaires and public meetings alone would not produce such a result. Instead, the consultants (the Community Engagement Team) recruited a team of 28 facilitators, mostly from within Regent Park, to serve as "community animators." They were chosen with an eye to ensuring representation of the main ethnic and cultural groups in the population. Their mandate, as the report describes it, was not just to inform community members of a plan for redevelopment, but to engage them in devising such a plan:

> Community-based workers would not be effective if they were simply employed as a friendly face on a standard consultation process. Efforts to mask the process do not engender trust. Employing people with the right colour skin or the right language skills is not sufficient to ensure cultural appropriateness. The process itself had to come from the community. The workers had to "animate" a discussion that was rooted entirely in the community.
>
> (Meagher and Boston 2003, 11)

Through a mix of face-to-face conversations, small group discussions and public meetings, the consultants surveyed residents and key informants to begin to consider what a revitalized community might look like. Ideas were collected, summarized, and brought back for further refinement in the groups that had first put them forward. Every animator's contact groups went through a three-phase series of focused conversations, each more specific than the previous one. Suggestions and complaints were circulated among planners and architects, who attended some of the meetings and participated in the drafting of successive plans. Animators working in different ethno-cultural groups were encouraged to adapt their approaches accordingly; in some, for example, they met separately with men and women. An informal survey of children, through art, proved effective at eliciting their thoughts (ibid., 36). In total, some 2,000 Regent Park residents participated in the exercise (ibid., 5).

The animators did not start with a blank slate. Their mandate was to find out how community members felt about the existing buildings and neighbourhood, how they imagined improving or replacing them, and how they reacted to the idea of building a mixed-income community. Personal security, streetscape, recreation, services and amenities were also on the list for discussion, addressing much of the criticism that for decades had been directed at the old Regent Park.

Residents Emphasize Diversity and Maintaining RGI

Reports from Phase 1 of the consultation indicated that residents were enthusiastic about their community and its diversity, but criticized the lack of facilities and amenities, from daycare and recreation to shopping, places of worship, and even mailboxes and pay phones. They spoke favourably about various community services, but had many complaints about the buildings in which they lived, and the way in which they were being managed. Crime and drugs were also frequently mentioned as concerns, along with a general sense that community safety needed to be improved. Participants in the discussions were receptive to the idea of more open streets. One report observed that "People from the outside neighbourhoods do not know about life inside Regent Park," and others spoke of the stigma that they felt was attached to the community. They accepted the idea of a mix of housing types, noting that market-level properties could be attractive to some families currently living in rent-geared-to-income (RGI) accommodation:

> Informants saw home ownership and market housing, both virtually non-existent in Regent Park, as welcome additions. Residents who found employment and saw their incomes rise found themselves effectively driven from their communities as they ceased to qualify for assisted housing but remained incapable of buying costly homes or paying the high rents in abutting neighbourhoods.
>
> (Meagher and Boston 2003, 41)

Respondents also emphasized that new market-level and RGI buildings should not be distinguishable from one another.

Early in the first phase of consultation, the groups drew up a set of Community Planning Principles that were accepted by TCHC and have been repeatedly cited throughout the subsequent stages of Regent Park redevelopment. Most are broad and imprecise ("design a safe and accessible neighbourhood," "minimize disruption for residents during relocation"), but two were of great potential significance for the development of the plan:

> 6. Create a diverse neighbourhood with a mix of uses including a variety of housing, employment, institutions and services…
> 8. Keep the same number of rent geared to income (RGI) units.
>
> (Regent Park Collaboration Team [RPCT] 2002, 19–20)

Point 6 can be read as an acceptance of the principle of an economically inclusive neighbourhood that contains market-level housing as well as a new array of amenities. Point 8, on the other hand, is a commitment that affordable housing on the same scale as the soon-to-be-demolished Regent Park will be maintained in the new community. Separately, TCHC also agreed to an ironclad Right of Return, so that any resident who was displaced would be able to resettle in Regent Park once new housing was available.

In the second stage of consultation, the agenda became more specific. When asked which buildings they liked and which they thought should be kept, participating residents offered few suggestions: "None" was a frequent answer. On the topic of security, the groups reported that "There were no streets that all groups felt safe on." Looking to the future, respondents were generally in favour of high-rise buildings, but wanted new ones to be safer and more attractive, with more community facilities. Some suggested that a mixture of ownership and rentals could have positive effects: "It would help create a safe building, and rent-to-own was mentioned as an important way of strengthening the community" (Meagher and Boston 2003, 48).

All the groups spoke favourably of busy, well-lit streets, but the idea of restoring a full grid elicited mixed responses, with some expressing strong opposition to through streets. In summarizing the results of this round, the consultants' report emphasized the ways in which it had challenged planners' expectations:

> The design implications were enormous. Through streets could not be a two-lane grid; a network of narrow one-way streets had to dominate. A host of new parkettes was not welcome, but buildings with internally shared courtyards were. A regional park should be placed at the centre of the

community to draw neighbouring communities in, not at the periphery to draw Regent Park residents out.

(ibid., 50)

It is worth noting that the final iteration of the Revitalization Plan, accepted by the consultation groups in the third phase of their work, matched in large measure the proposals that planners and TCHC officials had been contemplating.

Stage 2: The Social Development Plan

In 2004 TCHC commissioned a Social Development survey of services and facilities available to Regent Park residents before redevelopment. Researchers met with residents and with representatives of the various service agencies that were operating in the neighbourhood. It identified areas in which existing services were likely to need expansion, including daycare, skills and job training, and services targeting new immigrants (TCHC 2004). This was followed by a second survey addressing the question of how social inclusion could be achieved and encouraged as redevelopment went forward. The document not only reviewed existing programs, but commented on the potential effects of community associations and governance, faith-based and (immigrant) cultural organizations and informal activities such as community gardens. It recommended that some existing services be extended in order to address the needs of the expanding community; and it called for continuing consultation and full exchange of information between TCHC, residents, stakeholders, and community agencies (TCHC 2007a, 2007b).

Highlights of the New Plan

At the community level, the new plan is designed to overcome the insularity of the old Regent Park and, in an overused cliché, re-knit its successor into the urban fabric. The means for accomplishing this goal are: an altered streetscape; mixed land use; development of new community facilities that will be accessible and attractive to a wider public; and a mixture of housing tenures. The revitalization plan calls for replacing the former cul-de-sac lanes with well-lit through streets, and for new housing to be aligned along those streets. Sidewalks should be wide and streets well-lit (an issue that residents had complained about in the former Regent Park). These changes, the planners hope, will be an encouragement to pedestrian traffic and to more healthy interaction between residents. They may also, by promoting what Jane Jacobs called "eyes on the street," be a deterrent to criminal activity (Jacobs 1961, 35).

The attractiveness of streets will also be enhanced by the presence of retail stores, coffee shops, and related establishments that serve not only the immediate Regent Park vicinity but potentially a wider radius of city-dwellers. Expanded recreational facilities—among them a large indoor Aquatic Centre, a six-acre (2.5 hectare) park, athletic fields, a hockey rink and an arts-and-culture centre—are another attraction. If these innovations have the desired effect, they will make the Regent Park neighbourhood more permeable and, in sociologist Richard Sennett's (2015) term, "porous"—more accessible to outsiders, but also encouraging the community's residents to interact more easily with the wider urban environment and with one another.

Housing design in the new community will be, according to the plan, tenure-blind architecture, a "seamless mix of market oriented and TCHC units both horizontally and vertically" (RPCT 2002, 36). A visitor walking through the street should not be able to distinguish RGI houses from market-priced townhouses or condominium apartment buildings. In place of the uniformity of the old Regent Park, the new dwellings will be of various heights, designed by different architects. (Early drafts of the revitalization plan call for some buildings to include a combination of RGI and market units, but this has not been attempted in the first three phases of construction.[1] Another recommendation, that mixed-income non-profit cooperatives be included in the mix of housing, has also not been implemented in the first stages.) Market units, under the first version of the revitalization plan, would consist of one- and two-bedroom apartments—almost two thousand in all—plus 435 three- and four-bedroom townhouse units (ibid., 94).

The plan calls for RGI families with children to be housed in townhouses or on the ground or lower floors of taller buildings. There should be no more two-storey apartments in the high-rise towers. The new RGI housing will match the old Regent Park by number of rooms, but the rooms may be somewhat smaller in square footage.

Community Involvement

One more important difference between the new Regent Park and its predecessor is the increased emphasis on community involvement. In the 1970s the Ontario Housing Corporation, which was then managing the property, supported—for a time—tenant participation in a Joint Management Board, but this experiment was ended after a few years. Later community initiatives met, at best, half-hearted responses from officialdom in the 1980s and 1990s, and their leaders often found themselves in an adversarial relationship with Regent Park's management (Veronis 1999). But unlike their counterparts in Chicago and some other cities, Toronto's activists did not engage in strikes or confrontational protests. Community groups organized

Figure 4.1 "Consultation": Children playing in Regent Park with cardboard models representing housing units.

Source: L. Veronis

social events, published a newsletter, and took part in an unsuccessful effort to redevelop the northeastern quadrant of Regent Park in the late 1990s.

The collaborative team that drew up the new Revitalization Study and Implementation Plan in 2002–2003, emphasized the importance of long-term resident involvement in the planning and management of the new Regent Park. Their April 2003 Report to TCHC included a section entitled "Lessons from St. Lawrence," describing what they viewed as an outstanding example of a successful mixed-use, mixed-income community nearby in Toronto. Commending that neighbourhood for its stability and successful mix of tenures, and for the flexibility of its long-term development planning, the committee's report concluded with a series of recommendations including the following: a working committee including resident representatives, to advise on the revitalization process; a tenant management structure organized around "community housing units"; promotion of non-profit and cooperative housing as part of the new housing mix; integration of RGI units into non-RGI buildings as much as possible; and efforts by the Regent Park Residents Council to involve new residents in the community (RPCT 2003b, 15).

As the project moved ahead, the housing authority—in cooperation with other city agencies and the local councillor, Pam McConnell—has continued its efforts to inform and involve the Regent Park community in the redevelopment. Many public meetings were held, and were generally well attended. In the first years, when meetings were held in the old Regent Park

Community Centre, tenants had to arrive early in order to get a seat; seating became easier when larger meeting halls became available with the opening of the Daniels Spectrum building (2012) and the new Community Centre (2016). Meetings featured translation services for the languages most commonly spoken by residents. Childcare services and refreshments were provided. The typical format included presentations by TCHC staff and city officials, followed by question-and-answer discussion. In addition to meetings, TCHC has regularly distributed newsletters and other publicity to update residents on the latest developments (TCHC 2007b). Some observers have wondered, however, whether over time these meetings have come to focus more on presenting information, and less on open-ended consultations like those that took place in 2002–2003.

How is Regent Park Different from HOPE VI?

TCHC's commitment to one-to-one replacement of demolished housing, and its firm promise that tenants will have the right to return once new housing is built, both stand in sharp contrast to the HOPE VI experience in the US. In such cities as Chicago and Atlanta, only small minorities of original inhabitants have been able to return to redeveloped neighbourhoods. As well, US efforts at renewal under HOPE VI have usually involved replacement of demolished high-rise "superblocks" with a combination of townhouse and low-rise apartment structures. The influence of New Urbanist ideas of neighbourhood and community space has often led to a decrease in the density of settlement. The number of new housing units created was often smaller than the number razed. And among the new units the proportion of RGI occupancies was smaller still.[2]

Regent Park, in contrast, will resettle approximately the same number of households as it displaces, with preference given to returning former residents. This change will be accomplished through densification. By the time the project is complete, the density of the site will have approximately doubled, from a population of around 7,500 to somewhere between 12,000 and 15,000. The number of occupancies on the site will grow from just over 2,000 to 7,500 (by the latest revision—see below).

Returnees will, however, be living in a mixed-income community. RGI tenants will account for less than one-third of housing units, and somewhere between 40 percent and 50 percent of the neighbourhood's new population.

The often-criticized modernist towers of the old Regent Park South are being replaced by new high-rise buildings, some much taller than those designed by Peter Dickinson in the 1950s. Planners and developers have devised this strategy in the context of a broader trend in Toronto's downtown, in which new high-rise condominium housing has proven popular and marketable along the lakeshore and in neighbourhoods such as the Distillery District and the West Don Lands, a short distance from Regent Park. Despite the criticism that has in the past been directed against high-rise towers—especially in public housing—the planners and developers of Regent Park are betting that, in today's environment, the problems of earlier times can be avoided.

The Toronto planners' emphasis on community continuity has broad implications for Regent Park's future. Politicians and planners in many localities, including many who have actively promoted HOPE VI projects in the US, have often taken a "minimalist" view of public housing: They see it, along with other features of the welfare state, as something to be provided on a short-term basis. Subsidized housing is, in this view, a "helping hand" to people in temporary hardship, with the expectation that they will eventually become self-sufficient and outgrow their need for it. Some argue that, for this reason, public housing should offer only a basic minimum of shelter, lest its inhabitants settle in too comfortably. In places where residents have remained in place for a generation or more, critics have interpreted this as a sign of failure, turning public housing into a dead-end place devoid of hope. But RGI residents, not only in Regent Park but in many US jurisdictions, have described their communities in very different terms, as vibrant and cohesive. Many public-housing residents have also expressed strong attachment to the places where they live, despite the many shortcomings of those places. In encouraging residents to return, the authors of the Regent Park plan are acknowledging and even celebrating those feelings, making the pre-existing community an important element in post-redevelopment plans. If, at the end of the process, a mixed-income neighbourhood is successfully created, it may be one in which RGI- and non-RGI residents can teach and learn from one another.

Questions of Timing

Where to begin the long redevelopment process was a complicated issue. In the earliest plans, Phase 1 was to cover the northeast quadrant of the property, closest to the intersection of Parliament and Gerrard Streets. This proved technically unfeasible, due to the location there of a central heating plant that was servicing other sections of Regent Park. A second iteration of the plan proposed to begin in the southeast quadrant, near River and Shuter Streets. By January 2005, however, the planners settled conclusively on a third location as the starting-point: a sector bounded by Oak, Sackville, Dundas and Parliament Streets. One reason for favouring this location was that it would include commercial as well as residential uses—a major chain supermarket, a medical clinic, and two eating establishments.

The groundbreaking took place in February 2006. Phase 2, covering a tract along the south side of Dundas Street, began about two years later.

TCHC entered into a partnership with the Daniels Corporation, one of Canada's largest builder/developers. The corporation turned out to be more than a silent partner. Daniels President Mitchell Cohen and his staff became closely involved in many aspects of community life, well beyond the construction and sale of new condos. The corporation's contributions were in many ways a continuation of ideas that had been expressed during the consultation phase, but they were also an addition to the mix, especially with regard to timing. Cohen has repeatedly emphasized the need for flexibility as the broader Regent Park rolls out, and the need to listen to the ideas of the residents, but has also proposed new ways of supporting them:

> It's an iterative process for sure… One of the most powerful examples is that when we became involved there was no arts and culture centre in the plan… we looked at the plan and we also read this hugely important document, the Social Development Plan (SDP). Unfortunately there was a real disconnect… [T]he SDP [pointed to the importance of supporting the community's] rich cultural diversity, the heritage…the enormous number of different grassroots organizations that are doing: drumming, spoken word, storytelling, arts and crafts and cultural creations… We looked at that disparity and thought immediately, "we need to do something." So we approached Derek Ballantyne and the people of TCHC and said: "Let's start dreaming. What if?" … So, between Toronto Community Housing and ourselves and people in this neighbourhood, and then the engagement of Artscape to help put it all together, there is now this unbelievably important place in the heart of this community, Daniels Spectrum.
>
> (Cohen, personal communication, June 8, 2015)

Cohen described a second example, where community input combined with flexibility in plan implementation to accelerate and revise the plans for parkland and recreational space. According to the master plan, a large park at the very centre of the site was to serve as a focal point of community life, but would only come into being toward the very end of the redevelopment. After consultation, the timetable was advanced to ensure that the park was completed in Phase 2; it was officially opened in June 2014.

One more modification of the plan was a large-scale Aquatic Centre, featuring two swimming pools plus a wading pool for toddlers. Originally the revitalization plan had proposed a much smaller pool, to be located immediately off-site in a primary school. But funding for a larger facility unexpectedly became available to the City. The Parks and Recreation Department, working with TCHC and the local City Counsellor, Pam McConnell, produced a plan for an architect-designed facility that could become a showpiece of the neighbourhood (Rochon 2012). This entailed tearing down buildings that had, under the plan, been slated to stand for several more years. Additional tenants had to be relocated, some for the second time. Despite these inconveniences the new facility, which opened in 2012, has been welcomed enthusiastically.

The combined effect of new amenities—supermarket, coffee shop, arts centre, park, aquatic centre—was to make the new Regent Park immediately attractive and accessible, both to returning residents in Phases 1 and 2 and to prospective condo residents. Significantly, all these facilities are also designed to be accessible and attractive to Torontonians who do not live in Regent Park.

The Plan Evolves

Almost fifteen years have passed since the TCHC began its community consultation. The plans that were drawn up in 2003–2004 have been modified in certain respects, and there has been considerable change in agency personnel. Leadership of TCHC has gone through a series of upheavals in which senior figures were fired or were pressured to resign. A mayoral task force reported in 2016 that

> TCHC has had a tumultuous five years with three Boards of Directors, four CEOs and a significant turnover in senior management. A series of crises has caused priorities to shift on an ad hoc basis, often diverting staff resources away from tenant services. City Councillors, tenants, media and the public are asking whether TCHC is too large, too politicized, too bureaucratic or too inefficient to fulfill its mission.
>
> (Mayor's Task Force 2016, 19)

These changes were closely connected to political trends at City Hall during Rob Ford's turbulent term as mayor. Keiko Nakamura, who had previously held the post of chief operations officer at TCHC, was appointed CEO in 2010, but was dismissed a year later after Ontario's Auditor-General issued a report critical of TCHC's procurement practices (Alcoba 2011). Her successor, Gene Jones, was warmly supported by Mayor Ford, but lambasted by the city ombudsman in a report critical of his hiring practices, managerial style and apparent indifference to conflicts of interest. Over the mayor's objections, City Council accepted Jones's resignation in 2014 (Alamenciak and Pagliaro 2014). During this period, the Regent Park revitalization plan continued to move forward. But in ways great and small, the plans drawn up in 2002–2004 continued to evolve.

For example, the Regent Park Collaboration Team (RPCT 2003a) recommended working with "a number of different residential development partners," but in the end the TCHC entered into a partnership with just one, the Daniels Corporation. The first plan recommended that Phase 1 be located in the southwest corner of the property, but in the final version part of the northwest quadrant was the first to be redeveloped. The anticipated duration of the redevelopment was originally fifteen years, but has now been extended to twenty. The six phases of the original plan were reduced to five. In a plan as large and complex as this one, such adjustments are hardly surprising, and most elicited little reaction from residents. There were, however, four moments when a number of tenants objected to TCHC decisions and/or raised doubts about the consultation process.

The first addressed the issue of one-for-one replacement. Early into Phase 1, residents learned that TCHC was introducing a new concept that seemed to change the terms of Right of Return. A community meeting for residents held on December 18, 2008, presented an update on two types of replacement RGI housing units, those on-site and in "East Downtown" (TCHC 2008). The location referred to approximately 300 newly-built housing units, located in three sites each about one kilometre from Regent Park (see Figure 4.2: Map of Regent Park and Offsite Locations), which would be made available to returning residents, and treated as equivalent to new housing within Regent Park. Residents were shocked. One knowledgeable key informant, a non-resident, shared their reaction:

> it was very badly communicated by Toronto Community Housing, I was at the meeting when they first announced it. I was shaking my head, because instead of saying to people "look, we are going to have to think about the footprint as a little bit bigger," they said "we can't live up to Right of Return, the numbers just don't add up." And so people understandably freaked out, because they didn't know what the parameters [were] what this was for. Then they gradually rolled out the perimeter of the bigger footprint.
>
> (Tehara 2015, 108)

TCHC designated these sites—located at 92 Carlton, 501 Adelaide Street East and 60 Richmond Street East—as "East Downtown". Units in these buildings would be considered to be in the Regent Park area, and would qualify as replacement housing under the terms of the Right of Return agreement with tenants.

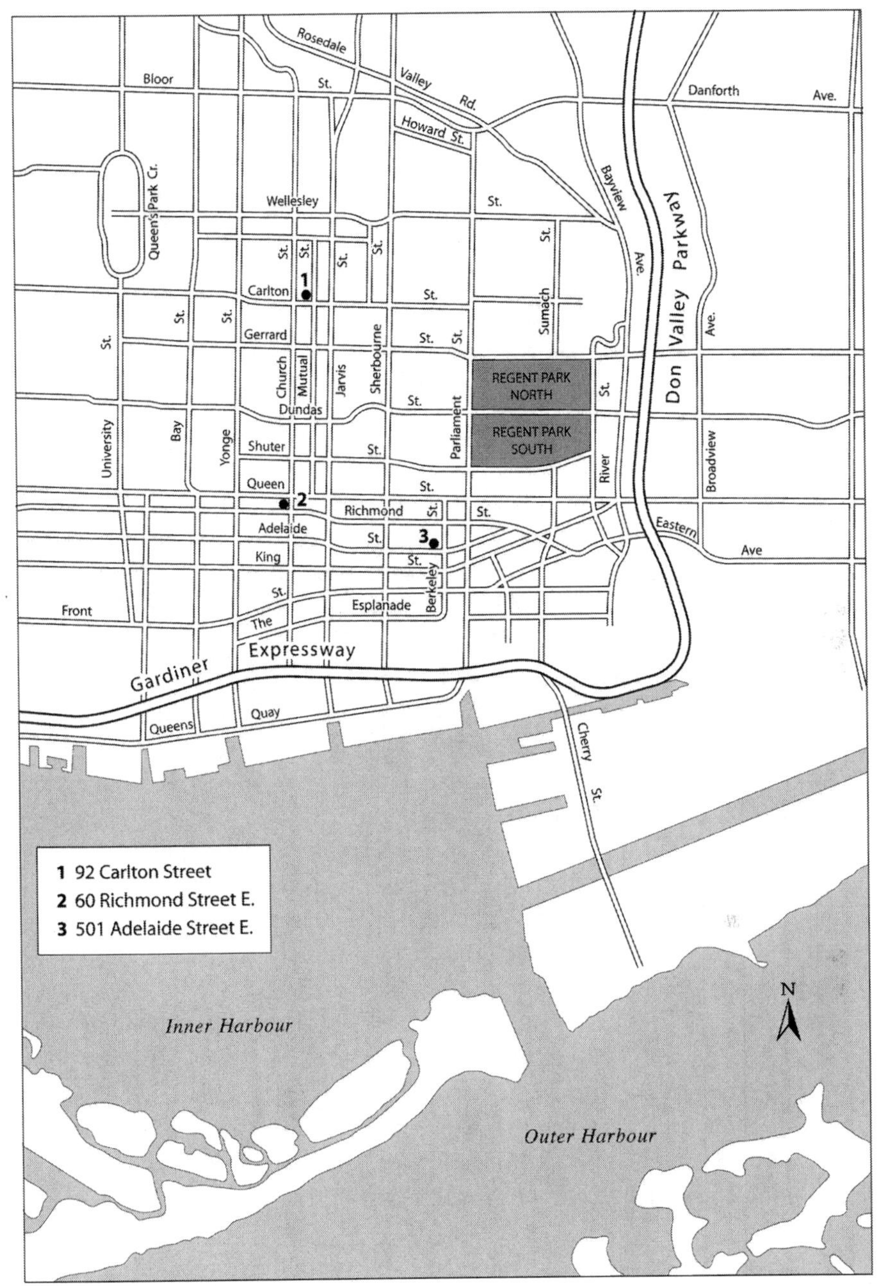

Figure 4.2 Map 3: Regent Park and off-site locations.

Source: B. Levely

Derek Ballantyne explained the change as follows:

> We were working through the business planning and it just dawned on me: Where are all the townhouses and who are they occupied by? And, the plan that had been created was a great plan, but every low rise building was a social housing building. So we were about to recreate a construct of physical form which was exactly what we were trying to move away from. And we spent a lot of time trying—Can we tweak this? Can we move this? Can we increase densities over here and create more ground floor?—but there were limits to what you could do on that site. And we had to make a choice. Were we committed to the principles that it would be... a well-mixed and not obviously social housing community, or were we going to say no, the primacy was get everyone on a ground floor unit and if it's all the townhouses and all the low rises social housing, so be it. You'd be back to having streets, and blocks, identified as social housing. We agonized over it a lot. And I said fine, I don't think there's another solution, you go do the meeting, cause we're not taking that message back to the community.
>
> (Ballantyne, personal communication, April 1, 2015)

Many tenants were unenthusiastic about moving to off-site accommodation. Some felt that TCHC relocation counsellors were trying too hard to convince them to take it. But the principle of free choice was still honoured, and some tenants did accept the offer. At a still later stage TCHC appeared to be reconsidering its earlier decision, with the result that all 2,083 RGI units may be replaced inside the boundaries of Regent Park (Gladki 2014, 14).

A second disagreement with TCHC arose over the fate of the Regent South Community Centre, located at 203 Sackville Green. This facility was the result of a long period of campaigning by tenants, who tithed themselves to raise some of the necessary funds. When, in the course of Phase 2 of redevelopment, TCHC proposed to tear down the old building and replace it, some in the community were opposed, wanting to keep a facility that they regarded as their own. That centre remained an important symbol of effective grassroots community engagement. Residents had fought City Hall and won! The issue was hotly debated in December 2008 at a community update meeting. One observer at that meeting reported:

> Residents who spoke on this issue felt strongly that the community centre is a symbol in the neighbourhood of the residents' capacity to organize and provide for themselves.... At the meeting, some residents relayed that the community centre has a long history and that residents "fought for it" to be

> built in the first place, so the idea of it being demolished was disrespectful to the history of the community.
>
> (de Schutter 2009, 58)

In this instance, critics' voices were not enough to alter the plan. The old centre was razed in 2015, and a new facility, larger and better equipped for a range of community uses, opened in 2016.

In 2012–2013, as preparations went ahead for Phase 3, two other issues arose simultaneously, in the context of amendments to the overall plan. The first concerned the preservation or demolition of an apartment tower at 14 Blevins Place. This was the last of five structures in Regent Park South designed by Peter Dickinson, the other four having already been torn down. Almost ten years earlier, the Toronto Preservation Board had recommended adding the site to the City's inventory of historic buildings, on the basis of its significance as a showpiece of modernism (Toronto Preservation Board 2004). Now a number of architectural conservationists came forward to keep it from being torn down. But when the idea was opened to public discussion on June 13, 2013, residents of the building lined up to complain about its many failings. Not only was it in poor repair, infested with mice and cockroaches. It was also, they said, poorly designed for family living. Many of the units were two-storey, with interior stairways that tenants found steep and narrow—inconvenient, for example, for mothers carrying young babies or laundry from floor to floor. Tenants spoke vehemently against rehabilitating the building, insisting that they would refuse to move back. Their complaints, which coincided with the preference of the TCHC to demolish, prevailed at City Hall, and eventually a demolition permit was issued.

At the same meeting (Marcusa 2013) the TCHC presented a much more controversial idea: The number of market-priced housing units in the overall plan was, it asserted, no longer sufficient to sustain the public-private partnership that was powering the redevelopment. Instead, the total number of living units was to be increased from 5,400 to 7,500, and the projected population from 12,500 to 17,000 (TCHC 2013, 18). All the increase would go to market units, with the number of RGI occupancies unchanged. The increase was to be accomplished by adding several extremely tall buildings, including one 120 metres tall (35–40 storeys) at the corner of Parliament and Gerrard Streets. At a series of public meetings, community members from Regent Park and surrounding areas listened to planners and city officials justify the change. Comments from the floor were mainly negative. Critics complained that the additional units would overcrowd the site, and that available infrastructure (especially public transit) would not be sufficient to accommodate the extra numbers. They also questioned the changed balance between RGI and non-RGI housing, pointing out that the City has a large backlog of applicants for subsidized housing. Lastly, they objected to the extreme height of several of proposed buildings, which critics feared would overshadow or overpower the landscape.

After some months, TCHC returned with an amended proposal (TCHC 2014, 8), which was presented to another community meeting with several hundred residents in attendance. The number of additional market units was unchanged, but the total would be differently distributed across the site. The tallest buildings in the previous version would be reduced in height—one from 120 metres to 60, and one from 88 to 77. To accommodate this change, several other buildings would be increased from 50 to 75 metres. While pleased with the changes in height, critics reiterated their previous objections to the overall density that the new numbers would produce. TCHC, however, insisted that no further changes could be made, and in due course the amended proposal was presented to City Council, where it passed.

To some community members, this episode raised questions about the place of community consultation in the planning process. The initial amendments to the official plan had, it seemed, been drawn up without input from residents, and the modifications, though they responded to one set of critics, made no concessions to the others. To a neutral observer, TCHC's decision may have seemed a matter of simple economic necessity.[3] But to some residents, it was a reminder of older patterns of decision-making. Community meetings were a forum for presenting a plan that, in its fundamentals, was already past negotiation. Was this what the 2002–2004 planning process had promised, or was a familiar, less consultative mode of planning being revived? Given the amount of turnover and controversy at the head of the TCHC, it seems reasonable to ask whether, among the later generation of leaders, some may not have fully shared the vision that was set forth a decade ago.

Notes

1 Ten years later, a TCHC 2013 Housing Issues report stated: "Toronto Community Housing is actively pursuing how to achieve deeper integration of Replacement Social Housing Units with market housing on the Regent Park footprint; in Phase 3 we hope to achieve a mix through integrating Replacement Social Housing Units with market townhouses. Toronto Community Housing will report on the success of this initiative in upcoming Housing Issues Reports" (TCHC 2013, 14).

2 For example, Atlanta's Techwood housing project originally had about 1,100 RGI units. Centennial Place, the development which replaced Techwood, includes 900 dwellings, of which 300 are RGI.

3 Senior planner John Gladki wrote in 2014 that TCHC's partnership with Daniels Corporation would capture "the increase in land value from higher densities… 2.5 market units will be built for each social housing unit to be replaced." TCHC's share of the profits would ultimately provide about 27 percent of the entire cost of replacing the social housing units (Gladki 2014, 21).

References

Alamenciak, Tim and Jennifer Pagliaro. 2014. "Jones Out as Head of TCHC." *Toronto Star*, April 25.

Alcoba, Natalie. 2011. "Housing board controversy opening doors for Ford." *National Post* May 11.

de Schutter, Jacqueline. 2009. "Community Consultation and Environmental Justice in the Regent Park Revitalization." Master's thesis, Faculty of Arts, Department of Psychology, Wilfrid Laurier University. scholars.wlu.ca/cgi/viewcontent.cgi?article=1968&context=etd. (Accessed January 10, 2017).

Gladki, John. 2014. "Inclusive Planning: A Case Study of Regent Park." In *Inclusive Urban Planning: State of the Urban Poor Report 2013*. Ministry of Housing and Urban Poverty Alleviation, Government of India. New Delhi: Oxford University Press of India.

Marcusa, Anthony. 2013. "Updated Regent Park plan flops at consultation Demolition of Blevins Place garners support." *The Bulletin, Journal of Downtown Toronto*. (June). thebulletin.ca/updated-regent-park-plan-flops-at-consultation-demolition-of-blevins-place-garners-support. (Accessed January 10, 2017).

Mayor's Task Force on Toronto Community Housing. 2016. "Transformative Change for TCHC." www1.toronto.ca/wps/portal/contentonly?vgnextoid=4184a1f9b4a72510VgnVCM10000071d60f89RCRD&vgnextchannel=102d30787e87b410VgnVCM10000071d60f89RCRD. (Accessed January 10, 2017).

Meagher, Sean and Tony Boston. 2003. *Community Engagement and the Regent Park Development*. Toronto: Toronto Community Housing Corporation. www.publicinterest.ca/community-engagement/community-engagement-and-the-regent-park-redevelopment. (Accessed July 22, 2016)

Regent Park Collaboration Team (RPCT). 2002. *Regent Park Revitalization Study*. Toronto Community Housing Corporation.

Regent Park Collaboration Team (RPCT). 2003a. *Development Vehicle*. (April).

Regent Park Collaboration Team (RPCT). 2003b. *Lessons from St. Lawrence for the Regent Park Redevelopment Process*. Toronto Community Housing Corporation. (April).

Rochon, Lisa. 2012. "Putting Regent Park in the swim of things." *Globe and Mail* September 14.

Sennett, Richard. 2015. "The world wants more 'porous' cities – so why don't we build them?" *The Guardian [Manchester]*. November 27. www.theguardian.com/cities/2015/nov/27/delhi-electronic-market-urbanist-dream. (Accessed January 10, 2017).

Tehara, Navroop Singh. 2015. "Tenants' Right of Return: Early Experiences from Toronto's Regent Park Redevelopment." Master's thesis, School of Planning, University of Waterloo, Waterloo, Ontario, Canada. uwspace.uwaterloo.ca/handle/10012/9739. (Accessed January 10, 2017).

TCHC (Toronto Community Housing Corporation). 2004. *Regent Park Community Services and Facilities Study*.

TCHC (Toronto Community Housing Corporation). 2007a. *Regent Park Social Development Plan*. Executive summary. (September).

TCHC (Toronto Community Housing Corporation). 2007b. Regent Park Revitalization Update. (April 3).

TCHC (Toronto Community Housing Corporation). 2008. "Regent Park Revitalization Community Update Meeting." Powerpoint presentation. (December 18).

TCHC (Toronto Community Housing Corporation). 2013. *Regent Park Revitalization, Housing Issues Report: Official Plan Amendment and Re-zoning Application for Phases 3, 4, 5, Lifting of the Holding Symbol Phase 3*. (September).

TCHC (Toronto Community Housing Corporation). 2014. "Staff Report, Action Required: 325 Gerard Street East—Official Plan Amendment & Zoning Amendment, Residential Demolition Control Applications (Phases 3-5)—Final Report. Ref. 13 127808 STE 28 OZ. February 13. www.toronto.ca/legdocs/mmis/2014/te/bgrd/backgroundfile-66817.pdf. (Accessed 30 July, 2016)

Toronto Preservation Board. 2004. "Toronto Staff Report:14 Blevins Place (Dickinson Tower) —Inclusion on the City of Toronto Inventory of Heritage Properties." November 9.

Veronis, Luisa. 1999. "Exploring the margin: the borders between Regent Park and Cabbagetown." MA thesis, University of Toronto. Ottawa: National Library of Canada. www.collectionscanada.ca/obj/s4/f2/dsk1/tape8/PQDD_0009/MQ46011.pdf. (Accessed January 10, 2017).

5
Residents' Perspectives on the Redevelopment

A survey of residents undertaken by TCHC's consultant team in 2004 prior to redevelopment indicated that most would prefer to return to a rebuilt Regent Park after reconstruction. Specifically, when the consultants asked a sample of almost 230 residents the question "When the reconstruction is finished in Regent Park, would you prefer to live: a) in Regent Park, b) nearby, c) somewhere else in Toronto, or d) Unsure," almost 80 percent answered that they would prefer to live in Regent Park (Tehara 2015, 77 and 164). To understand what return meant to the residents—what they wanted or expected in the new Regent Park—required a much longer, open-ended set of conversations.

Our study asked residents how they felt about their Regent Park community and their downtown neighbourhood—their expectations and hopes for its redevelopment. Did they share the critics' views about their community? How did they view the redevelopment plans? What would they change, or keep the same?

In addressing the responses to these questions, we will also consider the role that Phase 1 residents played in shaping and planning the redevelopment. We begin by looking at the perspective of young people from the community.

A Sense of Community

Early in the Regent Park redevelopment, when the first phase of the demolition was under way, a summer art workshop project recruited youth from the community to work under the direction of Toronto street artist/photographer Dan Bergeron, of Fauxreel Studios, on a series of mural portraits of residents. Under the auspices of Toronto's Luminato Festival of the Arts, the young people worked with Bergeron to produce about a dozen portraits of subjects, young and old. The greyscale photographic images were projected and copied onto the red brick walls of the buildings in which the subjects lived (TCHC 2008, 2). Each image was two storeys in height. In the early evening of June 10, 2008, at a public opening of the art installation on the Regent Park grounds, with refreshments dispensed free of charge from an ice cream truck, the young artists led group tours where they explained the significance of the giant portraits. Our tour guide explained:

> Each of these portraits represents someone who lives in the building. When the building is broken down, those portraits will crumble into rubble. We care about this community—even though the rest of the city feels it is a bad place. We made these pictures to illustrate that when these come down, parts of own selves will be lost. The rest of the city thinks this a dangerous and frightening place. For us it is home.

A photograph taken some months later depicts one of these portraits, of a young man, against a background of demolition equipment (Bergeron, personal communication, October 15, 2014). The backhoe setting depicts the scene of transition and the old neighbourhood's imminent demise (see Figure 5.1).

Local public schools developed curriculum to prepare Regent Park school children for the major changes that would transform their neighbourhood. Nelson Mandela Park School, a kindergarten through Grade 8 school in the heart of Regent Park, developed a week-long special program to inform the upper grades about the redevelopment plans. In the spring of 2007, experts from various local agencies and organizations addressed the classes, telling children about the history of their community and the way it would be

Figure 5.1 "Last Day": Demolition of building with occupant's portrait.
Source: D. Bergeron

changing. In interactive sessions, children had opportunities to ask questions of the visiting experts, and describe their concerns. A teacher who had helped to plan and organize this orientation program recalled the kinds of questions the children asked when a housing official came to their classroom:

> They had all kinds of questions, and really intelligent questions. There were questions about equity and how many of the units will be rent-geared-to-income… They asked a lot of questions about safety, and a lot of questions about facilities and what improvements will be made… The children are very aware that things are broken, that elevators don't work, there's urine, there's feces in the halls, garbage everywhere. They asked them if there will be recycling, [They asked] "Will there be flowers? Will it be beautiful?" Those are things that kids—that 10-year-olds—are asking. I think they're really important questions that maybe their parents wouldn't be able to ask in the way that they're asking them… [They also asked] about the process: "How will we know where we're moving?" and "How will we know for sure we can come back?" You know, like those types of things too. "When will we get the letter [saying we need to move]? How will we know?" … [Y]ou soon realize that they're taking responsibility at a young age that I never had… [O]ne of the boys who's going into grade 8 said "I'm not going to be here in the afternoon because I have to go line up at the housing office to see about getting my sink fixed." Well, [laughs], you know, you're 14-years-old! Good luck! "Can I help you with that?" "Oh no, it's okay, I can do it, it's not a problem." … Children grow up quickly here, and they have a different level of understanding and responsibility.
>
> (Key informant interview; Johnson and Schippling 2009, 18–29)

In addition to asking key informants from the community about children's feelings and their knowledge about the redevelopment, our Phase 1 research collected young people's views in a more direct fashion. Team members interviewed a sample of 29 young residents between the ages of twelve and twenty years, to learn about their experiences before and during the redevelopment.[1] Many of them were members of the sample of 52 households surveyed for the longitudinal study. The youth interviews were conducted individually, but in one instance two friends requested they be interviewed jointly; this request was accommodated. The resulting interview was very animated, as the two friends expressed and explored their areas of agreement and disagreement relating to the redevelopment.

Many of the young respondents were very positive about their Regent Park community, and expected that they would miss it if/when they had to move. While they acknowledged serious problems with the old Regent Park—the deteriorated physical infrastructure as well as crime and vandalism—they still valued the strength of community ties they experienced there. Some wondered whether that strong community feeling could be reconstituted after the redevelopment, with new buildings, new programs and new residents.

An eighteen-year-old emphasized the importance of historical continuity. She felt that this was the reason that her family, given a choice between staying in Regent Park and moving elsewhere, would opt to stay in Regent Park: "It has a lot of history and I think—because it's Regent Park, it's special."

A sixteen-year-old resident commented on the disconnection between the view the public has of Regent Park, and the reality that she knew. As with many of the young people interviewed, her vision of the community included the walkways, outdoor pool, and other open spaces—most of which will be sacrificed in the higher density redevelopment:

> I think a lot of people outside of Regent Park think it is a dangerous area where everybody hides in their little houses and doesn't talk to each other. But it's kind of totally different. Especially during the summer, outside on the sidewalks in the middle area. Everybody's there… talking to each other… People wouldn't think of that when they think of Regent Park.

Her friend echoed this sentiment, describing Regent Park as "pretty much one big community. Everyone knows one another, like everyone knows someone in here and everyone usually gets along."

Other youth from the study sample expressed concerns about the ways the new, higher density, re-built community might deprive them of public open spaces that they had previously enjoyed, and that reinforced the sense of community they associated with the old look of Regent Park. Most acknowledged that the buildings were badly deteriorated and in need of renewal, but still expressed attachment to those old dwellings, which for them were home. One fourteen-year-old who had lived for a decade at the same address in Regent Park described the sense of loss she felt on moving from that home:

> It feels like I spent my whole life there because… it was like I know everybody, and liked everybody. It was a comfortable place to live. You always felt safe because everybody was around you… even though the building was very old, it felt like a good place to be in… I just loved the building [and] the people living in it. Because everybody that lived on the same floor, like, I know everybody.
>
> (Johnson and Schippling 2009, 26)

Many young people from Regent Park had serious concerns about safety and crime. Some associated the poor state of repair with the unsafe conditions. One thirteen-year-old said that she liked her friends in Regent Park, but what she liked least were "all the drug dealers and the crackheads" (Johnson and Schippling 2009, 22). Comparing the relative weight of the poor building maintenance and the presence of drug addicts and dealers, youth generally found the addicts most troubling. As one seventeen-year-old reported, having "crackheads and drug dealers chill in my building" was associated with feelings of risk and danger (ibid.).

Positive Public Spaces

Danielle Leahy Laughlin, in her dissertation research, began exploring the attitudes of Regent Park youth toward that community's public spaces in 2004, before any of the physical redevelopment had begun. Using a photovoice technique, Leahy Laughlin asked Regent Park teens aged ten to sixteen years to record photographically the public places they considered more and less successful. Many of their chosen places were informal rather than institutional in nature. Murals painted on exterior walls and unpaved pathways exemplify the kinds of places identified by the youth as important.

The Boardwalk, a pedestrian roadway through Regent Park North, contained spaces the young people considered their own; places where they felt a sense of belonging. It followed the path of the former Oak Street (which, under the new plan, has now been reinstated as a through street), past an outdoor swimming pool and community centre. Benches were located at intervals along the path. In Laughlin's interviews, one youth, Farah,[2] described the Boardwalk as "beautiful when you see mothers walking with their strollers with their babies" (Leahy Laughlin 2008, 126). Another young woman, Cindy, described the Boardwalk as a place "where you could always find or go with

Figure 5.2 Boardwalk, 2008: Gathering place for young people.

your friends, walk, and hang out." Cindy felt that the Boardwalk is "mainly the perfect place for everyone to hang out to do whatever" (ibid., 126).

Another young person in Leahy Laughlin's study sample, Jessica, described the whole geography of the Boardwalk, with zones claimed by particular groups. She ascribed an overall purpose to the Boardwalk:

> There's sections of it. Up here there's the basketball courts and more of the athletic people. More in the middle is the little kids running through the poles and on their bikes and playing around. And down around the darker corners and at night and around the corner of the building at that corner is where the gangs are drinking and down more there's people playing baseball. So it's like everybody's there… It pretty much leads to everything.
>
> (Leahy Laughlin 2008, 126)

It was the walkways in general, and the Boardwalk, in particular, that the youth felt should be saved. One 16-year-old described the Boardwalk as "the spine of Regent" (Leahy Laughlin & Johnson 2011, 4). Young people were opposed to the idea of re-introducing through streets into Regent Park. They rejected a basic premise of the redevelopment—the need to renovate the streetscape to end the isolation of Regent Park. While these youth advocated some sort of heritage designation status for the Boardwalk, they recognized that it was badly in need of work to repair lighting and seating, and a general upgrade.

Figure 5.3 Oak Street, looking east, 2016: The former "Boardwalk" shown in Figure 5.2; new playground to the right.

Figure 5.4 "Streetscape 2008" showing wall mural and family.

Murals painted by residents were valued highly by both the youth interviewed in Leahy Laughlin's study and in our survey. One young woman in our Regent Park survey described how she had created her own photographic record of the murals to preserve that important memory:

> I took so many pictures of those murals. I took them because they were going to break it down. I think they're really beautiful… Like one of the townhouses has this beautiful mural and I don't think they should destroy it. They should just keep that chunk… People work hard on that, right?

In her study of residents relocated involuntarily from a sixty-year-old public housing community in Portland, Oregon, Karen Gibson (2007) found that they particularly missed the open spaces in that project. Open spaces in the low-density modernist housing project had helped generate valued social interaction among neighbours. In contrast, while Toronto's rebuilt Regent Park includes an indoor swimming pool, a large park and athletic fields, much of the space is heavily programmed, and may not allow for the kind of informal social interaction that was supported by the open space in the earlier lower-density design. What was previously the unpaved Boardwalk will now be the paved Oak Street, with two-way traffic, and official signage. For better or for worse, it is no longer a gathering place for teens (Leahy Laughlin and Johnson 2011). Whether the promenade in the new six-acre park will take its place, only time will tell.

One Big Family

It was not only the young residents who felt there were aspects of the old Regent Park community that they valued, and that they wanted enjoy in the future. The adults we interviewed, though they also identified aspects of the environment that were sub-standard, knew and appreciated the community's sociability. They wanted to recreate it in the new iteration. The interviews included questions designed to get residents talking about what they liked and disliked, and what they wanted to see in a renewed Regent Park. We invited residents to reflect on what they saw as desirable and undesirable outcomes of the redevelopment.

Residents generally agreed with the characterization of Regent Park as being like "one big family." Some talked about ties of friendship beyond racial and ethno-cultural groups. Others talked about their long friendships with neighbours, and ways they provided help to one another. Still others mentioned sharing of food with neighbours, just bringing over some new dish for neighbours to sample, and sometimes having tea together. This discussion got people thinking about the community-wide events that took place particularly in summertime. Not all the answers were positive. Some people cited crime, and gang behaviour. Others worried that the redevelopment would destroy the family feeling. Some mentioned the idea of social mix, and were concerned that introducing wealthier residents into Regent Park would diminish the sense of family that had prevailed.

Asked what they liked about the Regent Park community, residents generally said more about the location and the friendships, and the unique collection of local community-based services, than about the physical plant. Living downtown was a factor many valued highly. But some of the residents also expressed appreciation for some of the features of the old neighbourhood's built form.

The 2002 consultation raised the question of rebuilding Regent Park as a mixed-income community, and reported that members of the community accepted this approach as a necessary component of the plan (Meagher and Boston 2003, 41). But our own interviews found many residents poorly informed about this aspect of the redevelopment. Some were suspicious that the whole of Regent Park was being turned over to private uses, and that they themselves, once displaced, would be unable to return. Shauna Brail and Nishi Kumar, who conducted a similar interview project a few years later, encountered similar ideas. One non-resident in their study observed that "I don't think that there's a whole lot of people in that community who said 'Gee, I think we need some rich people moving in'." (Brail and Kumar 2015)

What's in a Name?

In a hypothetical question intended to tap residents' inner feelings about their neighbourhood and their ideas about the historical significance of their Regent Park community, our interviews asked the Phase 1 residents whether they thought Regent Park should be renamed following redevelopment. Most replied that the redeveloped community should keep the same name, and offered many reasons for preserving the history, revealing a strong depth of feeling for, and attachment to, the place. In the words of one resident,

> I don't think they should change the name. "Regent" has to be in there somewhere, I don't care where you put it… have it "Regency" or whatever… Because to take that name away, you are taking a lot of people's memories away and you are taking times, where people remember, some people have good times and stuff like that.

Another resident echoed the view connecting the name with its history:

> It does matter. I'd rather keep the name as Regent Park. It's just the name that just, people know… It's only in the minds of people that… It's just an area. I don't think that changing the name will make it any better, right? Just because you got new buildings coming up doesn't mean you have to change everything, right? Something should be the same, keep it like… if you change the name to like Rosedale [a wealthy area nearby] or something like that, right? It's just going to take the historical background of the area. So keeping the name as Regent Park will give it some history even though it's being basically torn apart.

Mitchell Cohen, president of The Daniels Corporation, the Regent Park private developer, echoed the residents' views about the need to preserve the community's original name. According to Cohen, very early in the marketing process, people he called "marketing gurus" advised Daniels on how to sell condominiums in a neighbourhood with a bad reputation. He dismissed that advice as being "off the mark," almost laughable:

> Some of the first recommendations were: Don't put the sales office in Regent Park. People will be too scared. Another recommendation: Get marketing gurus together and pick a new name for the community. We rejected those suggestions. First, we need to be in the community. So we made the sales and presentation centre in the middle. And we put community meeting space there, [saying] "Come on in." Many community groups used that space, before Spectrum [the new Arts and Culture centre] was ready. So

that was important. [We put it] right on Dundas [major street through the community]. Very visible. Glass walls [announcing]: "We're here, we're part of this neighbourhood." At first, we invited everyone in to dinner. Welcome!

About changing the name: OK forget about it. This is a community with deep, important history. Even if the media [view is] negative. The revitalization came from the people in the community. Here are the principles on which it should be rebuilt. Honour it. This is Regent Park, it will always be Regent Park.

(Mitchell Cohen, personal communication, June 8, 2015)

Residents' Role in Planning the Redevelopment

The interviews asked generally about residents' level of participation in planning the redevelopment. Among the sampled households, few had been actively involved, though many indicated, in retrospect, that they would have preferred to have had more input. Some felt the housing authority's community consultation was more window dressing than genuine participatory planning. In the words of one relocated resident: "They listen to us but they don't follow us." Another relocated resident reported: "The only thing they did was 'information sessions' not 'decision-making meetings.' It would have been better to allow the tenants to help with the decisions."

Many of the Phase 1 residents interviewed said they wanted a say into what elements were to be preserved, and what should be changed. The Boardwalk was the most prominent example of a site that many felt should be given protected status. The Regent Park South Community Centre, demolished in Phase 2, was another example that many respondents brought up. One youth, almost eighteen years of age, cautioned against demolishing the community centre. To do so would be a real mistake, he argued, because of its symbolic and historic importance: "A lot of people know about it, the way it was made, because people from the community actually created the funds for it, right? And that's very historic for Regent Park—it's a great story."

A number of tenants indicated that they wanted to help shape their redeveloping community—both the social planning and the urban design. In some cases they would have phased the redevelopment differently. In other instances, they would have altered the process of relocation. Youth as well as adults voiced preferences for more meaningful roles in planning the redevelopment. One young person offered the following assessment of the role they had played: "They didn't ask us. They just gave us notice. We never had a choice. They never asked us if we wanted our buildings to be broken down, if we didn't like them" (Johnson and Schippling 2009, 21).

TCHC, for its part, maintains that the community was widely consulted, and offers as evidence a long list of meetings and interactions with community members. What our interviews suggest is that not all community members were engaged in those conversations, and some felt they had been ignored. The negative comments that we heard can be taken as evidence of the difficulty of reaching out to a large and diverse community. Perhaps inevitably, some members only became aware of the redevelopment plans at a later date. Inevitably, too, there was no unanimity in community members' responses.

Cultural Meanings of Housing

Phase 1 residents wished the housing authority had paid more attention to their opinions on how the houses were designed—especially to cultural factors that influence residents' ideas about housing. For example, Regent Park has a substantial population who are immigrants from African and Arab countries. In the new housing the kitchens in particular do not meet some of these immigrant families' ideas of privacy and good design. In some of the new buildings kitchens are designed in an open plan, with clear sightlines from other living areas. This conflicts with traditional gender divisions, in which kitchens are regarded as women's space, and are segregated from the rest of a family's living quarters. One relocated Muslim resident explained how these units offended her family's sense of privacy: "We are [...] Muslim people... The kitchen is here, your living room is here, it's not good. You cook in front of the people, it's not good." Another relocated resident described how the mainly-glass exterior cladding of new units goes against her family's cultural preference for housing design that reinforces privacy: "We don't like it... they make it [with glass] it's no good... sometimes you don't want to open everything, but you can watch... I don't need it, I don't want it... they don't have privacy [in those] houses."

Given a choice between remaining in the ageing Regent Park housing unit her family currently occupies, and moving to one of the new glass buildings, that tenant stated she would prefer to stay where she was. She regretted that the family had no such choice, because all of the old units are to be razed.

The antipathy towards open kitchens was not confined to any one religious or cultural group. One Phase 1 resident who came from an Anglo-Saxon Cabbagetown background also criticized the kitchen designs planned for the new Regent Park units, based on their sightlines: "I don't like the idea of an open kitchen... God—someone walks into your door [and] you haven't done your dishes—the whole place looks like, you know! ... I'm not the cleanest person, but I do try to be!"

The subject is not simple; it raises important issues about how much public housing should cater to the ethno-cultural preferences of specific groups of tenants and how much tenants of public housing should get to choose the design of their housing units. This issue became controversial a few years ago in the Netherlands, when public opposition arose to what were called "halal flats" that addressed immigrants' preferences for dwellings with partitions separating women and men (*The Economist* 2013).

While the criticism of those open-plan kitchens was relatively widespread among the Phase 1 tenants interviewed, it was not universal. Some objected to the complaints about open kitchens; this view is reflected in the comment by one youth from an immigrant Muslim family:

> [A] lot of the members of Regent Park, they're very demanding. Like even when someone moved here they're complaining like "Oh my god the kitchen is open! What are we going to do? We need a door!"... [Y]ou should be glad you got this new place! It's completely new, new security and so forth. Yet you're complaining and there's too much demand as well. So I think, I kind of get what TCHC's kind of like, we can't take everyone's suggestions.

Cultural preferences in house design influenced planning ideas for other rooms as well as for kitchens. The gendered idea of private spaces led one Muslim household to suggest that subsequent development phases offer the alternative of homes with a second living room so that women and men could socialize in separate rooms. This suggestion has not been followed.

Some elderly respondents complained about bathroom design in the new seniors' complex. The units were equipped with specially-designed showers with seating intended to make bathing easier for elderly persons. But some elderly tenants were used to bathing in tubs, which they maintained were healthier for soaking. The new units did not offer this option.

One Phase 1 resident commented wistfully about an area where TCHC did take her suggestions seriously—bathroom fixtures. She reported that after moving into new Phase 1 housing, she had an opportunity to convey to TCHC her criticism of the design of the washroom sinks. "Storage space is very scarce in these new housing units," she said she told them, "so every opportunity for storage space should be utilized... Keeping a bathroom sink on a pedestal or just on legs, is a waste of useful space—you should enclose that space in a vanity, making room for cleaning supplies, toilet paper and the like." When she visited a friend in a newer Phase 2 housing unit, she discovered that TCHC had listened to her about the washroom redesign. She admitted she felt "a bit jealous" of her Phase 2 friend because TCHC had incorporated her good design ideas into the newer units, but not into hers.

Another Phase 1 resident described being part of a focus group consultation on designs for the new houses. She reported being asked what changes she might want in the plans. By her account, many people said they wanted more washrooms. She was pleased to report that now the larger units (those with four and five bedrooms) have more than one washroom. She said the residents were very happy that their recommendation was taken seriously.

In the early stages of relocation, a number of residents expressed the wish that the existing buildings be renovated individually instead of whole areas being razed. Such a plan, they argued, would have been less disruptive to their community. These views were not reflected in the numerous reports produced by and for TCHC in the planning stages of the redevelopment.

Lessons Learned?

TCHC did make an enormous effort to explore the wishes and complaints of the tenant population. Even so, judging from our interviews, a substantial proportion of Regent Park's population was not involved in the consultation process that produced the revitalization plan. This is probably inevitable, given the size and diversity of the community, and the doubts and mistrust that had arisen from previous interactions between management and tenants. Still, it seems appropriate now to ask what more could have been done to enlist the community. The housing authority could, for example, have undertaken more consultation and sharing once the overall revitalization plan was in place. Tenants could have been given a role in planning the system for allocating temporary and long-term accommodation to displaced tenants (Chapter 6). Better communication of planning objectives could likely have been achieved through additional workshops, oriented toward a multi-generational audience in which teenagers and their parents could participate together.[3] And crucially, the residents could have been given more of a voice in determining the fate of such community symbols as the Boardwalk or the Regent South Community Centre. The ultimate result would likely have been the same, but effective planning is about more than outcomes. No consultation will ever produce unanimous support for a plan, but a more sensitive and inclusive planning approach might have produced a greater degree of consensus.

Notes

1 Results of this youth survey are published in Johnson and Schippling 2009. A DVD of a half-hour documentary video, *Growing Up Regent*, is distributed with this research report.
2 All youth were assigned pseudonyms.
3 This multigenerational coaching approach was used effectively in a Regent Park effort to teach computer literacy and English language skills to immigrant parents.

References

Brail, Shauna and Nishi Kumar. 2015. "Community engagement and leadership after the mix: The Transformation of Regent Park." Paper presented at the annual meeting of the American Association of Geographers, Chicago, April 2015.

Gibson, Karen J. 2007. "The relocation of the Columbia Villa community: Views from residents." *Journal of Planning, Education, and Research* 27(1): 5–19.

Johnson, Laura C. and Richard Schippling. 2009. *Regent Park Revitalization: Young People's Experience of Relocation from Public Housing Redevelopment.* Ottawa: Canada Mortgage and Housing Corporation, External Research Program. (June). Catalogue Number: NH18-1-2/50-2009E-PDF.

Leahy Laughlin, Danielle. 2008. "Defining and Exploring Public Space: Young People's Perspectives from Regent Park, Toronto." Ph.D. dissertation, University of Waterloo. hdl.handle.net/10012/3737.

Leahy Laughlin, Danielle and Laura C. Johnson. 2011. "Defining and exploring public space: perspectives of young people from Regent Park." *Children's Geographies* 9(3–4): 439–456.

Meagher, Sean and Tony Boston. 2003. *Community Engagement and the Regent Park Development*. Toronto: Toronto Community Housing Corporation. www.publicinterest.ca/community-engagement/community-engagement-and-the-regent-park-redevelopment. (Accessed July 22, 2016).

TCHC (Toronto Community Housing Corporation). 2008. Regent Park Monthly Update (Newsletter). Regent Park does Luminato! (May).

Tehara, Navroop Singh. 2015. "Tenants' Right of Return: Early Experiences from Toronto's Regent Park Redevelopment." Master's thesis, School of Planning, University of Waterloo, Waterloo, Ontario, Canada. uwspace.uwaterloo.ca/handle/10012/9739. (Accessed January 10, 2017).

The Economist. 2013. "Race in the Netherlands: The Aftermath of a Football Tragedy." January 12.

6

Tenants' Displacement Experiences

From the perspectives of existing tenants, the experience of redevelopment can be examined and described according to three distinct stages:

1. Displacement, beginning with receipt of an official letter of notification that their unit will be demolished and giving a date by which they will need to vacate the premises, and including their selection of temporary alternative housing inside or outside the Regent Park boundaries.
2. Relocation, in which the household moves to temporary alternative public housing accommodation for the duration of construction of new housing for the households in that redevelopment phase.
3. Resettlement into a newly constructed Regent Park housing unit.

Chapters 6 through 8 describe each of these stages from the perspectives of the study sample of Phase 1 residents.

Moving Day

On the day in 2005 when the first households displaced by the redevelopment were moving their belongings out of their old Regent Park homes, a photographer sought to document the landmark day by putting human faces on the abstract idea of revitalization. He asked a large family if he could do a portrait of the family members with their boxes and other assorted packed luggage. He asked the youngest child to move his bike over to the side, outside camera range. The photographer posed the people around their packed boxes and suitcases and took a number of photographs. He did not, unfortunately, get any photographic documentation of the thief who stole the boy's bicycle while the family was posing. For the boy, that theft was the most memorable event marking his family's temporary displacement from their Regent Park home.

Being displaced from their old Regent Park dwellings was the Phase 1 tenants' first step towards being re-housed in brand new dwellings. In the view of tenants assigned to move in later phases, the Phase 1 tenants were the fortunate ones;

they would be the first to get out of the deteriorated housing stock; the first to move into a brand new home. They wouldn't be consigned to live for years on an active, noisy, gritty construction site. They would not need to occupy the decrepit "before" setting when groups of visitors were led on tours comparing the "before" and the "after" of the redevelopment. But, for their part, many of the Phase 1 tenants didn't feel so lucky. The prospect of moving was daunting. Moving possessions was one thing; switching children's schools, leaving friends and neighbours, places of worship, neighbourhood-based services and programs, nearby workplaces, transit routes, even familiar places to shop, were difficult. For those who were recent immigrants, there was the concern about leaving the community-based ties to their culture. Most difficult of all were the unanswered questions, the open-ended time frames that made it hard for the tenants to imagine how their lives would roll out over the coming years.

This chapter describes the Phase 1 tenants' displacement experiences. Based on interviews at or close to the time of their displacement, it looks at their decision-making among various options available for temporary housing during the construction of new Regent Park housing. It examines the housing authority's policies and procedures from the perspectives of this first cohort of displaced and relocated tenants. It considers what the interviews reveal about the relocation needs of particular age groups of households, including families with school age children and seniors. And it examines the factors influencing the Phase 1 tenants' preferences and choices for their temporary housing while they awaited their new housing.

Involuntary displacement from one's home is stressful, even if there is a promise of eventual re-housing in improved circumstances. Research in the US by Edward Goetz has looked at public housing tenants' experience of involuntary displacement in the course of public housing redevelopment. His research in the Minneapolis area found that even tenants living in the most deteriorated, most distressed public housing projects report they would prefer staying put over moving elsewhere (Goetz 2003). Recent immigrants—especially non-English speakers—and visible minority populations were especially reluctant to be uprooted (Goetz 2003, 202).

Our interviews with Phase 1 Regent Park tenants also found reluctance among youth and adults to being moved out. A local educator described bringing an elementary school class to a celebration marking the start of the Regent Park renewal. The ceremonial start of demolition brought home to his students the idea that they would really need to leave. According to the teacher, the promise of newer, better housing didn't make the prospect of their displacement any more appealing:

> Some people say, "what's the big deal [about relocation]? You're going to get a nice, new place, you know?" No. Home is home and [youth] view it in

> those sorts of terms: "They're taking away my home!"… I remember when they started the demolition. They had the mayor and everyone here… I brought my class to witness this. [For] a lot of them… it wasn't real until they saw the wrecking ball going into the building… and then some of my students started crying. It became more real to them… "Wow they're serious!" And so the question is: "When are they going to do my building?"
> (Johnson and Schippling 2009, 18)

Being displaced or evicted from one's home can make one feel rootless and vulnerable—the phenomenon Mindy Fullilove has written about in the context of urban renewal in US neighbourhoods (Fullilove 2009). Demolition of a neighbourhood can deprive that residential community of its common ground; residents can be deprived of their spatial identity (Goetz 2013, citing Venkatesh 2000). As Goetz observes, tenants of public housing, regardless of its poor state of repair, may feel a strong sense of place attachment to that housing community, the source of important social networks (Goetz 2013, 130). Our interviews of Regent Park residents found that their attachment to the neighbourhood was quite strong. Could it be sustained, however, over a lengthy period of disruption and relocation?

Displacement of tenants marked the first part of the first phase of the Regent Park redevelopment. As prescribed by City of Toronto regulations around eviction/termination, those tenants received notices at least five months in advance of the moving date, advising that they would need to vacate the premises (CMHC 2011, 68). The TCHC needed to find these 380 households temporary public housing accommodations for at least two years—if the initial timetable was maintained—while the new housing was constructed. As it turned out, most Phase 1 families lived in temporary quarters for much longer periods. Once new housing was ready, there might still be additional delays while tenants chose a particular unit of the size (measured in number of bedrooms) for which their household was eligible.

Tenants were assured they would have a choice about their temporary accommodations, including their location. In the expectation that many would choose to stay within Regent Park, the TCHC had been stockpiling vacant housing units in Regent Park for two years in order to meet at least part of that anticipated demand. A TCHC presentation at a community meeting early in 2005 laid out the terms of the housing authority's agreement with tenants. Under the heading "Coming back" residents were told of their "Right to move back when unit is rebuilt—usually about two years" (TCHC 2005). The whole Phase 1 displacement, relocation, resettlement experience was something new for all parties involved. Working out those logistics was challenging for landlord as well as tenants, since this was the first time TCHC had tackled a redevelopment of this scale.[1] The housing authority had to develop and refine a system as they went along. Their ad hoc approach seemed evident to the tenants, as various schemes were tried, revised, and tried again. By the later phases, a new system had been worked out that made dislocation more bearable and more predictable for the tenants, and more efficient for the housing authority.

Surprise Early Morning Line-ups[2]

Residents reported that they were told initially that temporary alternative housing would be assigned on a "first come, first served" basis. Phase 1 tenants understood that they would line up to choose from available temporary housing units. According to the terms in the housing authority's tenant agreement, "when tenants come back they will be able to choose their permanent units… in the order that they left their old units. The tenants who leave first are given first choice of units to return to" (TCHC 2005).

The first implementation of this system was, to tenants, disorganized and confusing, even chaotic. With no prior models to inform them, the Phase 1 tenants did not really know what to expect for selection of their replacement housing. Most had attended the public information meetings about the redevelopment convened by the housing authority. One such meeting, held in a community meeting room above a local public library branch, featured a three-dimensional model to give Phase 1 tenants an idea of what the redevelopment would look like. Those in attendance were more interested to hear about the projected timing of their moves into temporary and then new permanent housing. The tenants reported that they heard conflicting accounts and lots of gossip about redevelopment plans. School children brought home some information; neighbours offered still different accounts.

Despite attempts by the housing authority, local schools and other local agencies to spread the word and prepare the residents for moving, the Phase 1 residents' initial opportunity to choose alternative housing was a tumultuous scene. Many residents were surprised the first time a line formed in the early morning outside the Regent Park relocation office, a line for Phase 1 tenants to select their alternate housing. Residents thought they would have received more notice of the date and time they would need to line up.

Before the first light of day on a cold, early spring weekday morning (April 18, 2005), Phase 1 residents began to form a queue outside the TCHC's Regent Park relocation office. No lights were on in the office, but there was a commotion outside. According to one resident's account, people came running from several directions, trying to get a good place in the line. He said he was one of the early arrivals: "I was actually here at the office at three o'clock in the morning, by six o'clock there was 200 people in line waiting to take their choice."

Another resident recalled the experience, what she saw in the early morning, and how she coped:

> I just saw people are running. I told my children I'd just go and look… So when I go there, there was a big line, so I just stood in the line and I told [my daughter] "If I get late to come, you just phone my sister… and you go to school and she will come… and she [will] stand for me in the line…"

Looking back on the whole relocation journey, that resident remembers the first line-up for alternative housing as a low point: "I remember lining up. I remember the big crowd. I even remember my number from the line-up."

She recalls that tenants had not been prepared to stand in line to choose alternative housing. They had been told the system would be based on a first come, first served rule, and—a very important detail—that at a later stage their order of priority for choosing new units would be based on the order in which they moved out. She knew that her family would soon need to choose alternate housing. She had understood that they would have to make a choice among available alternate housing units, and would need to choose where they would live temporarily. She just didn't know how this would be done:

> I didn't know that we'd have to go early in the morning and have to stand in line. I didn't know that. I just thought we have we have to go to the office and select the house. So when I go there it was this big line, "Oh my goodness!" I was upset, "what's going on?" But there was no one I—I didn't know anybody there, there was all men, no women, so I just realized what's happening. I can see I just [had to] stand in the line, and that's what I did.

She was not critical of the way TCHC handled the whole Phase 1 relocation effort. In fact, she thought they did a good job, and she was pleased with the temporary housing to which her family was relocated. But she would have appreciated better communication, giving her more of an understanding of what would be happening, and when. She offered some advice to the TCHC about their way of working with the tenants:

> I think they should… contact people… if they're moving them… in future [the TCHC] should contact everyone on the list and they should make an appointment with them and they should meet, instead of lining up, because it's really hard for people.

As they waited, people were anxious, convinced that their family's future housing security depended on their place in that queue. At least one fight broke out over people seeming to cut into the line. A frequently-told tale about the first line-up features a Regent Park resident who, in an entrepreneurial spirit, offered cups of hot coffee for sale to those in the line.

In the background on this cold early morning were many frantic phone calls between tenants to spread the word of the line-up among neighbours, relatives and friends. Households had to plan which adults would join the queue, and who would deliver children to school, or travel to work themselves. Those who were ill or infirm, those with disabilities, and parents with very young children, found the situation particularly difficult.

The line-ups continued for some time. A parent with young, school-age children recalled those days, and how unpleasant and inconvenient they were:

> It was very hard that time, all the time. Very hard, you get up in the morning every morning, line up, stay there and you don't have anything to do, you know. They give a ticket at five o'clock in the morning, they give a ticket and they open the door at nine o'clock in the morning. It's too hard. You know with kids, you can't leave them alone…

A number of residents balked at the line system, saying it was an unfair and inefficient way to match households with available housing units. They objected that it discriminated against those who, for reasons of employment, family responsibilities, disability or health limitations, were not able to line up in the early morning hours. In the words of one tenant:

> They put rules that the one who moved first, he gets to come back first. They didn't consider time, they didn't consider that we are busy and they didn't make many apartments available to look for. They just wanted us to move; they didn't look at what we need. They didn't consider my situation.

Another resident said working people, in particular, were very inconvenienced by it. And she added that in Regent Park "most of the people are working."

A Phase 1 resident who had clearly understood the plans and procedures as explained by the Relocation staff still objected that it was unnecessarily difficult for the residents about to be displaced:

> I don't think it's a good idea waking up and lining up. The system is kind of [pause] the system is kind of African. That is how, back home, we used to do it. You line up and there is no system. This is now… [with] technology and everything, they know. It is not safe for everybody. Even I had to wake up early in the morning, 4 o'clock, to line up.
>
> (Schippling 2007, 70)

Changes in Line-up Procedures

Over time and with experience there was some refinement of the line-up system. In the later stages, Phase 1 tenants were asked to come on particular days, depending on the size of housing unit for which they were eligible. Two- and three-bedroom households were served on alternate Mondays and one, four and five bedrooms were served on alternate Tuesdays (TCHC 2006, 9).

The residents became accustomed to the routine, but it did not become easier. According to one tenant's account, eventually it was the TCHC that supplied the coffee and even donuts to those waiting. According to another Phase 1 resident, the procedure only became easier and more efficient when TCHC changed their practice by: first, dealing with households according to the size of unit (number of bedrooms) for which they had been approved; and second, by advance posting of a listing of available alternative housing units, by size. That way, according to the resident "when they started posting the list before… if you saw something that you wanted, then you could have gone. Then they broke it down [by bedrooms] doing it one day 1 and 5 bedrooms, then 2s and 3s."

Organizing the line-ups according to housing unit size made the process easier, more streamlined. However, it still was far from an efficient or considerate use of residents' time. Another tenant offered her criticism of that system:

> Finally, they separated it by bedrooms—this day one-bedroom, another day three-bedroom, whatever. They separated it into different days. I didn't go. I went the first day, I filled in the form, the relocation form you can fill, I filled that in and I went there. I couldn't find anything [on] the day I went. I can't [go so] early in the morning to line-up. [It was] First come, first served—that is why I end up the last.

Another resident described how the TCHC had eventually made changes in their alternate housing allocation system that made it somewhat easier for residents:

> The first day that they had it (the line-up), we went at four o'clock in the morning. Then the next time it was midnight. And the next [time] it was 11:00 pm, and then they put a stop to it and started posting it the night before. After about four or five times people were lining up they started posting the list before so if you saw something that you wanted then you could have gone. Then they broke it down to doing it one day was for one bedrooms, and [another] for five bedrooms, then two or for three or four bedrooms.

While such tinkering made the line-up system work more efficiently, many Phase 1 residents still objected to lining up to re-house their household. The message from their accounts was that the system was demeaning, an affront to their dignity. For many it exposed them and their family members to unnecessary hardship and stress. A system designed with respect for the tenants would not, they said, have had people rushing to join a queue to choose temporary replacement housing. It would not have had them making emergency phone calls asking neighbours and relatives to hold their place while they delivered their children to school or childcare.

From the outset it must have been clear to TCHC that their line-up system was flawed. Residents complained that it was inconvenient, degrading and inefficient. But as TCHC began to introduce still other procedures—such as a lottery system—residents became anxious at the changes in rules. At least with the old system, they felt they knew where they stood. If this procedure was changed, what other surprises might be in store for the residents? Some wondered: What about the promise of Right of Return? How secure was that?

TCHC, in its own survey evaluation of the Phase 1 relocation experience (TCHC 2006, 20) asked whether tenants had any suggestions about ways to improve the services provided to tenants. A report on the results of that evaluation included a sample of those suggestions. Two of the survey respondents offered suggestions with alternatives to the line-up—at least for the elderly and disabled. They suggested that TCHC relocation staff could call tenants or visit their homes to offer alternative housing choices.

The housing authority eventually got the message and ended the line-up system. A lottery draw allowed subsequent waves of displaced tenants to choose alternative temporary housing—and to select permanent replacement housing—without lining up.

Housing Authority Communication with Tenants

Phase 1 residents were given at least five months' notice of the date by which they would have to vacate the premises in which they had been living. These plans and timetable and the details of relocation were communicated to residents in mailings, meetings, workshops, and by way of newsletters available in the eight languages spoken most frequently by Regent Park residents. Since many residents were recent immigrants with limited English language proficiency, simultaneous interpretation was offered at the information meetings. Residents were given general information about temporary alternative housing, and were told that the housing authority would cover all their moving costs. They were eligible for an alternative housing unit of the same number of rooms as their current housing.

The temporary housing available to the residents was in one of three locations: 1) vacant units within the Regent Park public housing community that had been stockpiled for two years for this purpose; 2) other TCHC housing nearby in downtown Toronto; 3) other TCHC housing elsewhere in the Greater Toronto Area. The final figures showed that 40 percent of the Phase 1 resident households obtained alternative housing within the Regent Park boundaries, 48 percent moved to public housing downtown nearby, 8 percent moved to public housing elsewhere in the greater Toronto area, and 4 percent moved out of public housing at this point (TCHC 2006, 3).

As indicated in Chart 6.1, the distribution of temporary alternative housing units among the 52 sampled households followed a somewhat different pattern, with 65 percent of those households settling into units inside the Regent Park footprint, compared with just 40 percent of the overall population. This difference is likely due to the non-random selection by which households came into our study (as described in Appendix 1). Even so, the sum of "inside" and "nearby" resettlement was 78 percent in the study's population, not very different from the overall figure of 85 percent. For households moving farther away or leaving TCHC altogether, the differences were not great.

The moment of displacement was a key decision point for residents. Most saw it as an opportunity preceded by major inconvenience. They were signing onto a journey which would leave them living in temporary quarters for some unspecified time period no less than two years, and then resettle them in new housing in their Regent Park neighbourhood.

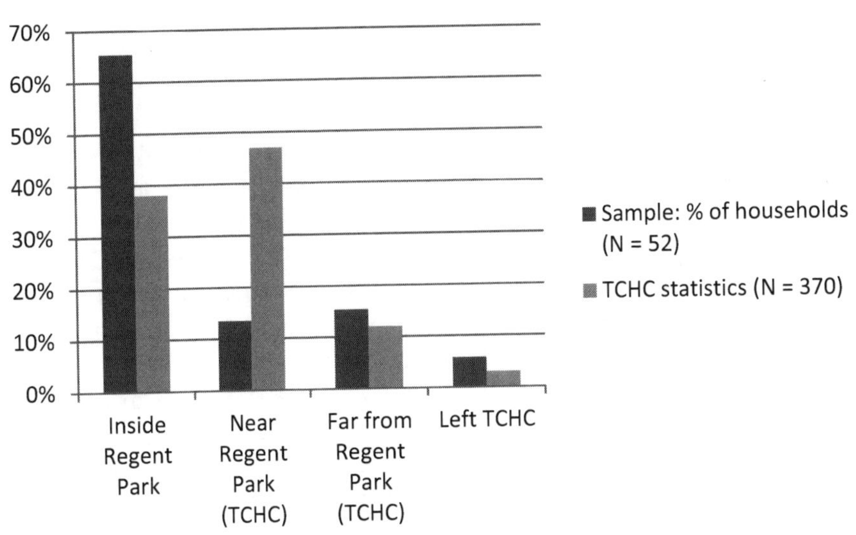

Chart 6.1 Destinations of Phase 1 tenants temporarily relocated.

Source: L. Johnson, interviews; Toronto Community Housing Corporation (private communication, 2014)

Housing within the Regent Park footprint was the favoured choice for alternative housing for many Phase 1 households. Some preferred that choice based on children's schools, not wanting to disrupt their education. Some wanted to stay close to other services, programs, or places of worship, as well as to remain near their neighbours, relatives and friends. Others, afraid of being "out of sight, out of mind," wanted to stay nearby just to be sure that they really did get rehoused in Regent Park when the promised new housing was built (many tenants were not convinced that the Right of Return would be honoured). In some instances staying in or near the familiar neighbourhood meant settling for housing in what they considered a poor state of repair. But respondents generally felt the trade-off was worth it.

There were some, however, who felt that the eventual opportunity was not worth the stress of being uprooted and moved at least twice. In our Phase 1 sample of 52 households, three chose to leave TCHC tenancy at this point. Their destinations included: purchased housing on the private market; private rental housing; and other non-profit social housing outside the TCHC's portfolio. Over the following seven years, a number of other relocated households left TCHC accommodation altogether. According to figures provided by TCHC in 2014, of the 381 households in Phase 1, 19 percent waived their right to return and an additional 22 percent "are no longer TCHC tenants" (TCHC, private communication, November 19, 2014). Our source gives no breakdown of factors to explain the latter group's separation, but it may include some tenants who were, by TCHC rules, not in good standing and therefore not eligible to return.

Some Requests Denied

Two specific aspects of the relocation plan particularly displeased some of the residents as they were about to be moved. First, some tenants asked for, but were denied, provision to be relocated alongside or in close proximity to their previous neighbours. Whether these clusters of neighbours were in larger or smaller groups, some indicated that they simply wanted to be settled into temporary housing near one another. In interviews they reported that they had told the relocation counsellors that they didn't care whether their temporary alternative housing was inside the Regent Park footprint or elsewhere in the TCHC's stock of available housing units—they just wanted to be housed close together. Living for years in close proximity to one another, these households had developed bonds of friendship and social support—ties that they wanted to preserve. One tenant described a failed attempt to obtain the housing authority's approval for the idea:

> [We wanted them] to move us as a group. And when we all went into [the relocation] office, [we were told] "Oh no, it's all individual." Because there were a group of us from [one address] that wanted the same building. They said they couldn't do it that way.

For many residents, the social bonds of community life were very important; for some their supportive relationships with neighbours compensated for the more negative aspects of their life in Regent Park. The TCHC's failure to take seriously these bonds of friendship, and their reluctance to even consider the residents' requests to be settled in temporary alternative housing close to their former neighbours, seemed to contradict the TCHC statements about the importance of community. We have not, in our interviews, found evidence of residents repeating this request when moving back into permanent units; but neither have we encountered any indication of TCHC offering such an opportunity to returning residents.

Secondly, some tenants felt that seniority, in the form of their and their relatives' number of years of tenure in their Regent Park housing, should be acknowledged in choosing temporary housing and in resettling them in new housing. Some expressed the idea that having been born in Regent Park, or having raised their own children there, should give them priority status in relocation and resettlement. Others felt that a long record of responsible tenancy should translate into a priority position when it came to choosing alternate housing during the redevelopment.

Residents reported that both of these requests were denied by TCHC. The first, they said, was refused on the basis of feasibility—relocation counsellors told them it was just too difficult to find clusters of available alternate housing of the sizes required. The second request was rejected on a policy principle. The relocation counsellors told residents that neither seniority nor record of tenancy would be used as a basis for housing assignment. According to the TCHC's expressed policy of Right of Return, all those in the status of tenants of the original Phase 1 RGI units at the time of notification of displacement, and who were tenants in good standing, would be granted equal access to replacement housing. All residents would be treated the same, regardless of the length of past tenure in Regent Park.

The Role of Schools

According to key informants, the local schools played an important role, serving as a channel of communication about redevelopment plans to families with school age children. Working with TCHC, liaison persons from local schools developed and delivered curriculum about the history and the future of

Regent Park. One teacher who had served in that liaison role described how she delivered information to her students within a unit on Regent Park's history and future. In her example, children between the ages of ten and twelve in Nelson Mandela Park School spent a week learning about the redevelopment plan. Some of the material in this special unit was delivered by their classroom teachers; invited visitors from other local community agencies also addressed the children about the kinds of changes that they could expect. Over the course of that study week they discussed their hopes and their fears about the upcoming changes. In one project the children illustrated what they liked and didn't like about their community. Their teacher created an album of their paintings and showed it during the research interview. One student's picture expressed the sharp contrasts she felt about her home: dark, muddy colours showed the garbage dumpster outside her building; bright sparkling glitter trimmed the front entrance to her building and the windows of her family's apartment.

That same teacher was asked to assess the Board of Education's role in the process of resettlement:

> I know that the [Toronto District School] Board has, and continues to have a policy and a procedure… that allows for students to stay in their home school even when they are moved, and given certain parameters there, they are allowed to be bussed, and TTC [public transit] tickets will be provided. So there is definitely an understanding and a desire by the TDSB to make this process as comfortable and as easy for students as possible. Remaining in your home school is certainly something that can help make that happen. But not all parents want that either.

Moving Out

Phase 1 tenants reported in interviews that they found the displacement and the moving very difficult. For families of any size—even solitary individuals—relocating was psychologically and physically taxing. The relocated tenants spoke about the challenges of packing and unpacking. Although TCHC provided the movers and covered all moving expenses, residents were responsible for organizing and boxing up, and later uncrating, the contents of their homes. One elderly tenant acknowledged that although the unpacking job couldn't easily be delegated, it was a demanding job:

> If somebody were to help you to unpack, all the glasses, the plates and the valuable stuff, they don't know where you want it. You know where to put it, you know where you want it, so, you know. With the big stuff it's okay

> they [move] it for me but, with the other stuff, they wouldn't know where I want to put it.

The order of people's departure also became a significant issue. Phase 1 tenants reported that they arranged their moving date according to the schedules of household members. In particular, parents of school-age children tried to avoid switching children's schools during the school year. Some households tried to delay moving out as long as possible. Without knowing much about the alternative temporary housing to which they would be moving, they preferred to stay for as long as possible in the familiar old home. Reflecting on that experience, several households reported that being the last occupants on a floor of an apartment building—or being the very last in a building—was unpleasant and unsafe. If the building appeared vacant or even seemed to be in the process of emptying out, those who remained could become the target of burglars and other criminals. Additionally, cockroaches and other vermin quickly found their way to apartments that were still inhabited. Being the last to leave was clearly not a good idea.

One resident with school-age children described her experience:

> Someone tried to break into our house because there was almost nobody else in our building. I called the police at about 4:30 in the morning. I yelled. I also made a complaint to the manager. We don't know who tried to break in. It was only me and one girl were left, the last people on our floor. They tried to break in, but they couldn't… I yelled. I couldn't see their faces—there was no light on the floor; it was too dark to see them. Then Security arrived. I was very scared by that experience. I was very uncomfortable living there. Because of safety, I very quickly chose available alternative housing, saying "give me anything".

Another resident stated that she knew it would be a bad idea for her family to be the last ones out of their old building. "As people started moving out, it got worse. Things were spreading out—the bugs go to other places." She made a point of checking in regularly with the relocation office staff to see what alternative housing options were available.

The larger issue, according to some of the Phase 1 residents, was the lack of maintenance and security in buildings that were being evacuated prior to their demolition. Cockroaches were only one symptom of overall neglect. One tenant said:

> The building became scary. You could not come at night because you wouldn't know if somebody had broken a window and gone inside. It was

> scary, the laundry room was dirty, the maintenance was also dirty, the elevators dirty, the hallway. They became careless.

Another Phase 1 resident voiced a different, more positive opinion based on his experience. This tenant looked on the brighter side of the absence of crowds in his building:

> To be honest it was pretty neat! Like I had a whole building to myself almost for like a week and a half. With nobody in the whole building the elevator was there at my convenience! If I stopped it on my floor it doesn't go nowhere because nobody else is using it. It was alright!

Despite having been moved into temporary accommodations, some quite far from Regent Park, many relocated Phase 1 residents reported returning regularly to their old neighbourhood. The reasons were varied. Some returned to attend classes or places of worship; take part in after-school programs or extracurricular activities; play sports; shop on nearby Parliament Street; or visit relatives or friends. Some found the experience jarring. One resident after relocating off-site, described her reaction of pleasant surprise when, upon returning to her former street, she discovered that her old building was still standing, and how she greeted it like an old friend: "My building is still up. [Now] every time I pass by it, I say 'Hi, how are you?' "

The Twice Displaced

Almost no one associated with the Regent Park redevelopment had anything negative to say about the new Aquatic Centre constructed early in the redevelopment. Bright, airy, spacious and beautiful, this addition to the community was welcomed by most community members. But the facility came as a surprise, added after the start of Phase 1. Funding unexpectedly became available for a new City of Toronto pool. The suggestion that it be built in Regent Park, adjacent to the large park in the very centre of the new community, was greeted with widespread approval from local residents and politicians. The only downside to the Aquatic Centre idea was that its proposed site—230 Sumach Street—was occupied by an apartment building and an adjacent row of townhouses, all designated for later demolition. Some of these units had also been assigned as temporary housing for about a dozen displaced Phase 1 households. In all, 55 households were living in the new path of demolition.[3]

Variously relabelled "Phase 1b" or "Phase 2a," the amendment to the plan for the new pool meant that families relocated to this site would have to move a second time, to different temporary housing. While the disruption and inconvenience earned these households top spots on the priority list for choosing new housing when that was built, they found that moving out twice was especially stressful, not just because of the extra work involved, but because it undermined their confidence that the housing authority knew what it was doing.

Flexibility by Design

A phased development allows for changes in procedures based on experience. At the time of writing (2016) the redevelopment project is in Phase 3 of the (revised) five projected phases. Some of the hard lessons learned over the displacement of Phase 1 tenants have produced change.

People no longer line up to choose temporary housing. Instead, choices are made by a lottery system, which has gone through multiple phases and re-invention. Now people make a random draw for their choice of temporary housing, and draw again for their ranking in selection of new housing when that has been built. Tenants' lottery numbers only come into play when there is a conflict with multiple households choosing one unit for permanent resettlement. In such a case, the one with the lowest number wins. Tenants acknowledge the fairness of the lottery system.

A TCHC staff member described the lottery system with enthusiasm:

> We have learned so much from the first time when we relocated people based on a first come, first served basis... Since we started with the draw system, we not only offer tenants a certain type of house, we offer you everything you are eligible for. It's up to you to choose what you want from the list. It is up to your draw number to determine whether you get that one. Now we are giving the same opportunity to everyone. It doesn't matter that you lived in a townhouse [before]. We are not promising that you will get back a townhouse. You can choose—it is fair because everybody has the same opportunity—the same chance… We came up with the draw system. I love it, and the tenants are getting to love it too. Because they will have one draw for their relocation, and another one for the new return. Everybody has a chance to be number one.

According to the staff member, the system has the advantage of being both public and fair:

> In Phase 1, it was the first time… it was a bit hard, because people did not want to move… After that relocation was done, that's when everyone got

> involved, and said "Let's do something, because this is not working." I remember… we started discussing a fair system that we could develop for the relocation and return process... We came up with the random draw number, where the choice is taken out of the [TCHC]—we do not decide where you [the tenant] are going to go, you are the one who is deciding. We created the system where you will get a draw number that is chosen in public. We put your name into a clear jar and in a public meeting we do the draw one by one. Somebody from the community does the draw. We don't want to be accused of anything, even though the community is looking.

Phase 2 and Phase 3 Changes

Another procedural change, more basic than the lottery replacing the line-up, is an attempt to skip the step of relocating households to temporary housing, and instead move them directly into new housing. This was begun in Phase 2, when almost 200 households followed that streamlined pattern. At a public meeting at the start of Phase 3, the TCHC's Acting CEO Greg Spearn pledged to speed up the building process in order to move households more quickly into new housing.

Still another change designed to lessen the negative impact of displacement is a pledge from TCHC not to displace any households with school age children while school is in session. This means that those families will have a right to be moved only in the summer months of July or August.

Some staff in the housing authority have a keen interest in minimizing residents' stress over relocation for the redevelopment. When the procedures for selecting and occupying alternative housing have been problematic from tenants' perspectives, TCHC has been flexible and willing to change those procedures in subsequent redevelopment phases. This experience will undoubtedly inform that agency's plan for future redevelopment of other housing elsewhere in the city.

Lessons Learned

Some of the difficulties experienced by this first cohort of tenants seem to be rooted in failures of communication between the TCHC and the residents. The idea of people running around, joining a pre-dawn line-up without knowing the rules or the expectations does seem to represent such a breakdown. Some of the problems can perhaps be traced back to longstanding antipathy between some tenants and housing authority staff. One TCHC staff person whom we interviewed made that point, saying that some of the tenants have a long history of dealing with "Housing"—sometimes going back twenty years or more—and it hasn't always been a positive experience. Now that staff and tenants are beginning a new endeavour, he cautioned, the housing authority is going to have to earn the tenants' trust. Improved communication may develop as that trust is built up.

Had the residents been given a more active (or proactive) and responsible role in their relocation, that first Phase 1 morning line-up exercise might have looked quite different. A system more like the lottery system that was eventually devised might have been utilized from the outset. A by-product of such a process might have been an increased feeling of trust among the various parties responsible for Phase 1 relocation. Decreased stress levels for residents might also have resulted from such a process.

Perhaps some amount of miscommunication and confusion was inevitable, given the scale and novelty of the new project. With practice, the system does seem to have been improved in later phases. It can be expected that it will continue to improve with time, and that other phases and other redevelopment initiatives will not need to start from scratch.

One way to benefit from the early learning from the Phase 1 experiences is to build in some continuity of staffing. Expertise can be maintained at the level of supervisory staff who manage the relocation counselling function. In addition, at the community level, TCHC has begun hiring Phase 1 residents, who have been through the experience of relocation and return, as community animators. Their role is to explain the process to tenants who are now beginning relocation. Along with helping with translation as needed, those Phase 1 returnees are able to empathize with the concerns of the still-to-be-relocated residents, and can facilitate community engagement.

The unmet request of residents to be moved as a group to their temporary alternative housing is worthy of closer consideration. Some tenants want to be re-housed in a cluster of dwellings in close proximity to one another. The neighbours, who already have the means of communicating via social media, have indicated that this sense of community is important to them—more important even than where they actually are housed at this stage in the relocation process. It is likely that only a minority of tenants would make such a request. In the spirit of promoting community, TCHC could consider developing a means of accommodating such requests. At the very least, this could be tried on a pilot project for one phase or sub-phase of the redevelopment, and expanded if the experiment is determined to be successful.

Finally, for the tenants, the early stage of the redevelopment is the most difficult and challenging. Asked to put a label on it, they come up with words like "stressful" and even "nightmare." If they can have confidence that the procedure is workable, and that at the end, they can be rehoused in new units that really meet their needs, their experience of relocation will be eased considerably. And if some can settle, at least temporarily, near to their old neighbours, they will have an improved relocation experience.

Notes

1 TCHC had recently undertaken a smaller-scale redevelopment less than one kilometre from Regent Park; Don Mount Court, a public housing community built in the 1960s, was transformed into a mixed-income development renamed "Rivertowne," with 232 rental units and 187 condominium ones. Planning commenced in 2000 and the work was completed in 2012.

2 This description of tenants' lining up to choose temporary alternative housing is based on Schippling 2007.

3 Figure based on information conveyed by TCHC staff, personal communication, March 25, 2008.

References

CMHC (Canada Mortgage and Housing Corporation). 2011. Research Report, Distinct Housing Needs Series: Case Study Research on Social Housing Redevelopment and Regeneration. Part A: Overview. Report prepared for CMHC by SPR Associates Inc. Case Study #5: Regent Park, Phase 1 (Toronto, Ontario) Toronto Community Housing Corporation (TCHC). (October): 63–84.

Fullilove, Mindy Thompson. 2009. *Root Shock: How Tearing Up City Neighbourhoods Hurts America, and What We Can Do About it.* New York: Random House.

Goetz, Edward G. 2003. *Clearing the Way: Deconcentrating the Poor in Urban America.* Washington, D.C.: The Urban Institute Press.

Goetz, Edward G. 2013. *New Deal Ruins: Race, Economic Justice, and Public Housing Policy.* Ithaca, NY: Cornell University Press.

Johnson, Laura C. and Richard Schippling. 2009. *Regent Park Revitalization: Young People's Experience of Relocation from Public Housing Redevelopment.* Ottawa: Canada Mortgage and Housing Corporation, External Research Program. (June). NH18-1-2/50-2009E-PDF

Schippling, Richard M. 2007. "Public Housing Redevelopment: Residents' Experiences with Relocation from Phase 1 in Toronto's Regent Park Revitalization." Master's thesis, School of Planning, University of Waterloo, Waterloo, ON. uwspace.uwaterloo.ca/handle/10012/3028. (Accessed January 10, 2017).

TCHC (Toronto Community Housing Corporation). 2005. Regent Park Revitalization, Tenant Agreement, PowerPoint presentation. (February).

TCHC (Toronto Community Housing Corporation). 2006. Regent Park Redevelopment Phase 1 Relocation Evaluation Report. Cargnelli, Jennifer. (May).

Venkatesh, Sudhir A. 2000. *American Project: the Rise and Fall of a Modern Ghetto.* Cambridge, MA: Harvard University Press.

7
The Challenges of Temporary Relocation (2006–2011)

On June 11, 2014, at the start of Phase 3 of the redevelopment, Greg Spearn, Interim President, Chief Executive Officer and Chief Development Officer of TCHC, addressed a well-attended community update meeting. He acknowledged that after completing two of five phases of redevelopment, the TCHC now knew what was the most challenging phase for tenants: temporary relocation. He promised to accelerate construction of new Regent Park replacement units so that more households could move directly from old into new housing. A letter under the heading "Our Three Promises to Regent Park Residents" was distributed at the meeting. It spelled out a commitment to treat all residents with respect, fairness and empathy, to not give anyone preferential treatment during relocation, and to increase the pace of construction of new rental homes. The letter pledged to build 900 housing units in four years—enough to house all remaining relocated tenants as well as those who would be moved in the rest of Phase 3.

How well did Spearn understand the challenges faced by displaced households in the early redevelopment phases? Would his proposal to speed up the relocation phase make the revitalization easier for displaced families? How feasible would it be to skip the temporary housing stage, and move households directly to new housing immediately upon displacement?

Our interviews with tenants from Phase 1 confirmed that relocation was often difficult. The lack of clarity about the timing or the duration of their temporary stay made life hard. For families with young children, making decisions about school enrolment and access to community-based services was complicated. Even decorating was hard. People were reluctant to invest in new furnishings, preferring to wait until they moved to new housing. Some reported that since their relocation was just temporary, they didn't really get to know new neighbours.

This chapter reviews two sets of relocation accounts, organized according to whether their temporary replacement housing was located inside or outside of the Regent Park boundaries, and examining the ways distance affects their lived experiences of relocation. Some of the households are families with children of school age, and these stories present the parents' perspectives on the relocation experience, with some input from teenage children.

It should be noted that the Tenant Agreement for Regent Park set out the terms of the relocation from the tenant's point of view (TCHC 2006). According to that document, under the heading "Choosing your Neighbourhood" tenants were told:

> When it's time for your part of Regent Park to be taken down, there will be a relocation process to help you find a new home. You can stay in Regent Park if you want to, or you can live nearby. You can also move farther away if you want to.
>
> (TCHC 2006)

The Agreement also describes the process of "Choosing your Unit":

> You will be allowed to choose the unit you want to live in during relocation. You will be able to look at a list of vacant units in Toronto Community Housing buildings across Toronto and pick one. You can also have a person from the Relocation Office choose a unit for you.
>
> (ibid.)

Most of the Phase 1 tenants ended up relocating to temporary alternate housing inside or near the Regent Park footprint. Fewer than 10 percent settled more than a few kilometres away (see Chart 6.1 for the distribution of their alternate housing).

Following the sample of the first cohort of tenants through relocation, we asked how their real life experiences with relocation conformed (or did not conform) to that agreement. Tenants described what had happened to them and their neighbours, friends and acquaintances, and drew their own conclusions about how the redevelopment plan was working. Views of local community agency staff were also reviewed, along with tenants' suggestions about how the system might be improved or redesigned to lessen the burden on households. Part of the housing authority's rationale for doing this redevelopment in phases is to be able to apply the lessons learned from earlier phases to subsequent ones.

"Temporary" Accommodation

The first redevelopment plan (TCHC 2003) called for the entire project to be completed in eleven years, with demolition beginning in 2006 and the last new housing units completed in 2017. Predictably, the work took much longer than the projected timeframe. By 2015 construction had begun in the third of five projected phases, with the ultimate deadline now estimated around 2025.

Inevitably, this change affected the tenants' experience of relocation. At the beginning of redevelopment, tenants were advised that "everyone who is relocated from a unit in Regent Park will have the right to move back into Regent Park when their unit has been rebuilt, approximately two years from the day you move to your temporary unit" (TCHC 2006).

But the experience of our respondents was quite different, with displacement often lasting more than twice as long.

From our interviews with sampled Phase 1 residents, it was possible to calculate the length of time from displacement to return for twenty-five of the sampled households. The mean duration was 56 months (4.7 years). Ten households were displaced for five years or more. The longest period of displacement was 95 months, from 2005 to 2013. The shortest duration was 45 months.[1] (Our calculation of duration of residents' relocation in their temporary housing is similar to that reported in a 2011 case study of housing redevelopment and regeneration conducted for Canada Mortgage and Housing Corporation [CMHC] of Regent Park Phase 1 residents' relocation experiences. That study reported that households experienced "a 4–5 year turnaround time between moving out and moving back" [CMHC 2011].)

Living for so long in temporary quarters presented relocated households with serious challenges in many spheres of life. Members of displaced households reported that their ties to schools (including extracurricular activities), work, places of worship, local community organizations and friendships all suffered from the open-ended nature of the relocation.

Young people in relocation recalled the easy socializing they had enjoyed previously in the old Regent Park environment. The combination of having been moved themselves, and their friends' families having also been relocated made it hard to keep in contact. One sixteen-year-old female reminisced that previously "all my friends were just a building away and we'd just walk by, and you would see them and say 'Hi.' Now they're all scattered throughout Toronto" (Johnson and Schippling 2009, 29).

For the youngest among them, distance was a barrier to keeping up with friends after relocation. One mother from a family relocated outside Regent Park, but still walking distance away, described how she regularly accompanied her young school-aged son back to a playground where they had lived, so that he could play with his old friends. She explained that he is a shy child, and doesn't make new friends easily, and really missed his Regent Park friends.

A thirteen-year-old reported being unhappy about the redevelopment

> because a few of my friends that moved out of the places that are already broken down moved far away—like to Jane and Finch [a TCHC property located almost 20 miles to the north and west of Regent Park]. So I can't keep in touch with them that much.

If given the choice between redeveloping the houses and staying with friends, her allegiance was not with the houses. She reported "I wanted to stay with all my friends" (ibid., 28).

For older teens, the Internet was a partial compensation. Interviews with youth from displaced families revealed that they were able to use telecommunications technology to maintain their social networks. One twenty-year-old described how his cell phone allowed him to keep in contact with friends:

> I've had my same number for a couple of years now, so they all know my number and even people I haven't talked to in a while, they call me back a year later, and "Hey, what's up bro?" Plus there's Facebook… As long as you don't change your phone number, everybody's going to find you.
>
> (Johnson and Schippling 2009, 28)

Adults, and some seniors in particular, found that distance interfered with social contacts with friends and relatives who had previously lived close by. One older resident said she had made friends with only one neighbour in her temporary accommodation. On occasion she travelled back to Regent Park to visit friends still living there, but found that the travel was burdensome. While she didn't regret the move to temporary quarters, observing "it's worth it, you know, to move back into a new place," she acknowledged: "It's hard work to move from there to come here—I'm here about four years now—and then to move back again. It's a big job."

Residents complained about the burdens of living for so long in a temporary residence, as well as the challenges of unpredictability and missed deadlines. Displaced residents expressed frustration when they were given unreliable moving dates by the housing authority. Not being able to plan ahead meant more than inconvenience. Parents of school children needed to know how moving dates would relate to times when children would be starting in a next level of school, possibly in a new school. Parents' own jobs were sometimes sabotaged by the "moving targets" of their resettlement plans. One Phase 1 resident recounted the story of a neighbour whose home-based employment as a childcare provider had been unnecessarily terminated: The caregiver told clients she would be moving on the date assigned by TCHC, then learned that her moving date was to be delayed by six months. She tried to renew her arrangement with those clients, but discovered that they had already replaced her with another caregiver. In the words of the neighbour:

> She was doing home childcare at her [temporary] house. They [the housing authority] told her "You are moving in June." [It was delayed] from June to December – she lost all her [babysitting] clients, saying "I will be moving soon"… [S]he packed everything and she lost her job.

While regular daily routines were difficult in the temporary alternative housing, some found holidays particularly hard. A displaced, relocated Phase 1 resident described the difficulty of observing the Ramadan holidays with fasting and visits from relatives amidst her pile of cardboard moving boxes:

> We were fasting that time, it was Ramadan, and you don't invite [guests to] your house [full of] the boxes. This is a holy month that we are fasting. It was kind of horrible. I don't remember how we passed those days with all the boxes. I piled them in the living room like we will be moving and stuff. It looks horrible. You don't want to invite anybody to see your house piled with the boxes. There is no place to sit… It is so devastating.

During the first phase of the redevelopment a staff person from a local community service organization worked with community residents to try to ease their burden of relocation. He acknowledged that there were some for whom it was particularly onerous, observing that "the weariness of moving is such a very, very hard thing" (key informant interview). He made it a point to arrange visits to relocated families to see how they were doing. He quantified the health costs, indicating the seriousness of the toll, noting that there had been "seven deaths from Phase 1."[2]

Phase 1 tenants' relocation experiences depended to a great extent on how close they were living to their original Regent Park address. In general, those who managed to find alternative housing inside Regent Park tended to have an easier time being relocated. Following are two sets of accounts of relocated households, starting with some that moved outside the footprint, and then looking at residents relocated to temporary housing within Regent Park.

Group 1. Households Relocated Outside Regent Park

1.1

One household was relocated outside Regent Park after long residence in the neighbourhood. Family members had many close friends and activities in the community. The mother described her reaction when she first heard of the redevelopment plan, worrying that there would be no place for them in the rebuilt community: "I was panicking; I was thinking they [TCHC] were only building a new building for private, not for Toronto Housing. When they actually sent me back, I was surprised."

This family's preferred temporary housing arrangement would have been a vacant three-bedroom unit inside another section of the old Regent Park—or at least close to the familiar neighbourhood. "I really wanted to have a house in Regent Park, [but] I couldn't find any." Despite lining up numerous times, the mother reported that she couldn't find an appropriately sized unit available inside the boundaries or nearby. She described making regular phone contact with the offices of Toronto Community Housing until she located the house into which they moved.

The basic costs of the RGI housing they moved to were the same as in Regent Park, except for increased utilities costs. At Regent Park their utilities were included in the basic rental, but in other TCHC properties this is not always the case. She described the difference:

> It was more expensive living here, because there I didn't pay hydro [i.e., electric power], here I have to pay for utilities… Costs depend on the month, and how much you use. Air conditioning takes a lot, and heat in winter. And washing machine, dryer, the lights, everything here.

The mother recalled how she felt:

> For me, it took me far away from the community and the place I used to know. When we moved in we had to start a new place, new life. It's different… You don't know anybody, you have to make new friends. The kids can make new friends. To start, it's hard.

After moving, the family's children transferred into schools in the new neighbourhood. They made new friends but they also stayed in contact with their old friends from Regent Park. What this parent missed most from the old home in Regent Park was the sense of neighbourliness—especially in the form of people watching out for each other's children as they would for their own. She missed that shared sense of responsibility in the new "temporary" neighbourhood: "[In Regent Park] we know each other, we are so close… If you see your neighbour's kids outside late, you can say 'Go home, it's late.' Here, nobody knows you, nobody can say anything."

More than "difficult" or "challenging," "nightmare" is the word she used to describe the whole experience of displacement and relocation:

> I finished my nightmare. I was thinking: "When are you going to move? When are you going to move? When are you going to move? Which building are you going to move into?" Now I'm ok. Now I'm settled. Right now, everything is finished.

Five years would elapse before they moved back home into newly built Regent Park housing. Members of that family are now pleased to be resettled into new housing in their old community. In the mother's view Regent Park—more than many other places—really does function as a community.

1.2

An elderly resident who had been relocated in Phase 1 from Regent Park to alternative public housing a significant distance away discovered how much she missed the busy, noisy, family atmosphere she had left behind. Sometimes, she said, until you miss them, you don't recognize the important things. To this tenant, whose alternate temporary housing was in the midst of a well-to-do community including many older people, too much peace and quiet did not feel like home:

> When I just moved in here, it was a little bit too quiet for me, because I was used to hearing babies cry… people walking, people talking, you know... I didn't like it at first, but now I get used to it, it doesn't bother me.

While she eventually grew accustomed to the quiet of her temporary neighbourhood, she was pleased to have received a delivery of moving cartons in which to pack her belongings for the move back to new housing in Regent Park.

Other tenants who were relocated away from their original Regent Park neighbourhood remarked on the difficulties of shopping away from their familiar collection of stores. This was a major inconvenience for the aforementioned senior, who regularly returned to Regent Park to shop in the local affordable stores. In the temporary neighbourhood, she noted, most prices were higher. Moreover, her (mainly wealthier) neighbours travelled by car to do their grocery shopping. They didn't tend to walk to shops, nor did they travel with a shopping cart for the groceries.

> What bothers me is that there's no supermarket [in the temporary neighbourhood] to run to. [It] has just one little store that is very expensive. I still have to go back [to] downtown Toronto to the "No Frills" [discount supermarket] to do my shopping, and when I go grocery shopping I have to pay $12 for a taxi back here. That's why I feel happy to be moving back downtown to Regent Park.

Interviewed again upon her move back to Regent Park, this resident was particularly pleased to find a new supermarket built very close to her new home. Resettled into new housing back in her old walkable neighbourhood she said: "Here you see everybody with their shopping cart. There you see nobody with a shopping cart."

1.3

A mother in a large family household recalls that, years earlier, she rejected the idea of moving from a suburban basement apartment to a unit in Regent Park. She tried to decline, saying she and her husband and family preferred to stay in the suburbs, but the decision was made for her:

> Then they said, "Sorry, the only available place we have is at Regent Park". I didn't know what's Regent Park. They said "It's in downtown, go take a look and then come tell us." Then I have no choice because I wanted the [public] housing because it's cheaper than the private rent. Then when I came at the beginning, I liked it because everything was close—shopping, the school was just across the street.

But once having settled there, the family was very pleased with Regent Park and determined to stay there. Their household included school-age children in early grades of elementary school through to high school. At the start of redevelopment, the family's clear preference was for temporary housing inside the Regent Park boundary. When informed that nothing was available that could accommodate them, they accepted a unit in another public housing project not far away. They agreed to move to the alternative, temporary housing unit because of its relative proximity to the children's schools and community-based recreation programs. While living in Regent Park their children were active participants in various neighbourhood and community program activities during the school year and the summer season. It was the mother's understanding that eligibility for those programs—particularly tutoring—would continue after their move outside Regent Park, but according to her account this turned out not to be so: She was unable to enroll her children in some programs that were restricted to Regent Park residents.

Even before they relocated, they regretted their decision. The family tried to get the relocation staff to allow them to change their choice, but that request was denied.

During the interview in the relocation premises, the mother and one daughter recalled their first days in the temporary housing, which was lacking most of the things that they appreciated about Regent Park. Feelings of safety and the presence of familiar faces among their neighbours were of prime importance. Less important but still troubling to them was the apartment's dark and drab appearance. At least, they thought, they could make a trip to a nearby discount store and get some inexpensive curtains and other brightly coloured housewares to liven the place up. Shortly before their scheduled move, they did this, leaving these purchases on a kitchen counter in the locked and vacant apartment. On the following day they discovered that someone had broken into the house and stolen this bit of badly needed cheer. The teenage daughter describes their unhappy beginnings with that temporary housing unit, and their stages of settling in:

> When we first wanted to move we were excited, I don't know why. And then we moved here and then we got mad, and we're like, "We don't like it here" and then we just got over it.

The family's complaints about the temporary housing dealt with matters they considered really basic, such as issues of safety, security and noise. At the time they were moving in, that one distressing incident of the robbery in particular symbolized their unfortunate housing predicament. The family members speculated on how someone might have accessed their apartment and stolen their purchases. It was at that point they had tried cancelling their lease on the replacement housing, but to no avail.

1.4

A large family with children ranging from elementary to high school ages had lived in Regent Park for almost ten years. Their first choice for alternative housing would have been a unit inside Regent Park. However they failed to find one that suited the family's needs. The mother recalls how disorganized the TCHC's allocation system was. On several occasions the relocation staff gave them leads to addresses of housing in Regent Park, but there was no housing located at the addresses they had been given: "There was nothing, no such address. And when they gave us another [it was] the same thing—the street is there, the number isn't."

The family was eventually assigned to a unit in the Regent Park vicinity. They were led to believe that their stay at that address would be two years; in actuality it was almost five years.

The main difficulty in this family's relocation experience was the change in school for the youngest child. According to the mother, the child's previous school had been very close to their Regent Park home; their alternative housing was closer to another school. The younger daughter was unhappy with the move to a new school, missing her friends, her teacher, her sports teams, and the old school itself. At first, when the mother took her to the new school, the daughter would cry, saying how much she missed her friends. In time, she made new friends and eventually came to quite like the new school.

Group 2. Households Relocated Inside Regent Park

2.1

A young family with two parents, a toddler and a young school-age child moved to temporary housing in fall 2005. According to the father, their first choice had been to relocate to somewhere outside Regent Park while the new housing was built. His wife explained that this preference was based on the negative stereotype they felt people had of Regent Park:

> Most people think of Regent Park in the negative. People all the time think that people living in Regent Park are… bad people… [They think] this area is not safe and most of them [think] that there is a security problem. That is why we were thinking that we have to move from here.

However, her husband reported that through the relocation process they had not been able to find anything satisfactory outside Regent Park. They settled for a comfortable two-bedroom apartment near where they had been living. While he had some criticism of the relocation process, overall he gave good marks to the relocation staff:

> We got lots of official notice to relocate to this place and office management provided all the information and they gave us the choice. We decided to move here. Myself I didn't [want to] move too far because I wanted to live close to this place. We have the same things as we had before so now we feel very comfortable over here. So the relocation team and the management, they did a good job.

Although they described what they considered a roadblock in their access to their preferred housing unit—which they secured eventually after some delay—these parents counted themselves very fortunate in the temporary housing they obtained. The mother described their unit in positive terms, comparing it favourably to their previous apartment, noting that the substitute was overall "a more convenient place for the school, groceries, shopping." She continued, "in this building we have a daycare, so it's good for me… we have the same things we had before, so now we feel very comfortable over here… We know the people on both sides..."

She felt that knowing neighbours on both sides was a particular bonus, making her family feel welcome in their temporary housing. She joked: "Now we are in the middle! … We just knock."

2.2

In 2006 the father in this family household stood in line to arrange for alternative housing. He reported that he took the first available unit of the size for which the household qualified. The replacement unit seemed to be similar in size and building style to their previous Regent Park housing, but turned out to be in worse condition. Besides the unit not being clean, the refrigerator was in need of repair, as was the unit's balcony. When the family reported these problems, the building superintendent did not address their complaints. But the family also noted some good aspects of the move. Neighbours in the new place were friendly, and the location inside their old Regent Park community meant that they could stay in touch with friends and neighbours.

The family settled into their temporary housing, until they were informed by TCHC of a change in the phasing of redevelopment: Their new building was among those that would now be demolished several years ahead of schedule, for construction of a new Aquatic Centre. The family members expressed a preference to again stay inside the Regent Park boundary, a request the TCHC was able to accommodate.

The mother [who had limited English language proficiency] and the teenage daughter [who served as the mother's interpreter] recalled their move into the second temporary replacement housing:

> Mother: "This was our first choice. When we made that choice, when we first came here, we discussed the house [which] was in very bad condition. When we told TCHC they said 'Ok, ok, in one month we'll fix it.' When we moved, no nothing. Then we fought them, and then little by little, the things were fixed. Not everything [but] now it is ok, not bad."
>
> Daughter: "They didn't do all the things that they needed to fix."
>
> Interviewer: "What kind of things were broken when you moved in?"
>
> Mother: "Do you see the [interior] doors? All three doors were broken—there were no doors."
>
> Daughter: "There was no door there [pointing to doorway leading to the kitchen]. All the things that we needed fixing, they didn't respond."

The family was told that, in compensation for their inconvenience of two relocation moves, they, along with twelve other twice-relocated households, would be placed at the top of the list when it came to choosing their new permanent housing—a promise that was honoured when the new housing was built. The family reported that the first move was handled better by TCHC. The teenage daughter said the first move was "well organized—and they let us know what was happening." In contrast, the mother recalled, for the second move it was just "You have to move, and they didn't even tell us anything about it."

Asked whether, in hindsight, they might have regretted their expressed preference for replacement housing inside the Regent Park boundary, the mother said, "No. It is right in the downtown. The schools are nearby, mosques, groceries, everything is nearby, so it is familiar." Unanswered phone calls to the superintendent and unfinished repairs aside, the trade-off for this family was to remain in their familiar neighbourhood.

Relocation Stresses

When something major happens in a large, close-knit community, it is not surprising that rumours arise and circulate. Despite the housing authority's efforts to keep Phase 1 tenants well informed of the progress and status of the redevelopment, some tenants report that they experienced an information void. When the Phase 1 relocation began, and moving companies started shifting tenant households to destinations unknown—at least to their neighbours—stories began circulating about death and illness. Some of these stories were echoed in the accounts reported by a community service worker we interviewed. According to this account, residents associated the involuntary displacement with their neighbours' compromised health status.

These themes were prevalent in interviews with residents as the relocation began—particularly among residents of one of the buildings slated for Phase 1 demolition, in which the tenants included some seniors and persons with disabilities. Stress-related illness was another theme that came up in interviews. Still another was loneliness. Displaced and relocated residents discussed these as conditions associated with the relocation process, and believed them to be causes of mortality among some of their neighbours. One tenant reported: "A lot of people died from that building because of loneliness. And now look at, since they've moved, people are dying more… I think a lot of the problems is the stress put on people."

Another tenant attributed people's distress to the disruption of the family feeling that had prevailed in the building that had housed many seniors and persons with disabilities: "It was like an entire family. Everybody knew everybody… It was like a little community in itself. Three people have died over this that I know of."

Some of the stories that circulated about residents dying or becoming increasingly ill were undoubtedly based on reality. But it is unclear and impossible to substantiate the extent to which these accounts were attributed correctly to the redevelopment. Some mortality would be expected statistically, based on the age and health status of this population, regardless of whether or not they were moving. Nevertheless, the high level of concern and anxiety among tenants was a reality: The first phase of the redevelopment, demolition and rebuilding of their community, and the uncertainties associated with it, were a source of uneasiness and confusion for a number of residents.

Other Phase 1 residents found the experience of moving so difficult and so distressing that they were loath to contemplate a repetition. These included some older residents and some with health problems. For them the idea of staying permanently in their alternative housing was preferable to packing up and moving again. The TCHC gave them that option, which some exercised.

According to the terms of the redevelopment, and as specified in the Tenant Agreement for Regent Park, under the heading "Protecting Tenants," tenants were assured that, "You will continue to have the right to live in social housing as long as you continue to follow the rules of your lease and pay your rent" (TCHC 2006).

This pledge was reiterated at many public meetings, and in numerous written communications to tenants before and after displacement. Despite these assurances, fear persisted among relocated tenants that the housing authority was screening out what it considered "undesirable" tenants. Officially, no such screening was taking place.[3] All original residents who were, in official parlance, "tenants in good standing" had been granted a Right of Return. Furthermore, they could take their time in exercising this right. If they didn't find housing that they considered acceptable in a particular phase, or if their originally scheduled resettlement date turned out not to be convenient for their household, they could defer their Right of Return until a subsequent phase of construction was completed and new units were available. Nevertheless, rumours to the contrary continued to circulate. They may have been fuelled by one high-profile story that was picked up by the daily press, of a tenant—the very last occupant of 14 Blevins Place—who went to court to fight eviction (Hasham 2014).[4]

For those Phase 1 tenants relocated to temporary housing away from Regent Park, the reception they received sometimes added to the challenges they faced. For some, Regent Park's reputation as a rough and dangerous place preceded them. News media and the rumour mill combined to spread stories of Regent Park tenants bringing bedbugs and gang violence into their new neighbourhoods. A teacher in a local Regent Park school, interviewed in 2007, described issues facing some of the Phase 1 youth who had already been relocated:

> Kids don't have a lot of power over their surroundings or what happens in their lives, and for a lot of them who are a little bit older, and in particular boys—teenagers of any gender really—going into a community coming out of this community with the stigma that's attached to it is very difficult. I know several students, or several young people, who had really, really big problems… when they moved communities… if you're a teenager coming from Regent Park and moving to Jane and Finch [a neighbourhood in

> northwest Toronto], which also has its own set of expectations or stigma—it was, for some, very dangerous and I know for some it didn't go well at all, and it continues to be problematic… Regent Park is a community that has a lot of social agencies and programs and people who work in Regent Park make a big effort to reach out into the community and connect with families, so a lot of the families that move have moved to an area where maybe there aren't the same types of supports and so suddenly, they're floating alone and socially isolated. Not connected in the way that everyone's been.

The teacher concluded by observing that with the redevelopment structured into phases, there was an opportunity for the housing authority to learn from—and improve upon—early mistakes from the initial phases. She was aware that TCHC had acted upon that learning:

> Well, I think one strength of the relocation is that residents are given a choice. So that is a very important part, and that is sort of the foundation of the mission… Has it always worked out that way? I'm not sure that it has. I think another strength would be that they seem open to learning from mistakes from the previous phases. I know things have changed a little bit. I think that's because they've realized that.

A community worker who had kept track of the relocated Phase 1 households, making home visits and providing assistance as required, described a mindset in which some of those households were so focused on returning to a rebuilt Regent Park that they avoided getting to know their new neighbours. In looking at these tenants' experiences moving into a new community, he focused on the temporary nature of their community connection, and considered how that might serve as a barrier to their integration into the community in which they were living:

> Some of the households that I've visited out in Scarborough or in Etobicoke [Toronto suburbs], they have found it difficult and so they'll come back [to Regent Park] once a week and every few months because this is a part of their connection. Some have found the new environment very… welcoming, because they're closer to schools… and so that has gone very well for them. Other people… have found that moving to new areas has been particularly difficult because their mindset has always been to coming back and initially it was going to be three years out, or three and a half years out. They're looking at coming back next year, it'll be four years. So there's a dynamic about not wanting to invest their lives in developing new relationships and new ways of being in the new places because that becomes

> a new place of loss, and so they've just bided their time. Some people have, some households have said it's been really difficult developing new relationships but that's maybe also part of the process. There's an unconscious resistance to developing those new relationships.

This community worker, who established regular contact with displaced tenants, identified their difficulty forming informal social relationships as a key challenge of the relocation process. This problem is an important theme running through the various interviews with relocated tenants, regardless of age or family structure. Temporary living arrangements with open-ended timeframes make it hard for the relocated tenants to get to know new neighbours.

Another key informant working in a community agency expressed his apprehension about the level of communication between the housing authority and the relocated families. Having maintained contact with many of the relocated youth and their families during their relocation, he voiced concerns about the level of preparedness of relocated families, particularly as they approached the time to return:

> Quite honestly, I don't think the community is as prepared as they should be in terms of… ensuring that, "How do I remain informed around coming back?"… Some people have now been out of the community almost three years. The redevelopment process is behind [schedule], so potentially it could be four years before I'm actually able to move back. There's a lot that could have happened in my world in four years, right? It would be interesting to know… "Okay, I'm coming from a three-bedroom townhouse or apartment. Four years later, I've had two more kids and my family's increased. I now need more space".

According to TCHC personnel, this latter issue is being addressed under their practice of "right sizing" accommodations for households returning to newly built housing. Families that have gained or lost members during relocation will be assigned to new units that match their current household size. A housing authority staff member described that process, which can be easier in the context of vacant new buildings. In a stable community like the old Regent Park, such a family would have to spend an unpredictable amount of time on a list, waiting for a suitable unit to become free:

> This "right sizing" is part of the relocation process. If you have five kids, and meanwhile you are waiting, you will come back to a big unit that your family is eligible for. It doesn't matter that when we moved you out you were living in a one bedroom with three kids… You are coming back with

babies, it is really hard to get the bigger units when you are on a regular transfer waiting list. [But] with this process we are right sizing.

Lessons Learned

The Regent Park tenants' experiences were not exceptional. Studies of public housing redevelopment elsewhere underscore the challenges faced by uprooted tenants (Goetz 2013). The experiences, the difficulties and challenges that tenants have encountered are a story in themselves, with more than one lesson for future phases and other redevelopment initiatives.

This chapter began with the community update meeting at the start of Phase 3 of Regent Park redevelopment, at which Greg Spearn, promised residents that TCHC would accelerate the pace of building new housing. In his open letter to residents, he acknowledged the particular difficulty of relocation. It was, he observed, the area where the housing authority needed to make some changes to ease the burden for residents.[5] According to the new plan, many of the tenants would be able to move from their original housing directly into new, permanent housing. That revision of the plan should go a long way towards reducing the types of difficulty Phase 1 residents experienced in the relocation. The overall changes should ease the burden on households. Moreover, it will demonstrate to new phases of relocated tenants that—at the very least—the housing authority really seems to be taking seriously their concerns and their suggestions for change.

To the extent that the housing authority can speed up the rate at which new housing is built, and can thus move households directly from old to new housing, the burden of relocation will be significantly lightened.

Temporary relocation can be difficult for families awaiting the rebuilding of their housing. Moving is difficult for most people, regardless of circumstance. Moving based on involuntary displacement is particularly difficult—especially when the timing for moving back remains open ended. Families with young, school age children face a particular burden when moving homes also means moving schools.

Clearer communication between the housing authority and the tenants—e.g., about key dates in the moving process—would ease the tenants' lives during relocation. But communication entails more than dates and timing. Rumours and gossip channels convey considerable information—often inaccurate—within a close community such as Regent Park. Fuller sharing of accurate program information by the housing authority in a timely fashion will help to reduce tenants' reliance on the rumour mill. Use of social media channels may be an efficient way for interactive communication between TCHC and tenants.

Changing children's schools is difficult. In 2014 the TCHC made a commitment to families with school age children that they will not be required to move during the period when school is in session. Moving families with children only in the summer months of July and August goes a long way towards more family-friendly relocation planning.

Some relocated households are in need of support services while awaiting re-housing in rebuilt homes. In 2014 the TCHC, in partnership with the Regent Park Community Health Centre, successfully completed a six-month pilot project to deliver social work support services to vulnerable tenants relocated during the Regent Park redevelopment. In September 2014 a TCHC Community Update Newsletter announced the start of a new program making available the services of a community support worker to assist households during their relocation. That support worker should now be available to assess residents' service needs, and to help them to maintain current supports or access any needed services and supports. While not all relocated households will require such supports, a minority does, and this new program should ease relocation for those households (TCHC 2014).

Notes

1 In estimating duration of displacement, an approximate date was assigned to those cases where the information was incomplete: For example, if only the year was given, a date of June 30 was assigned.

2 Comprehensive statistics on mortality among Phase 1 tenants are not available, leaving only anecdotal evidence. In other localities, relocation has sometimes been associated with high mortality: Of 26,000 households—about one-third of them elderly—displaced by the Chicago Housing Authority in 1999, 2,073 exited public housing by 2007 due to the death of a member (Vale and Graves 2010, 9, citing T.D. Boston's unpublished data).

3 Note, however, comments of several police officers at a community meeting in 2016:

> Some new Regent Park residents… asked after the previous residents, wondering where they had gone post-relocation and whether they would be returning. 'Everyone that was moved out, has the ability to apply to come back,' said Sergeant Craig Somers [of 51 Division], 'If they're part of a problematic family, we talk to housing and work on not bringing back combinations of people who in the past have caused issues'." Inspector Dave Rydzik observed that "It's a handful of people who wreak havoc. It's not just those people who live there, it's all the other people they attract.
> (Geary 2016, 12)

4 In the TCHC's eyes, she was not a tenant in good standing. Hasham reports she was accused of having kept multiple firearms in her apartment, and of being in arrears in her rent. The tenant, according to the news story, claimed the guns had been placed there without her knowledge by an ex-boyfriend, and that TCHC had arbitrarily raised her rent as if the boyfriend (who was just an occasional visitor) was a member of the household.

5 Greg Spearn, Interim President and CEO, and Chief Development Officer, Toronto Community Housing, Letter distributed to residents at the start of Phase 3, "Our Three Promises to Regent Park Residents," June 11, 2014.

References

CMHC (Canada Mortgage and Housing Corporation). 2011. Research Report, Distinct Housing Needs Series: Case Study Research on Social Housing Redevelopment and Regeneration. Part A: Overview. Report prepared for CMHC by SPR Associates Inc. Case Study #5: Regent Park, Phase 1 (Toronto, Ontario) Toronto Community Housing Corporation (TCHC). (October): 63–84.

Geary, Siobhan. 2016. "Corktown isn't a big problem: 51 Division." *The Bulletin: Journal of Downtown Toronto* XVIII: 1. (January).

Goetz, Edward G. 2013. *New Deal Ruins: Race, Economic Justice, & Public Housing Policy*. Ithaca, NY: Cornell University Press.

Hasham, Alyshah. 2014. "Single mom refuses to budge from Regent Park highrise slated for demolition." *Toronto Star* October 3.

Johnson, Laura C. and Richard Schippling. 2009. *Regent Park Revitalization: Young People's Experience of Relocation from Public Housing Redevelopment*. Ottawa: Canada Mortgage and Housing Corporation, External Research Program. (June). NH18-1-2/50-2009E-PDF.

TCHC (Toronto Community Housing Corporation) 2006. *Tenant Agreement for Regent Park*. www.regentparkplan.ca. (Accessed November 22, 2006).

TCHC (Toronto Community Housing Corporation) 2007. Regent Park Revitalization Update. April 3.

TCHC (Toronto Community Housing Corporation) 2014. Community Update Newsletter, Regent Park Revitalization. (September).

Vale, Lawrence J. and Erin M. Graves. 2010 "The Chicago Housing Authority's Plan for Transformation: What Does the Research Show So Far?" Department of Urban Studies and Planning, Massachusetts Institute of Technology.

8
Tenants' Resettlement (2009–2013)

It is challenging to evaluate a project as large and complex as the total redesign, rebuilding, and redevelopment of an ageing public housing community on a vast, downtown site. Many criteria could be used as measures of success: financial balance sheets, estimated demand for market housing, scale of job creation, design and planning prizes awarded and other recognition of success. But from the point of view of 2,083 low-income households, the most telling evaluation is social. The most important issues focus on how the members of those original households fare in the course of the redevelopment, and how they assess the outcome.

Comparing Regent Park's resettlement experience with that of many cities in the United States, the differences are striking. By the narrowest definition, 40 percent of displaced Phase 1 residents returned to the community they had left. Taking the "East Downtown"—housing units located barely one kilometre from Regent Park—into account, the TCHC argues that 60 percent of residents were resettled in or near their former homes. And a further 10 to 20 percent found alternate permanent housing in TCHC units. Contrast these figures to Chicago where, in Lawrence Vale's description, of 26,000 displaced households that were offered a Right of Return, fewer than 2,000 actually found housing in the mixed-income communities that replaced their former public housing neighbourhoods (Vale 2013, 305).

This chapter describes the Phase 1 tenants' resettlement experiences. Throughout our longitudinal research, household interviews were conducted with the person most knowledgeable about housing issues for the family. The study sample respondents were mainly a mix of single-parent and two-parent households. Regardless of household composition, it was generally the woman who answered our questions: She was the one closest to decision making about housing matters. Yet this matriarchal pattern was not followed at the important pre-return interviews with the TCHC's Regent Park relocation counsellor. If there was a man available for this meeting, it was often he who was sent as the family's representative, under the assumption that he could be more assertive in conveying the housing preferences. This was the moment to present the family's choices among the available newly-built units. According to informal gossip within the community, the relocation counsellors could be tough and assertive, and could forcefully urge applicants to reorder their choices as directed. Families that had endured relocation for periods from three to five years wanted to be sure their actual choices were recorded in the order of the family's real preferences, and reflected in the meeting's outcome. If the meeting turned adversarial, they wanted to be sure that person representing them was the one best able to push back. In the judgement of many families, this was a role for a man.

A particular concern of some family households was to avoid being permanently settled into housing outside Regent Park. Early into Phase 1, residents learned that TCHC had introduced a new concept that changed the terms of Right of Return. A community meeting for residents held on December 18, 2008, presented an update on two types of replacement RGI housing units, those on-site and those in "East Downtown" (TCHC 2008). The off-site location referred to approximately 300 newly-built housing units at three different sites within a radius of about one mile from Regent Park (see Figure 4.2) which would be made available to returning residents and treated as equivalent to new housing within Regent Park. TCHC designated these sites—located at 92 Carlton, 501 Adelaide East and 60 Richmond East—as qualifying as replacement housing under the Right of Return agreement with tenants (TCHC's rationale for this change was discussed in Chapter 4; at a later date TCHC appeared to be reconsidering this policy, but at the time of writing the ultimate outcome is unclear).

While a minority of the sample of displaced Phase 1 households accepted this new off-site option, a number of those interviewed questioned this change. Most displaced and relocated Phase 1 tenants expressed a preference to stay within the footprint of what they considered the "real" Regent Park. As the selection process wore on, some expressed anxiety that they might be pressured to resettle in those off-site areas. Having heard stories of some of their neighbours who had settled in new East Downtown housing, and who subsequently were lobbying to move back into the original Regent Park neighbourhood, they didn't want to risk that course. If it took having a husband taking time off from work, this seemed to the women to be in a good cause.

Guaranteeing original residents of Regent Park a Right of Return to redeveloped housing is one of the key features of the redevelopment. Other jurisdictions have experienced difficulties with Right of Return. In a number of cities in the United States, housing authorities have promised displaced public housing tenants that they could return once their neighbourhoods were rebuilt. But the actual nation-wide rate of return has been estimated at less than 15 percent (Marquis and Ghosh 2008, 405). The Regent Park experience is very different, with a Phase 1 return rate between 40 and 60 percent.

By 2014, most Phase 1 tenants in the study sample had left their temporary quarters and either returned to Regent Park or settled elsewhere. Chart 8.1

shows the pattern of settlement as recorded by TCHC and compares it to the experience of our sampled Phase 1 households. The outcomes are quite similar. In both cases, approximately 40 percent of families returned to housing inside the Regent Park footprint, with an additional 15 to 20 percent moving permanently into the "East Downtown" off-site buildings described above. Four of the sampled households (8 percent of the study sample)[1] deferred their decision about returning. As of 2013 they were still waiting for their preferred type of housing unit, or for a better time to move. One-fifth of households left TCHC housing altogether—to rent or purchase housing in Toronto or some other jurisdiction. And between 10 and 15 percent moved to other TCHC housing elsewhere in Toronto.

Once the resettlement process was complete, residents could begin to assess whether it was worth the effort. Was it worth packing up their belongings and moving temporarily to alternative housing within the Regent Park community, or to temporary housing nearby or farther away? Was it worth having their children switch schools? Was it worth the stress and uncertainty of relocation? Was it worth the other required changes in residents' lives, routines, and separation from their networks of friendship and informal social support?

Who chose not to return at all? What are the tenants' reasons for their respective choices? What are the influences, if any, of their temporary housing choices on their decisions about re-housing? What are the influences of disruption and social mix on neighbourhood ties?

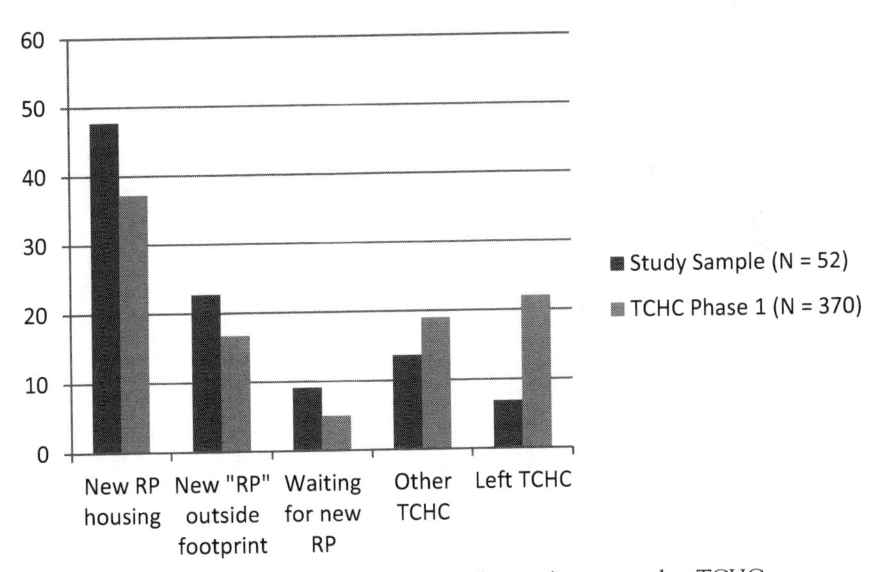

Chart 8.1 Relocation Statistics for Phase 1; study sample compared to TCHC.

Source: L. Johnson, interview data; Toronto Community Housing Corporation (private communication, 2014)

In evaluating Regent Park's experience in Phase 1, we must consider both the incentives and the disincentives that tenants faced: What factors enabled them to return, or led them to move elsewhere? How helpful or unhelpful was the TCHC in providing tenants with information and facilitating their resettlement?

Choosing a New Housing Unit

According to the approved TCHC procedure for choosing replacement housing, Phase 1 residents began by drawing a lottery number from a random draw. The draw was held at a public meeting. A community member—not a TCHC employee—drew numbers from a clear jar, assigning each household a place in the order of priority, from 1 to 400. Households would be given their choice among available units based on this ranking.

Relocation counsellors provided descriptions of the new units to the eligible households. Households were given printed floor plans of available accommodations of the size (number of bedrooms) for which they were eligible. When they met with counsellors the household's designated member would indicate housing choices, in order of preference. They would also have an opportunity to seek any additional information they required to make their choices.

As a researcher, Laura Johnson was given an opportunity to spend a morning early in 2009 in the revitalization centre, sitting in on six of the tenants' meetings with a relocation counsellor (with permission of the counsellor and each of the tenants). Upon entry to the centre, visitors were greeted by a large sign reading: "Welcome to the Revitalization Centre. It's a place where tenants who moved out of buildings in Phase 1 can meet with staff, get information about the new buildings and begin the process to move to a new home being built as part of the revitalization project." A recurring theme in the interviews was whether the tenants would consider including among their choices any units in three new off-site housing alternatives in the East Downtown.

Among the key informants we consulted, there is some disagreement regarding the nature of the Right of Return. Some assert that the right has been exercised as soon as an original displaced tenant household signs a lease on a new replacement housing unit, regardless of whether that unit is located inside the Regent Park footprint, or in designated replacement housing in nearby TCHC properties. According to that view, such housing fulfills the TCHC's obligation on tenants' Right of Return. Other key informants consulted assert that displaced tenant households who settle elsewhere continue to have a Right of Return to housing inside Regent Park—in perpetuity: They can exercise that right whenever they wish, regardless of whether or not they have accepted alternative replacement housing. Without delving into the particulars of legal interpretation, Phase 1 residents took very seriously their decision as to whether to return inside the footprint of their original neighbourhood, or to move to an alternative downtown location outside that footprint.

Further complications arose over tenants' right to refuse whatever housing was available. Under the rules that TCHC adopted for Phase 1, anyone who declined all the options offered to them would not only remain on the next list for new units as they became available, but would automatically go to the top of that list. Members of this group account for a large proportion of the "still waiting" category in Chart 8.1. A TCHC staffer commented:

> Regent Park is the only location where we let people defer, again and again. It was a mistake, because it's not fair for the other people. We are relocating new groups but we always have to go back to this first group who are going to pick and choose. They are always at the top of the list.

Another issue that tenants considered was whether the housing was configured as a single level apartment unit or—in the cases of townhouse-style units—had interior stairways connecting multiple floors. Households could also choose what floor of a building they wanted, and often, what exposure they preferred. They could opt for a balcony, or instead could have more floor space inside the unit. In the six interviews observed, households sent just one representative to register their housing preferences. Some tenants were clearly proficient at reading the floor plans, others less so. Some came to the appointed meeting with many choices of acceptable units; others had few. Some chose only housing inside the Regent Park boundary; others included some off-site units.

In one of the aforementioned meetings, a relocation counsellor urged a tenant seeking a three-bedroom unit to include some off-site housing among his choices. The tenant said he didn't know. Before making such a choice he needed to make a phone call to his wife. After a brief phone conversation, he confirmed their original choices, telling the counsellor they only wanted to consider housing inside Regent Park, as his wife was very active in volunteer work in the community and was only interested in housing right there. Among those available units within the Regent Park footprint, he indicated further that his family was only interested in a unit with a balcony.

A second resident came to the interview to register his household's exclusive interest in a particular apartment layout in one particular building. When told that his family was unlikely to receive one of only ten units available in that size, he agreed to wait for a subsequent phase of construction: If their preferences combined with their lottery number didn't land them the apartment they wanted, they would stay in temporary housing until the next selection round, hoping to obtain a similar apartment in a different building.

Another tenant was seeking a unit in a high-rise building for seniors. Uncomfortable with heights, she specified that she only wanted a unit on one of the lower floors. Still another tenant seeking a three-bedroom unit was amenable to a unit either inside or outside the Regent Park footprint. Four possible building choices were mentioned, and all were acceptable to him. But he specified that the family preferred a balcony—south facing—and also needed parking.

When residents in our survey's semi-structured interviews discussed the process of selecting new housing, several confessed that they had difficulty reading the plans they had been given. Some had enlisted the help of older children or friends to help them read those plans. Others just hoped that they understood the plans, and that they had registered the right choices in relation to their actual preferences. One relocated resident who knew how to read plans for the new units described how she extended a hand to help a neighbour visualize the space in an apartment she was considering:

> I took green painter's tape and marked out the floor in the living room because I had a bigger living room than her. I said "This is your living room and kitchen", and I marked out where the sink would be, the fridge… the sofa and everything… she visualized it that way… They [TCHC] handed out these papers… yet they couldn't do a three-dimensional video thing of these apartments? ... Some people just can't understand it when you look at a piece of paper.

For those who had difficulty reading two-dimensional plans, it was important to find another way to visualize and compare the new living spaces that were offered to them. Several of the residents interviewed wondered why computer visualization wasn't made available by TCHC to help them choose among alternative floor plans by means of more user-friendly, three-dimensional images.

No model suites were available for viewing. Moreover, TCHC rules prohibited tenants from viewing the interior of any of the new units until their choice had been made, their tenancy had been approved for that unit, and they had signed a lease. Thus it wasn't possible for tenants who were just considering a unit to get access to view it; tenants would not receive a key until fully committed to a unit.

One Household's Resettlement Experience

A resettlement interview was conducted with the mother of a young family of four (two parents, one pre-schooler and one school-age child) in summer 2011, a year after they had moved back into new housing inside the Regent Park footprint. The move—the mother said it was hopefully the family's last for some time—was recent enough that their decisions about their new housing were still fresh in her mind.

Her family had a very strong preference for new housing within the Regent Park footprint. Schools and friends were all there and grocery shopping was now nearby. "Why," she asked, "would we want to move elsewhere?" When making their selections among new housing alternatives, she recalls feeling pressure from the relocation counsellor to consider new housing outside the footprint in one of the three buildings known as East Downtown. "They just want to push me go to 501 Adelaide." She says she resisted that pressure, and held out for housing inside the Regent Park neighbourhood. In her words, she told the relocation counsellor, "When you find something in Regent Park, then call me."

Once they had indicated their general preferences by building and apartment type, they were given a set of apartment unit plans to rank according to their priority. In their case, there were eight possibilities for the three-bedroom apartments to which they were entitled. They ranked the eight units according to their preference. But while she thought the family had understood the plans, they had not. When they ranked their choices in order of preference, they ranked last the unit into which they eventually moved. When, on moving day, the family got to see that "last choice" unit, they knew instantly that it was the perfect apartment for them, and that it should have been their first choice, offering the best use of space, and affording them a view that gave the new apartment a feeling of home. That view, she noted happily, was the same that her household had enjoyed in their original—and now demolished—Regent Park home.

Even though the relocation counsellors had provided basic instructions on reading the plans, she admits she got it wrong. In the end, she reports, it was only through good luck that her family was assigned a unit that turned out to be perfectly suited to her family's needs and preferences.

Moving to New Housing Inside the Footprint

As difficult as the displacement and relocation phases may have been, households that moved into new units inside Regent Park seem, from our resettlement interviews, generally to have forgotten those trials. Most respondents were enthusiastic about their new housing and—for those who had relocated temporarily elsewhere outside the Regent Park footprint—their return to the neighbourhood that they considered home.

One older resident who moved into the new seniors building extolled its virtues. As one of the first tenants to occupy the newly-constructed units, she was surrounded by mostly vacant apartments up and down her hallway. She observed that it was pretty lonely there. She admitted finding that isolation somewhat uncomfortable, but she acknowledged that it was temporary. It didn't really bother her, as she knew the other units would soon be inhabited. We rode the elevator to another floor where she proudly showed off the bright, airy and well-furnished lounge with laundry machines for the building's residents. Despite the on-going construction, she felt comfortable in this familiar, accessible neighbourhood, the place where she was living close to her friends, her place of worship, her health centre, and familiar shops whose goods she could afford. She particularly appreciated the Regent Park neighbourhood's walkability and accessible public transit.

Another household that returned was a fairly large family that had moved into a duplex townhouse unit on two floors at the base of a taller building. Interviewed at an earlier stage in the redevelopment (in 2010), a teenage daughter from this family had expressed doubt that they would actually succeed in moving into one of the new units in Regent Park. She was sceptical that TCHC would really honour its commitment to rebuild all the units of RGI housing units that it had demolished and offer them to the original tenants displaced by the redevelopment. Her comments are indicative of the uncertain and apprehensive mood of many tenants in the early stages of relocation. Following is the text of her comments in that earlier interview while her family was occupying temporary housing:

> Youth Participant: "My family's pretty sure that they are not going to be able to move back because a lot of people around Regent Park are like 'Even if they've told us that they are going to relocate us back into the building, it's going to be pretty impossible.' "
>
> Interviewer: "Because?"
>
> Participant: "Because of all the plans for it to become condominiums. The thing is, it's going to be pretty hard to move back into that area when there's a high demand from much more—I guess—people from higher economic status. A lot of people, even the ones who haven't yet moved, they are kind of thinking that once they've made the new buildings, they are not going to move back. It's going to be hard to move back, so it's going to change everything... I remember when I was back in elementary school, I was thinking the government is selling the area for money. Basically with all the area for the stores and they are selling it to their company. It's going to be hard. Would you rather choose to take someone in who is going to pay you a lot of money, or take someone in who is only going to give you a little bit? So it's hard to compete with that sort of people."

We re-interviewed the family once they had moved into the new Regent Park housing. Asked how they liked it, the father replied with a question, "What wouldn't we like?" When pressed, he came up with only one design suggestion that could have improved the layout—all of the washrooms were located on the upstairs level by the bedrooms. It would have been preferable, he said, if a powder room had been located on the ground floor with the living room and kitchen. Similarly, the construction workers walking by outside their windows didn't really bother them—the family joked good-naturedly about their temporary lack of privacy. But they knew that those workers would only be there while the construction was completed. Overall, the family expressed their pleasure with the unit, the design, the finishes, the landscaping, and the quality and the environmental sustainability of the construction materials. They understood that the new building they occupied was certified LEED Gold (signifying Leadership in Energy and Environmental Design), indicating its high rating in terms of the sustainability and efficiency of its construction and operation, and appreciated this feature. After years of living with dumpsters outside their front entrances as their only means of disposing of household garbage they welcomed the opportunity to participate in recycling.

Other tenants who had moved into new housing inside the original neighbourhood were generally very pleased with the housing and the new services, amenities, and facilities in the neighbourhood. There were some complaints that the sizes of rooms in the new units were smaller than in their old housing. For some that meant a need to replace their furniture with smaller scale pieces. They acknowledged, however, that such was the way with new apartment housing.

Kitchen design was an area in which a number of the returned and resettled households wished that their suggestions from their landlord's focus groups had been followed. Having registered their preferences for an enclosed kitchen option, they were disappointed that their proposals had not been implemented. Kitchens in the Phase 1 units were designed as open, in a way common to new North American apartment housing with limited space. As a result, there were clear sightlines into the kitchen from elsewhere in the housing unit, even from the front doorway. Some residents (Chapter 5) preferred having privacy for doing kitchen work. As one resident observed on her move into her new Regent Park housing, "In some of these new apartments, the minute you open the door, you can see right into the kitchen." The woman observed that while it might work to install some sort of curtain as a screen to enclose the kitchen, the tenants had been instructed by the TCHC not to install any such hardware onto the walls of the new housing units.

A preference for enclosed kitchens was expressed by only a minority of residents. One newly resettled tenant expressed her personal preference for an open plan kitchen, but acknowledged that her neighbour disagreed:

> I love the open kitchen. It makes bigger space and I can see everybody, the small children, while I'm cooking. But for my neighbour, she's told me every time, "I hate this house, I hate…" I said what's wrong with it? and then she said "I don't have privacy when guests come." … Then I said "You can make the room like a guest room."

As suggested by one of the tenants interviewed, some sort of flexibility, possibly with optional adjustable panels, might enable those who wish to enclose their open kitchens to make that modification easily without changing the basic structure of the housing unit. Perhaps that will be possible in subsequent phases of the Regent Park redevelopment.

Kitchen stoves in the new housing units were another source of dissatisfaction for some of the newly resettled residents. They complained that the stove temperature controls did not permit them to cook at the very high heat that they preferred. Some immigrant households in particular felt that this kitchen equipment prevented them from following culinary traditions that required oil and spices to be cooked at high temperature. Complaints to management produced no change, and there was a sense among these residents that their landlord was overstepping its authority and dictating how they should live their lives.

Such complaints about the appliances were far from universal. Other newly resettled Phase 1 residents expressed appreciation for what they considered to be environmentally sustainable, energy-efficient new appliances, and the well-designed kitchen cupboards. The stoves, while they took a while to heat up to the desired temperature, were generally considered very safe to operate. Residents praised the large refrigerators—in one resident's words, "you can see through the glass drawers, you can see the fruit and vegetables, and it's deep—the freezer too."

In general, residents who moved into new homes in their old neighbourhood were pleased with the design and construction of the housing units and the community amenities and design. Most expressed their appreciation for the rebuilt housing. Some of the resettlement interviews with Phase 1 tenants who had moved into new housing inside the Regent Park footprint describe how their relatives and friends were positively impressed by the newly redeveloped neighbourhood, with its park space, shops, and services. One resident, now living in a new unit in Regent Park, tells a story of a relative from an outer suburb of Toronto who rarely visited her in her old Regent Park apartment. On those prior visits the aunt made sure to leave her young, impressionable children at home, lest they be lured into the criminal lifestyle that she felt Regent Park represented. Now, the respondent observed with a mixture of amusement and pride, her suburban cousins look for opportunities to visit the new Regent Park, and each time they do so, they find new attractions.

Moving to New Housing Outside the Footprint

Ten of the 52 households in the Phase 1 study sample resettled into new housing in the three East Downtown buildings. Interviews with these tenants indicated that half of them had moved away from Regent Park by choice. They were pleased to have the option of living in brand new housing, still with the convenience of living downtown, but outside of Regent Park. The other half had settled for new East Downtown because they had grown weary of waiting for permanent housing inside the Regent Park footprint, because they objected to features of the available housing stock there, or because of dissatisfaction with the process of assigning people to housing units within Regent Park.

One participant described feeling pressured by relocation counsellors to accept the East Downtown housing. Residents, she said, were miffed at the pressure to move to one of those alternative locations. She mimicked what she said were the words of the relocation counsellors directed at the Phase 1 tenants who were holding out for the One Oak rental building inside the Regent Park footprint: "Adelaide [one of the 3 off-site locations] is ready, you can take it or not." The interviewee turned down this option but described how one of her former neighbours from Phase 1, who had been impatient to move into more permanent housing, had been convinced by that pressure to move off-site. The neighbour wishes now that she had waited until the housing inside the footprint was ready.

Another participant who moved into new housing outside the footprint had very mixed feelings about leaving the old Regent Park community. She missed the old place, became tearful at the thought of leaving it behind, and said that she still kept a souvenir brick from the old building. But she appreciated the new building, its location and its new appliances. Contrasting her experiences in the old Regent Park and the brand new replacement housing she said,

> they were old apartments and they didn't keep up with things. Different things broke… And here, so far, they have been different… I've always wanted a brand new apartment that nobody lived in before I did. And I'm so happy here. And I like the location… I like it here… the people are very friendly and… I'm going to be here a long time because I don't want to move again.

A young woman in another household that resettled into one of the new East Downtown buildings outside the Regent Park footprint expressed very ambivalent feelings about her family's choice. They had intended to resettle in a new Regent Park building. When choosing their temporary relocation housing, they deliberately opted for housing inside the Regent Park footprint because they believed that, "If you stayed in Regent Park, there's more likely a chance of getting one of the new apartment buildings… Like if you moved outside, you would probably be the last to be told that there's new apartment building." She often visited friends living in new housing inside the Regent Park footprint, and felt much more of a sense of community there. Although apartments in her new off-site building might be more generous in size, she noted that the area was missing the kind of rich community supports that she was watching reappear in Regent Park. While she acknowledged it might be good for her family to live without support services, she missed some of the programs she had attended previously, and the community feeling she had enjoyed in the old neighbourhood:

> I would say that moving out, it does build some kind of confidence. But at the same time, as a person, you're like "I kind of miss some of the things that were there and some of the supports that were there." But now that I've moved out, I guess that support is not there. And you can't step outside and say you're going into the community. Because [here] when you step outside, it's just a road, not a community any more. It's just this one building.

Her new building, she noted, did have some continuity with the old Regent Park neighbourhood. She encountered many familiar faces from Regent Park in the hallways and riding the elevators. People greeted one another like old friends.

The study interviewed a young man, a few months away from his eighteenth birthday, whose family had moved to another of the new buildings located outside the Regent Park footprint. On the basis of a week's experience in the new building, sitting in the midst of some of the family's not yet unpacked boxes, he compared the new place with the Regent Park South high-rise where he had spent his childhood. He observed that in this new building "You're not growing up in a neighbourhood, right? You're growing up in a city." It is unlikely that these young people, who were living in different off-site locations, had compared notes. Nevertheless, they do seem to agree that the Regent Park living environment offers a supportive neighbourhood that cannot be matched by otherwise equivalent off-site accommodations.

Lessons Learned

In the case of Regent Park, the promise of return has been more or less honoured, albeit with considerable delays and complications. Statistics from the more recently completed Phase 2 (Chart 8.2) suggest that the proportion returning has risen significantly. Fully 65 percent of displaced households in this phase had moved back to Regent Park by 2014, and an additional 22 percent were waiting and expecting to return (in Phase 2, tenants were no longer being

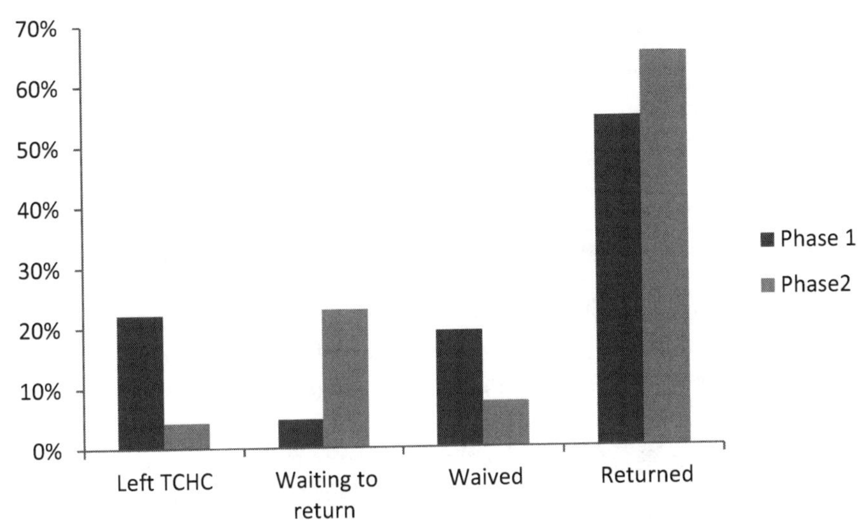

Chart 8.2 TCHC statistics on relocation of Phase 1 and Phase 2 households.

Source: Toronto Community Housing Corporation (private communication, 2014)

offered "East Downtown" alternatives). Of all displaced households in Phase 2, barely 10 percent had permanently moved away and/or waived their Right of Return. For some of the Phase 2 sub-phases, the return rate exceeded 80 percent. When these figures are combined with those for Phase 1, they produce an overall return rate of 60 percent (TCHC, personal communication, November 19, 2014).[2] These figures suggest strongly that tenants remain committed to living in Regent Park, and that TCHC remains committed to the Right of Return, and may have overcome some of the obstacles that Phase 1 returnees encountered. TCHC personnel report that during Phase 2 a number of families were able to move directly from their old apartments to newly-built units—a sharp contrast to the long periods that Phase 1 residents spent in temporary housing.

Some of the stories we heard from Phase 1 households ended in full satisfaction. Having endured difficult conditions of displacement and relocation, a large proportion managed to resettle in new housing that is very well suited to their needs and their preferences. In some cases, that fortunate outcome happened through good luck. Luck is not an optimal way of matching tenants' housing preferences with the housing stock available. Nor are home-grown solutions—such as tenants having to make masking tape outlines on a floor to indicate the dimensions of a unit in question—an ideal way of helping prospective tenants to understand the choices they are offered. With tenants who are well informed about housing options, and with TCHC relocation staff working hard to place tenants in appropriate housing, it can be anticipated that there will be good matches between tenants and available new housing. If the housing authority's policy of not showing model suites or allowing access to vacant apartments continues, TCHC could still consider using readily available, user-friendly computer visualization software to provide realistic three-dimensional views of the various housing options.

Relocation counsellors have a difficult job to do in conveying to tenants all of the information required to make sound choices about their new housing options. The housing authority's current use of a lottery system builds fairness into the system. With experience, the housing authority progressed a long way from the early days of line-ups and first come, first served. Clearly some organizational learning about resettlement procedures has occurred. But some tenants still report feeling pressured by relocation counsellors to choose particular housing options. The tenants should not feel that they must make particular choices, or that they need to—as some tenants report—make sure that they send a man, or some other forceful advocate, to the resettlement interview to ensure that their housing choices are communicated in an authoritative and convincing manner.

The issue of agreeing to accept new housing outside of the Regent Park footprint has been the main point of contention between tenants and relocation counsellors. The tenants were assured at the time of displacement and relocation that they enjoyed a Right of Return to Regent Park. Our respondents understood that to mean a right to return to housing within the footprint of the original Regent Park community. Some reported that they sought legal advice in order to guarantee that right.[3] While some households moved willingly—even enthusiastically—into new housing off-site, others held out for their Right of Return to the place they lived previously. Recall the words of the young woman whose family accepted new housing outside the footprint: When she steps off the curb in front of their new building, she is just "in the road;" when her friends who insisted on new housing inside the rebuilt Regent Park step out of their homes, they are stepping into a community. Many of our respondents say they want that community. They understood that Right of Return is intended to protect their continuing enjoyment of that community. They felt that they should not need legal services to guarantee that they receive the Right of Return to which they are entitled, and which is a hallmark of this revitalization project.

A central lesson from the collective experiences of these Phase 1 households is that temporary displacement and relocation are difficult. They ought to be avoided if at all possible. The approach that the housing authority has taken in the second and third phases is to build new housing on an expedited schedule so that RGI households can move directly into new units, without off-site relocation. If they can't skip the stage of living temporarily in alternative locations, it can at least be reduced from the four to five years that Phase 1 residents endured. The main lesson is to build new housing first if possible.

Notes

1 According to TCHC reports, the comparable figure for all Phase 1 households was 5 percent.
2 This figure includes those households in Phase 1—8 percent of the overall total—that accepted housing in the "East Downtown," outside the Regent Park perimeter.
3 Throughout the Regent Park redevelopment process the TCHC worked with Neighbourhood Legal Services, a local non-profit community based legal clinic, and advised tenants to consult that agency as required.

References

Marquis, Gerald P. and Soumen Ghosh. 2008. "Housing Opportunities for People Everywhere (HOPE VI): Who Gets Back In?" *Social Science Journal* 45(3): 401–418.
TCHC (Toronto Community Housing Corporation). 2008. "Regent Park Revitalization Community Update Meeting." Powerpoint presentation. December 18.
Vale, Lawrence J. 2013. *Purging the Poorest: Public Housing and the Design Politics of Twice-Cleared Communities*. Chicago: University of Chicago Press.

9
The Revitalized Regent Park Community

By 2015 most of the relocated Phase 1 households who chose to resettle inside Regent Park had done so. Phase 2 resettlement was also virtually complete. The fact that, despite all the difficulties discussed in Chapters 6 and 7, more than 40 percent of the displaced Phase 1 households managed to return to Regent, and another 20 percent to nearby TCHC housing, is indicative of the residents' attachment to this community and their determination to remain there. For Phase 2, the rate was significantly higher. These statistics also suggest that the TCHC, in contrast to most of its American counterparts, did a pretty good job of honouring the Right of Return.

At this mid-point in the projected revitalization, what did returnees find? Can we speak of a viable and continuing community? Land use has changed to make the area economically diverse, including new retail and service facilities—many of which are sources of on-site employment opportunities.

Figure 9.1 "Old and New" Sackville Street 2013, showing original apartment building in foreground, new tower behind.

The site's population has increased with the addition of about 3,000 condominium residents. At the ten-year, half-way point in the community's redevelopment, we can begin to assess the first returnees' experience of mixed tenure and social mix.

Continuity and Discontinuity

During the displacement phase, tenants who were temporarily relocated to housing elsewhere in the city often reported travelling back to the Regent Park neighbourhood to shop or participate in community-based programs, and to visit with relatives and friends. For some it was a short journey, for others it could take an hour or more on public transit. The fact that they were able to return demonstrates an important feature of the redevelopment plan: Regent Park's phased approach to demolition stands in contrast to the all-at-once policy followed in some other jurisdictions. Successive sectors of Regent Park were razed, but the rest remained standing and occupied. The reasons for this timing were mainly economic, but the net effect—whether intended or not—was to promote continuity. There was still a neighbourhood—and potentially a community—for displacees to return to. The process of dislocation was undoubtedly disruptive and often painful for tenants, but it allowed a community to continue through successive phases of construction. Displaced households from Phases 1 and 2 eventually moved back into new homes, but the surroundings—with three more phases ahead—were still largely familiar, as were the neighbours who were waiting their own turn to move.

Some households minimized or avoided displacement altogether. Many Phase 1 residents were able to stay in temporary housing inside Regent Park, and some Phase 2 residents moved directly from their old units into new permanent housing, with no separation at all from the residential community.

Pre-existing community organizations and institutions have been able—at the very least—to operate continuously through the redevelopment. Some, in new spaces, have been able to expand their mandates significantly. Outside the periphery of the development, retail establishments that cater to specific sub-groups in Regent Park's population—for example, halal butchers and African-Canadian hair salons—have continued to operate on nearby streets, apparently without losing their clientele. No such shops, however, have yet moved into the newly-constructed retail spaces of the Regent development; it remains to be seen whether the new rental spaces will be affordable and accommodating to such businesses.

Our study has found numerous indications that the strong bonds of community that characterized Regent Park previously have not been diminished by the ongoing demolition and construction. One returning

Figure 9.2 Lower Parliament Street retail, 2016: These shops are located along Dundas Street, west and slightly south of Phase 1 of the new Regent Park.

respondent, a decade-long resident in Regent Park now resettled, summed up this feeling: "The kids grow up in the same neighbourhood and [attending the] same school… playing like brothers and sisters. They grow up together, that's why they say [we are] one community."

Another respondent said that while she hadn't met any of the new condominium residents, she had many activities that put her back in touch with the people who used to be her neighbours. She described her participation in programs sponsored by a century-old local settlement house with a tradition of offering community recreation and support: "Thursday afternoons twice a month we have a workshop at Central Neighbourhood House, and we have a yoga program [there] on Wednesdays, and sometimes we do Tai Chi. We have a women's group."

A different TCHC tenant described neighbours' interaction occasioned by a fire alarm in a newly occupied building on a cold winter night, when residents had to stand outside waiting for an "all clear" that would let them return to their homes:

> It was actually a fire alarm in our building in December, I believe, or January and it was really cold and we had somebody from the next building… opened their door and they called a lot of people to sit inside, which was like, wow… they were very nice.
>
> (Fernandes 2014, 124)

In the spring and summer of 2015 the Daniels Corporation produced *The Journey*, a musical show meant to highlight "a living history of the Regent Park revitalization." With songs written by Mitchell Cohen, performed by a cast composed mainly of Regent residents, the production was designed as a tribute to the robust community, its past battles ("Grannies on a Mission," on the building of the Regent South Community Centre) and attachment to place:

> Maligned in the city, so misunderstood,
> It's my piece of the city, both the bad and the good,
> I know it ain't pretty, but it's my neighbourhood.

Planners and advocates of renewal in such cities as Chicago and Atlanta took a negative view of public housing communities, referring to them as ghettos or even "concentration camps of poverty" (Goetz 2013, 135).[1] "The one thing we're not going to do," declared Renée Glover, head of the Atlanta Housing Authority, "is go back and rebuild a newer version of something that has failed" (Goetz 2013, 112). Journalist Malcolm Gladwell offers a more nuanced view of this issue, based on an assessment of the experiences of New Orleans families after Hurricane Katrina: Those who left the city's high-poverty neighbourhoods for other cities were seeking better schools, better jobs, better housing and health care; those who remained and tried to rebuild devastated areas were motivated by an attachment to family, friendship networks, and a distinctive culture. Gladwell sees something gained, something lost:

> In the past ten years, much has been said, rightly, about the resilience and the spirit of those who chose to rebuild the neighborhoods they had lost. It is time to appreciate as well the courage of those who, faced with the same disaster, decided to make a fresh start.
>
> (Gladwell 2015, 37)

But must these two paths be seen as an either/or choice? In Regent Park, the TCHC has offered tenants the opportunity to move elsewhere, but guaranteed the Right of Return. By matching the demolished public housing units with new RGI ones on almost a one-to-one basis, the agency has taken a very different approach from, for example, Chicago's Cabrini-Green/Parkside or Atlanta's Techwood/Centennial Place, where only a small minority of displaced residents could return. Instead of squeezing occupants out of the neighbourhood, TCHC and Daniels Corporation seem to be committing to a long-term RGI presence—a minority of housing units, but a near-majority of residents. The new Regent Park will include almost as many subsidized occupancies as the old one, and the evidence from Phases 1 and 2 suggests that a substantial majority of dislocated households is choosing to return.

In this new context, the planners hope, the negative aspects of the older community can be overcome without losing its many positive features. Ten years on, what is the evidence?

Streetscape: Feelings of Safety or Lack of Safety

One of the most conspicuous changes in the neighbourhood has been the altered streetscape and landscape. The former isolation of the area has been addressed by the re-creation of a grid of through streets. Those that were previously closed to through traffic have been opened, and other streets and lanes created or restored—among them the former Oak Street, once a symbol of the original Cabbagetown (NFB 1953). Residents' guests can more readily find their addresses, as can taxi drivers and pizza deliverers. Public opinion is somewhat divided as to the impacts of the reconnected streetscape on neighbourhood safety. Where Regent Park was formerly described as a "gated community" of poor people, it is now open and accessible to pedestrian and vehicular traffic. Whether this is a positive change, and whether it has created an inviting environment, are questions that still await answers.

At the time of their resettlement interviews, the sampled Phase 1 residents had been living for a relatively short time in their new Regent Park homes. But most of the residents interviewed had been back long enough to have opinions about the changed streetscape. Their reactions are mixed. Some feel that the reconnection of their streets to the world outside facilitates intruders' entry into the community. One respondent suggested that the brand new network of paved streets might actually serve the interests of the criminal element, giving them easy access into and out of Regent Park: "Maybe it will be great for the people who do crime, because they can go anywhere. It's open… They do crime when they can leave faster… they can hide anywhere." She described how she carefully chooses her routes when walking through the neighbourhood after dark, avoiding empty places.

Another, who said she could see both advantages and disadvantages to bringing back the grid of streets through the neighbourhood, expressed concern that it might be the drug dealers who would reap the advantages of the new streetscape: "It will be an improvement to have those through streets. It's good. But we're concerned about the drug dealing—it will be much easier. It will be more convenient for them [drug dealers] to get around… just drive in."

Another recently resettled resident worried that the increased traffic through the neighbourhood created an unsafe environment for children. She expressed concern that her school-age child and his friends were at risk from irresponsible drivers: "All drivers are not safe drivers. Some are rushing. Our kids, they don't know—they are rushing too… Sometimes it's not safe for kids."

But other residents credited the new streetscape and the increased automobile traffic with increasing their feelings of safety. According to one resettled resident, "In this area, if you go to visit someone, now you don't feel like you did before—unsafe... Because there is a road here, a busy road… the cars are going all the time."

These Phase 1 resettlement interviews were conducted relatively early in the redevelopment—probably too soon for a valid measure of how the new streetscape may change people's lives or perceptions. As long as construction continues, traffic will move slowly and the full effect of changes will be hard to discern. One respondent, recently resettled, predicted that increased density will come in the latter phases of the redevelopment, and that feelings of safety will increase as streets became busier. She felt that would be an improvement, noting: "I don't like quiet places."

Still another respondent decided to move to one of the three off-site locations, in part because of the busy flow of pedestrian traffic she found there at all times of the day and night. She said, "I liked that there were people walking around the streets at midnight unafraid." As a shift worker who travelled to work via public transit, she felt safer at night time walking on crowded streets than on empty ones. She was not prepared to wait until the new Regent Park is fully settled, to see if it can provide the same lively street scene.

"A Well-resourced, Mixed Use Community": The Evidence So Far

Amenity spaces and facilities have been a priority for this project. Planners and residents sense that the project is on display, and that communities across the globe are watching to see if it succeeds in meeting its various objectives. The developer and the housing authority as well as the municipality have all been pressing for early completion of amenity spaces that make the new community attractive, not just to former residents but to condominium purchasers and the wider urban public (Chapter 4). Plans were revised to complete some facilities earlier rather than later: an Aquatic Centre, a large park at the centre of the neighbourhood, the Daniels Spectrum arts and cultural hub. A new community centre opened in 2016 and additional athletic fields are also complete. Significantly, some of these facilities are starting to attract a clientele from across the city, making Regent Park a destination for people who would previously have shunned the area.

The new **Aquatic Centre**, which is quickly becoming well known across the city of Toronto, is an innovation that has been particularly successful at improving the public image of Regent Park. Its reputation was enhanced in

2013 when it received the Toronto Urban Design award of excellence for Public Buildings in Context.[2] The jury explained why they selected the pool:

> The Regent Park Aquatic Centre is a refreshing and bold contemporary civic gesture for Regent Park and the city as a whole. Its use of glass and intriguing form create a pavilion-in-the-park quality that integrates gracefully with the emerging public realm in Regent Park. From the street, the building is inviting and has an unmistakably civic presence. The Regent Park Aquatic Centre is set to become a new source of pride for this community transformation.
>
> (Toronto 2013, 12)

The Aquatic Centre building is admission-free, and operates year-round. It contains three pools: a full-sized swimming pool, a smaller therapeutic pool and a shallow water-play area for children. There is also a water slide. The centre offers a range of classes, starting with pre-schoolers and extending to first aid and Bronze Cross. It also includes women-only swim days. A distinctive feature of the glass-clad building is its adjustable screening, which can be used to cover the windows, assuring privacy to women while they swim.

Media coverage of the new Aquatic Centre has been very positive, emphasizing the excellence of its design as indicative of the superior planning that has been invested in the rebuilt Regent Park community (Hume 2012). Journalist Tabatha Southey, in a column in *The Globe and Mail* newspaper, wrote enthusiastically about her own experience using the Aquatic Centre pool:

> I tried out the pool during a ladies-only swim, something Regent Park's sizable Muslim population makes essential. I assumed it would be quiet. I was wrong. The blinds were drawn, and the place went wild. They let us use the Tarzan swing. There's a water slide and a fountain.
>
> (Southey 2014)

She concluded that the City of Toronto had taken a bold step toward building a great city.

The pool is easily reached by public transit, and all Toronto residents are eligible to use the facility. Regent Park RGI residents, especially those with children, appreciate that the absence of program fees makes the pool accessible to their families. Some, however, have expressed disappointment that the new centre, which they saw as their own, is now being used by many people from across Toronto. They report that the crowds and the competition for swim classes make it somewhat less appealing. They feel that local residents should have priority in accessing the Aquatic Centre and its instructional programs.

They would prefer not to have to get on line at 5:00 a.m. to register their children for swim classes. Space in the Aquatic Centre is also available on a rental basis for private events such as children's birthday parties. One of our informants, a condominium resident, saw this as a positive development in that the pool was attracting people from other parts of Toronto and integrating Regent Park into the metropolis. But here, too, RGI residents may feel ambivalent.

Another highly-touted facility is the **six-acre park**, sometimes jokingly referred to as "Regent Park Park," in the very centre of the community. Located adjacent to the Aquatic Centre, the park includes a mall or esplanade of play areas geared to children of various ages, with ground-cover cushioned for safety. Swings, slides, teeter-totter and other active play equipment are among the amenities. The park also includes grassy play areas, a dog run, community gardens and an outdoor oven. Mitchell Cohen notes that the latter was a recent addition: "… the park was going to be grass, but the community said 'We need more than grass, we need… something to bring people together.' "

The community-building function was illustrated, in the summer of 2015, by the creation of a weekly outdoor market located in the centre of the park. The outdoor cooking facilities helped the organizers to offer low-cost meals with menus reflecting the many ethnic communities that make up the neighbourhood.

Cohen points out that the park prompted further community consultation, and was a stimulus to additional ideas that were taken up by the municipality and his own corporation. With new adjustments to the overall site plan, a set of athletic fields was added in another location:

> what also came out of it is that people said, "We need active playing fields, the kids need a place here to run and to play and to have soccer and to have a cricket pitch, and to have basketball". Because the cricket team for example from Regent Park travels three TTC [public transit system] transfers to get to their cricket pitch in [suburban] Scarborough where they play. That's crazy! … collectively, with the neighbourhood, with the local councillor, with Toronto Community Housing and in this case, with Maple Leafs Sports and Entertainment coming to the table… collectively we were able to move density around and create an opportunity for the Regent Park athletic complex [completed and opened for use in 2016.]
>
> (Cohen 2015)

Daniels Spectrum is a three storey 60,000 square-foot building providing space for music, dance and other instruction and performance. It includes a large auditorium as well as smaller meeting rooms, and a lobby furnished with couches, chairs and desks that is open to community members for study and conversation at all times. The lobby is WiFi-equipped, and also includes a piano with the caption, "Play me, I'm yours." A refreshment bar operates during concerts and other public events; it is embellished with a large illuminated sign salvaged from the former Root Burger shop, a momento of the old Regent Park. The third floor offers—on a rental basis—flexible co-workspace that serves as an incubator for starting community-based businesses. That space is managed by Toronto non-profit urban development agency Artscape, which operates several such community-based incubators elsewhere in the city. Other spaces in the building, including the auditorium, are available on a rental basis to the general public, and have been used for various purposes such as fashion shows, art exhibits and historical displays.

The Paintbox Bistro, a combined café, food service and employment training program, performs a dual function. Besides providing a venue for dining and musical performance, it serves as a classroom for training in the food service industry. This restaurant combines a for-profit with a non-profit organization. In one recent project, Chris Klugman, chef and partner at the Bistro, began working with a catering collective of some 50 Regent Park women—most of them recent immigrants to Canada—who were seeking to develop commercial catering skills to prepare and sell foods from their homelands (Somalia, Ethiopia, Pakistan). With access to the Paintbox's full commercial kitchen, the group members are learning food handling skills and cookery techniques from Klugman in this community economic development initiative. According to Regent Park community engagement worker and project founder Sureya Ibrahim, interviewed in media accounts, there are already some 100 waitlisted names for this popular catering collective (CBC 2014).

While many involved with the community redevelopment laud the Daniels Spectrum building, expressing pride in its design and satisfaction that such a community arts and culture hub actually came to fruition early in the project, some of the original residents feel excluded. Yes, some events there do not charge admission, and welcome all community members: for example, the annual Regent Park film festival, or community update meetings on redevelopment. Other activities, however, are priced beyond the means of the returning low-income social housing tenants. In some cases subsidies may be offered. But some RGI parents fear that in other cases they may have to tell their children that programming is beyond their reach. Just the appearance of well-dressed guests at events in the Daniels Spectrum, or of patrons at the Paintbox Bistro arriving on one occasion by limousine for a gala event, makes some residents feel like outsiders in what they thought of as their own neighbourhood. One young RGI resident summed up his feelings:

> I have to say… it hasn't really struck me as a positive vibe they're giving to the community. It seems to be more outside events that come to the Daniels Spectrum pretty much daily, and not too much community participation.

> So I don't know how much that centre is community friendly... I think especially with Daniels, they could do lot more to invite community participation... a lot of the times it seems like corporate events going on there and very little authentic community events are in that particular building.
>
> (Fernandes 2014, 106)

On a smaller scale is the **TD Centre of Learning and Development** (formerly East End Literacy, a project that began operating in Regent Park in 1979), located at street level in a new Regent Park building on Dundas Street. With ties to local post-secondary educational institutions, it provides instruction in the form of courses, lectures and workshops. Posters in the Centre's windows invite visitors to sign up for or just attend scheduled programs or meetings. One recent example was a course to address the needs of immigrant parents who, while working to improve their English language skills, realized that they also needed some basic computer skills. The Learning Centre offered a program of multi-generational computer coaching in which school-age children helped their parents to become computer literate. The Centre of Learning's sponsored series, "Ask a Professor," provides opportunities for dialogue between community members and experts in various fields such as entrepreneurship, health and immigration. The Centre offers workshops in digital storytelling and recently helped to launch the aforementioned catering collective as a community-based business.

Another long-established Regent Park program is the **Christian Resource Centre**, which has been refining and redefining its role and methods of service delivery in the context of other changes in the community environment. Founded in the mid-1960s as a social justice initiative of a United Church group, the CRC had a long tradition as a part of the original Regent Park public housing community. The CRC was a place of worship, a food bank, and a drop-in centre and shelter. As Regent Park redeveloped, so did the CRC. They constructed a new building in Regent Park, known as 40 Oaks, with a large church, kitchens and dining room facilities, and 87 affordable supportive apartment units housing some 100 people. The agency's most recent program addition, opened in 2014, is the Regent Park Food Centre, which serves healthy, nutritious meals sourced from fresh, local food, free of charge, on a drop-in basis (TCRC 2015). In 2015, this program provided support for a weekly outdoor market in the central park, which offered produce for sale at near-to-wholesale prices. Two more long-standing community groups are the **Regent Park Focus Youth Media Arts Centre** (established in 1990) and the **Regent Park Community Health Centre** (1973). The media centre operates a local radio, video and closed-circuit TV station to serve the community. It also provides young people with training in radio and television production skills.

Other longstanding educational programs such as **Pathways for Education, Parents for Better Beginnings, Dixon Hall Neighbourhood Services** have continued and in many cases expanded their operations over the course of Regent Park's transformation. Agencies with a broader mandate such as the **Salvation Army** also continue to play an active role in the community. Some of these are now giving particular attention to finding ways of bringing together the RGI and non-RGI populations of the new community.

Retail facilities. Regent Park was historically defined by its exclusively residential land use. Save for a chip shop and convenience store, and a truck selling vegetables, the Regent Park community had virtually no places to shop or to sit down for a cup of coffee or a meal. Residents and outside experts agreed that this should be changed, and mixed land use became one of the guiding principles for designing the new Regent Park. The neighbourhood now also includes a range and variety of commercial land uses located on its main streets. The largest new enterprise is a FreshCo supermarket, located on the western edge of the neighbourhood at the corner of Dundas and Parliament Streets. A part of the Sobey's chain of grocery stores, it emphasizes discounted prices; for some products this means a narrower range of choices, but the store also makes a special effort to meet the various ethno-cultural preferences of the community. In interviews, neighbourhood residents commented favourably on having such a store within easy walking distance—a quality-of-life improvement, especially for those with busy schedules.

Another new arrival that is especially popular with the original social housing tenants is the neighbourhood's Tim Hortons coffee shop. Not special, not unique, this most typical of Canadian coffee shops pleases residents precisely because of its normalcy. It is new, clean and ordinary, which is just what many of the residents want in a neighbourhood. One of the consultations with residents conducted prior to redevelopment reported: "One of the most compelling comments heard from residents of the existing community, was their wish that the new development look much like that of other downtown neighbourhoods" (Rowe 2004, 20). As recent immigrants to Canada, or as multi-generational residents of this downtown neighbourhood, community members appreciate having such an ordinary business as Tim Hortons on their doorstep.

Other newly-opened establishments include a bank (the first new financial institution to open in or near Regent Park in more than fifty years), a wireless phone dealership, a birth centre and a walk-in medical clinic, as well as two pharmacies. In addition to providing convenience to residents, these enterprises have brought employment opportunities to the area. Most but not all of the new local retail businesses that opened so far are associated with large retail chains. One exception is a food shop, the Sultan of Samosas, which sells South Asian pastries to eat in or take out. The owners boast that their establishment has brought street food to Toronto's East Downtown.

Just outside the borders of Regent Park, and especially up and down nearby Parliament Street, there has been for many years a diverse assortment of retail establishments, some catering to lower-income residents, some to specific ethnic communities, and some to the more affluent Cabbagetown community. As of 2015, that diversity remains. Dollar discount stores and ethnic grocers exist side-by-side with gourmet food shops. Pubs and restaurants abound. Sumach Espresso, a small and independent but upscale establishment opened in late fall, 2015 on the site of a former corner convenience store, across the street from Phase 3 of the redevelopment. It may be a sign of a new trend among retailers, addressing the emerging community of Regent condominium residents. Looking to the future, when Regent's redevelopment will be complete, one must wonder how the balance among retailers will change: Will there be affordable space within the boundaries of Regent Park for a range of retailers focusing on different parts of the mixed-income community? Will small, independent shopkeepers be able to hold their own against large chains and up-market competitors? Whether nearby properties remain as they are will be a question of how the redevelopment of Regent Park alters the real estate that surrounds it. Planners and developers who hope to build a thriving new community might reflect on Jane Jacobs's oft-quoted adage: "New ideas must use old buildings" (Jacobs 1961, 188).

Job Creation

Prior to the start of redevelopment, consultation with residents had identified job creation as one of the goals associated with rebuilding their community. In the set of twelve community planning principles guiding the redevelopment, number six was "Build a diverse neighbourhood with a mix of uses, including a variety of housing, employment, institutions and services" (TCHC 2010; Gladki 2014, 8). The City of Toronto established an employment centre in Regent Park to facilitate job placement and training. The goal is to create new employment opportunities for residents in new services associated with Regent Park, including positions in the construction trades. The tally of jobs created is part of the housing authority's ongoing evaluation of the redevelopment. Under the heading "Revitalization by the Numbers," the Regent Park redevelopment section of the TCHC website contains a running tally of jobs created, and is updated regularly. By late 2015, the total surpassed 1,100. Those jobs are in new retail establishments, including the supermarket, coffee shop and bank, as well as in the ongoing construction. They include a combination of full- and part-time employment; some of the positions are seasonal.

The Condominium Perspective

"Kiss that idea (and others) goodbye." That was journalist John Barber's pessimistic assessment, in October 2008, of Regent Park's proposed redevelopment. The financial crash that had just occurred in world markets, triggered by the US sub-prime mortgage crisis, had apparently put an end to Toronto's real estate boom—and with it the prospect of selling condos in Regent Park. Barring a miracle, he opined:

> the new tower now rising at the corner of Dundas and Parliament will be the last evidence of the much-anticipated revitalization of Regent Park, Canada's largest public-housing project – and the city's most ambitious attempt to use condo sales to finance social policy.
>
> (Barber 2008)

This gloomy prophecy turned out to be incorrect, not just for Regent Park but for the city's overall real estate market. Although the number of sales in Toronto fell slightly, home prices held firm through the crisis and have climbed steadily ever since (TREB 2015). Condo sales in Regent Park, far from collapsing, have met or surpassed the expectations of planners and developers. All the units built in Phases 1 and 2 have now been sold, and the prospects for the remaining phases seem (as of 2015) quite favourable.

Although the present study is more concerned with RGI tenants and their views of the redevelopment, the story would be incomplete without some examination of the non-RGI housing and the people who have chosen to live there. Apart from some statistics on sales and rentals, our evidence is anecdotal. But the comments of a small number of condominium residents can be matched to the observations that we gathered from their neighbours in TCHC occupancies to produce at least an impressionistic picture of the overall community after a decade of change.

In all, four condominium buildings were completed up to 2014, and a fifth is nearing completion. The first four have been completely sold—a total of 1,591 market apartments and townhouses (*Toronto Star* 2014). Unfortunately we have not had access to first-purchase prices, as these transactions were not recorded in the available database. We are able, however, to track resale prices; Chart 9.1 shows the trend in in these since 2009. We see a slow but steady upward trend, with overall growth of just over 10 percent for both sizes of unit. Over the same period, average Toronto real estate prices rose by a little more than 30 percent. In the first eleven months of 2015, the Multiple Listing Service recorded 177 sales of single-bedroom units in Regent Park, and 38 of two-bedroom ones; prices were consistent with those recorded in previous years, and the average number of days-on-market was just above 30 for both

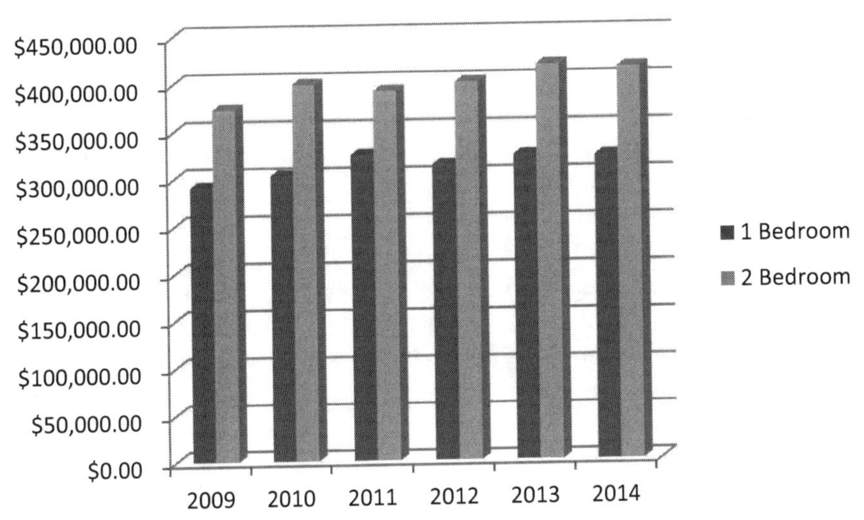

Chart 9.1 Average resale prices of Regent Park condominium units, 2009–2014.

Source: Toronto Real Estate Board, Multiple Listing Service, courtesy of Nicholas Humphries, Sales Representative with Sage Real Estate Ltd.

sizes of unit. In the third quarter of 2015, the average price of a condominium (all sizes taken together) in the City of Toronto was $405,865, and in Regent Park, $358,827. Taken together, these numbers suggest that the market for units in Regent Park has been solid, but not quite booming in the way that some other neighbourhoods have been.

The condos that have been built to date have been mostly studio apartments and one-bedroom units. Just 30 percent have two bedrooms, and only 5 percent have three. This stands in contrast to the distribution of unit sizes among the RGI occupancies (including townhouses as well as apartments), where 54 percent have three or more bedrooms and just 12 percent are one-bedroom or bachelorette. The small size of the condo apartments makes them ideal for single people or childless couples, but also helps to define the population that will choose to live there. Judging from the comments of our respondents, the number of condo households with children is not large. On the other hand, Mitchell Cohen of Daniels Corporation sees an emerging trend among some of the residents:

> People who have bought in Phase 1 are having children and want to move into a larger unit. And I don't have the numbers, but I know anecdotally… [they] are saying to us, "Build bigger units." And we are now in Phase 2 and 3, building more three-bedroom units, and as we go forward … because we have a very important proof of life, if you want to call it, that the community

> is alive, it is growing, it is evolving, and it is a place for families as well as single people.
>
> (Cohen 2015)

Looking ahead, the presence or absence of children in the non-RGI population may influence the amount and variety of social interaction that takes place within the mixed-income community of Regent Park. Schools, and the parental involvement that sometimes occurs in them, can play a major role in bringing people of different backgrounds together. If, as Cohen believes, condo owners who start families choose to remain in Regent Park, schools and child-centered activities may bring them into closer contact with their neighbours. If, on the other hand, they regard their Regent units as "starter homes" and move on, the opportunities for interaction will be lessened.

Another important aspect of the condominium sector is the presence of rental tenants. Absentee owners who have invested in these properties for rental income and/or future resale have accounted for about 20 percent of all sales (Daniels Corporation 2015). The proportion of investors is higher among the newer buildings than in those that were first offered for sale. Judging from condo residents' comments, the number of owners who rent their units to tenants may be larger still; one estimated that more than half the occupants in one building were renters rather than owners. Based on realtors' listings (which may not be typical of the larger population of rentals), the average price in 2015 for a one-bedroom unit was $1,514/month, and for a two-bedroom, $2,136. These figures are 10 to 20 percent lower than the citywide average.

The number of renters is another factor that may influence the shape of the future community. If they move in and out with great regularity, they may be uninterested in making any kind of connection with neighbours, whether from condos or from RGI occupancies. On the other hand, the below-average level of rents (and also the lower purchase price of units) suggests that the condominium population is not especially affluent. Perhaps the economic gap between them and the RGI population is less than some members of the old Regent Park community imagined when they tried to picture living next-door to "rich people." At a recent job fair, hiring staff for the soon-to-open drug store, RGI and non-RGI tenants lined up together to apply.

A Mix of Tenures

TCHC's 2002–2003 revitalization study spoke of a "seamless mix of market oriented and TCHC units," and as plans became more complete the Corporation commissioned a strategic review to suggest strategies to bring this about (Connelly 2004). Here the objective was to find ways "to diversify the range of available housing options, from almost entirely rent-geared-to-income to include a mix of affordable rental, affordable ownership and market ownership" (TCHC 2014, 2). Eventually two different mortgage-assistance schemes were introduced. The first, supported by the City, province and federal government, was marketed by the Daniels Corporation under the name "Boost." It was designed for first-time home buyers with an income below $82,600: If they were able to come up with a 5 percent down payment on a condo purchase, the program would provide an additional 10 percent in the form of an interest-free loan, repayable if the unit is resold, but forgiven in entirety if the purchaser resides there for twenty years (Daniels N.D). As of February 2013, 176 mortgages had been issued under this program (TCHC 2013, 6).

A second subsidy was offered specifically to Regent Park RGI tenants under the "Foundation Program," supported by a total of $1.6 million in federal funding channelled through the City of Toronto. This program offered second mortgages of up to 35 percent of purchase price, on terms much the same as the Boost program. To qualify, a household's combined income had to be no greater than $81,000. The purchasers also had to be able to contribute, by the time of closing, a 5 percent down payment. Like those in the Boost program, these mortgages were interest-free, but if the purchaser sold the unit they would be required to repay the full 35 percent plus 35 percent of any gain they made on the sale. As of July 2014, 15 households had secured mortgages through this plan.

TCHC also offers "affordable rentals" to other qualifying households. These are different from rent-geared-to-income in that the tenant pays a fixed amount of rent, set at 80 percent of CMHC average rents in the city,[3] but not varying according to fluctuations in income. To qualify for affordable rental, the tenant household's gross income must not exceed four times the annual amount of the rental (TCHC N.D.). As of 2015, 210 such units were built, with another 100 expected to be completed with a year.

These categories of rental and purchase have, to some degree, blurred the line between market-level condominiums and rent-geared-to-income occupancies. As already noted, the physical design of the new Regent Park is intended to have the same effect, by making housing units architecturally "tenure blind"—i.e., making TCHC housing indistinguishable from private market units.

The units are, however, still grouped together by category—market occupancies on one side of a street and TCHC on the other. Even without external markings, residents soon come to know which are which.

Early versions of the revitalization plan called for mixed forms of tenure in individual buildings, on the grounds that this was more likely to promote social integration. Apart from the small number of subsidized-mortgage purchases, Phases 1 and 2 of the Regent Park redevelopment have no mixed tenure in any of the newly constructed buildings. At the start of Phase 3, there

Figure 9.3 Cole Street, 2013, an example of "tenure-blind" architecture: one side of street is RGI, the other market.

is as yet no plan for mixed tenure in subsequent phases. There has been no further public discussion of any plan for mixed tenure buildings in future phases of the redevelopment. Absent from the plan, in particular, is any form of cooperative housing, which the collaborative team identified in 2003 as one of the great strengths of the widely-admired St. Lawrence neighbourhood, where self-management was seen as a source of resilience over a period of some forty years:

> the healthy level of community involvement... is directly linked to the large number of cooperative and condominium buildings in the neighbourhood. [Residents] feel that the co-op philosophy encourages community engagement in each individual board level. ... [and in] the neighbourhood association.
>
> (RPCT 2003, 13)

The St. Lawrence cooperatives were created at a time when such projects were eligible for large-scale federal and provincial support. Those subsidies no longer exist. But that need not prevent today's planners from exploring alternative means of establishing self-governing, non-profit associations that enable renters to exercise real control over their environment. Condominium residents already possess such rights under the Condominium Act, which vests governance in elected boards, accountable to the members of the association.

Assessing Social Mix

In the public-private partnership that is Regent Park redevelopment, social/tenure mix is the instrument being used to finance the construction of replacement RGI housing. In simplest terms, the development portion of the original site is being sold to pay for new public housing construction.[4] But proponents of the redevelopment plan argue that the mixture of market and rent-geared-to-income (RGI) tenures is more than an economic "alliance of convenience." In support of the policy of social mix, they see social advantages in a community that integrates residents of various income levels and tenure forms. Those alleged advantages include social network contacts for low-income residents, upgraded community services and amenities, and safer streets. According to this view, an economically mixed neighbourhood will possess advantages that an income-segregated public housing community does not possess. Toronto's St. Lawrence district is often cited in support of this argument.

In Canada and elsewhere, social mix/income mix is a growing trend in public housing redevelopment. Toronto's recent task force on overhauling TCHC recommends using social mix as the basis for reorganizing the agency's entire housing portfolio (Mayor's Task Force 2016, 25ff.). Social mix is seen in that report as a way of creating a positive social environment and moving to a positive cash flow. This approach is being embraced despite a lack of conclusive evidence of the efficacy of social mix.

The literature on public housing includes numerous critics of the social mix/tenure mix rationale (Hackworth 2009; August and Walks 2012; August 2014). In this view, the true goal of redevelopment is gentrification. Partnership with the private sector makes the state an agent of this process, leading sooner or later to the displacement of low-income residents—often to housing that is far less desirable than the now-demolished public housing.

Results from other North American cities where income-mix has been introduced show relatively little social interaction among higher and lower-income neighbours (Silver 2011, 74), but some reports from New York City (Bloom 2008) and the Biljmermeer and Slotervaart districts of Amsterdam (Saunders 2010, 292–300) are more positive. A recent longitudinal study of poverty in the US (Chetty and Hendron 2015) concluded that changing neighbourhoods can have a positive impact on children's future earnings, as well as on other social outcomes; results were not immediately apparent but could be discerned over the course of several decades. (Here the focus was on families that moved from one neighbourhood to another, whereas in Regent Park families are remaining in place while the neighbourhood around them changes.)

Residents of different income levels who live close to one another do not automatically socialize, and the social benefits that some advocates predict have not often appeared. Robert Chaskin and Mark Joseph recently completed a six-year interview project in three Chicago sites that were redeveloped by the Chicago Housing Authority. They concluded that low-income residents, far from becoming economically and socially integrated into their new neighbourhoods, were in a state of "incorporated exclusion:"

> Relocation has for the most part neither led to significant cross-class interaction between public housing residents and their higher-income neighbors nor significantly enhanced social networks for them... [Despite offering some material benefits] these new communities expose poor people—and particularly relocated public housing residents—to different kinds of disadvantage and have generated new forms of exclusion.
>
> (Chaskin and Joseph 2015, 224)

Anthropologist Sharon Kelly conducted twenty months of fieldwork in Regent Park in 2009–2010, interviewing more than 40 condo and RGI residents (Kelly 2013), around the time that the first residents in both groups were moving into new units. Her overall observation was that relatively little communication was taking place between the two populations. Condo purchasers, she observed, arrived with enthusiasm and the expectation that they would be part of a social experiment. But after living in the neighbourhood for a few months, they were finding few opportunities to connect with their RGI neighbours. One compared her own unit to a "ghetto in the sky," separated by an "invisible line" from the rest of Regent Park. Another spoke of fellow condo owners going "into their little bubbles." Kelly found the RGI tenants, for their part, to be indifferent to the presence of up-market residents: "... it seemed that many Phase 1 residents, to the extent that they pay attention to the condos at all, are on board. Their concerns about the redevelopment centred upon other issues; the social mix piece received little criticism" (ibid., 188).

Our own survey asked returning TCHC residents whether they have met any of the people moving into the condominiums—newcomers to the community. Most said they had not had occasion to meet them. But there were some exceptions. One high school student from a returning RGI family, for example, recalled that when they initially moved into their new unit there was not yet any functioning WiFi service available to her. A classmate and friend who lived in one of the new condominium units invited her to work with her in that condo's lounge, and share the WiFi available there. Without invitation, such common spaces in the buildings are available only to residents and their guests; those spaces are not locations to promote social interaction between residents of various tenure. But in this instance, the line between RGI and private-market residents was crossed.

Some of the new community facilities are perceived by returning residents as sites of social interaction across income groups. The father in one recently-returned family with school-age children observed how the new retail businesses and the redesigned streetscape served to open up the formerly isolated Regent Park. He is pleased that their community is no longer isolated from the rest of the city:

> If you look at the part that's revitalized you know it's open. You will see many people that are not from Regent walking around in front of our door. Have their cars parked here. And the business… we have a Tim Hortons there… where people of the condo owners and the TCHC people [are] coming together and also a FreshCo [supermarket] where you know the people from condo owners are going and shopping… We are proud of having such things.

In addition, there are volunteer activities at the neighbourhood level, including community gardens; these are open to all and are intended to serve as meeting places for neighbours from market and social housing. There have now been two attempts to organize a weekly outdoor market. The first, in the summer of 2014, drew farmers, bakers and other vendors from many parts of the city, including some Regent Park residents offering freshly prepared foods from various cultural traditions. But the prices of most goods proved too high for many residents. A year later another market was organized as Taste of Regent Park, in cooperation with the Regent Park Community Food Centre. Its mandate was to offer, at cost, fresh produce purchased from food terminals, and to serve locally cooked affordable meals in cooperation with several other neighbourhood organizations. Both markets drew a mix of RGI and non-RGI residents, but the first leaned more toward the latter group and the second toward the former.

A residents' association, Regent Park Neighbourhood Initiative (RPNI), was created in 2002 as a forum for discussing the revitalization plan and advising TCHC on its implementation. It helped, for example, to draw up the 12 principles of revitalization (Chapter 4), and strongly supported the Right of Return. When condominium residents began arriving in the neighbourhood, they were welcomed into the association. RPNI received modest financial support from TCHC. But after a few years the organization began to run out of steam. When, in 2013, TCHC brought forward a revised plan that increased the number of condominium units, RPNI was not among the groups that offered comments. By this time its membership had dwindled significantly, and in 2014 it was dissolved. As of June 2016, efforts were under way to organize a new Residents' Association that would represent condo dwellers and TCHC tenants alike, but these have not yet come to fruition (McConnell 2015). Neighbourhood informants suggested to us that any such group, to be effective, should remain fully independent of both TCHC and the Daniels Corporation.

The argument for income mix is sometimes depicted by critics as a kind of missionary colonialism, in which higher-income residents provide uplifting role-models for their lower-income neighbours to emulate. Based on our interviews and observations, neither group in Regent Park would accept or aspire to such roles. At a more mundane level, social mix does offer some possible advantages, and also some risks. The condominium residents may—though we can't confirm this—expect and receive higher levels of municipal service (e.g., trash collection), with results that benefit the entire community. Local schools—to the extent that the higher-income residents send children to them—can also be a forum that brings together parents of different backgrounds, with different skills to contribute. Policing of the community, however, raises other issues. If the non-RGI residents make new demands of the police, this may not promote social cohesion. Although most in the neighbourhood favour cracking down on illegal behaviours, many low-income residents (young men in particular) object to being stereotyped and—in their view—harassed for behaving in ways that, though legal, offend the sensibilities of some of their new neighbours. Loud music is one example. "Hanging (or chilling) out" is another.

To call what we are seeing in Regent Park "social engineering" would be an overstatement. The neighbourhood is going through a series of changes and "growing pains" without a predetermined outcome. Many residents as well as planners and service-providers are trying to encourage the emergence of a community that is not split or fragmented—on economic or any other lines. Martin Blake of Daniels Corporation put it this way:

> What we want to do is recreate cities like cities have been built for years and years, decades, millennia… where people with money and without money live in the same neighbourhood and are not thrown into ghettoes… I don't need to know if it's going to work, because it works everywhere else in Toronto. Why in the entire world would there be one spot where normalcy doesn't work?
>
> (Kelly 2013, 179)

These comments point to a vision of a diverse civil society composed of many groups—economic, racial, linguistic, cultural—that coexist in the same space, acknowledging and tolerating their differences and, if all goes well, sometimes learning from one another. The TCHC and Daniels Corporation are helping rebuild a community in which RGI housing will be a permanent feature. The wishes and past experiences of the tenant population have been treated with respect, even though their proposals have not always been accepted. Efforts to promote cooperation and dialogue among the various members of the new Regent Park community have sometimes been clumsy or unsuccessful. There are bound to be crosscurrents, disagreements, and feelings of ambivalence among the participants, but this does not justify dismissing the effort as inappropriate.

Stephanie Fernandes, who studied social mix in Regent Park in 2014, spoke with a number of residents and key informants about their impressions. She was especially interested in the sentiments of one young man who had grown up in Regent Park and expressed his feelings about redevelopment in a poem. Here is Ismail Afrah's poem (with permission): "In Between Love and Hate Lies Home, Poverty, Arts and Culture, Confusion and Gratitude, and Possibly a Contradiction:"

> I love Toronto Housing.
> I hate Toronto Housing.
> I love because I have a home.
> I hate because it will never be mine.
> I love Regent Park because we are a community.
> I don't like Regent Park because poverty makes me live here.
> But post Regent Park is post poverty and an even greater community to live in.
> Look at arts and culture, at the Daniels Spectrum. All of that is really nice, I can personally testify.
> But who is Daniel and how long will it be his centre?
> You are confused. Yes, but I am equally grateful. Seriously.
> I love that this is not a contradiction.
> And guess what, I hate that it is a contradiction.
>
> (Ismail Afrah)

Fernandes comments on her own interpretation of the poem, and relays some explanation from the poet:

> The Daniels Spectrum was built as an Arts and Culture Centre as identified as a need in the [social development plan] SDP (TCHC 2007). In this way, the space was created through resident involvement in the decision making processes. However, this poem illustrates the changing community and that both positive and negative things accompany this change. Look particularly at the line "But who is Daniel and how long will it be his centre?" It illustrates a perspective that redevelopment is changing the ownership of Regent Park; what was once a community led development initiative and grassroots organizing is now happening alongside a larger project that is being imposed on the community. In explaining this poem, he said:

> "What that poem was talking about was having to be in a community you identify with, but at the same time, because you see the total changes that is happening, the new rises in the buildings, the new activities that's going on at the arts centre. It feels at the same time that this is not an output you're giving. This is not coming from within the community. The community itself is poor. So this is coming from an outside investment, an outside interest. So even though you might feel a sense of gratefulness, a sense of joy, that things are changing, and you see a lot of positive things, at the same time you're concerned that these are not for you, or this is going to impact you in some sense. It's a fear, and at the same time a sense of gratitude you might say".
>
> (Fernandes 2014, 104–105)

Lessons Learned

This chapter has reviewed the built form environment into which the original Phase 1 residents resettled within the Regent Park footprint, and the social environment that accompanies it. The area's re-zoning for mixed use has resulted in new commercial establishments bringing convenience to the residents. Many original residents express their pleasure at the ordinary businesses, particularly the new supermarket and established chain coffee shop, which—besides having the convenience of close, walkable services—makes their neighbourhood feel like a regular, normal neighbourhood. New premises for old and new services are also welcome additions. The income mix and the increased density of the neighbourhood bring an array of facilities.

In accordance with the Social Development Plan (TCHC 2007), the Regent Park redevelopment recognizes the original low-income tenants' claim to their neighbourhood. Those residents are given a voice in the redevelopment planning, and a Right of Return to their rebuilt community. The original public housing residents of Regent Park should enjoy, in principle, what Henri Lefebvre (1996) terms, a "right to the city." As used by Lefebvre, that term involves the idea that all residents, regardless of housing tenure or income level, should have influence in planning the urban environment that is their home. The original tenants are, however, trying to claim their "right to the city" in a community where their households will eventually be outnumbered at least two to one by middle-income neighbours in market-rate accommodations.

Uncertainty, confusion and contradiction may be an inevitable part of Regent Park's story, both past and future. The neighbourhood has its own complex history, identity and loyalties, including many features that today's residents would like to banish from their future. Planners and developers also have a long history that includes, by today's lights, massive mistakes that disrupted people's lives and caused more harm than good. Looking toward the future, we should not be surprised to find disagreement and contention (not to mention suspicion and animosity), not just between residents and planners, or between RGI and market residents, but also within each of these groups. What has been accomplished in ten years is, however, an impressive start toward a new synthesis of housing forms, and a new effort to build a civil society. The test of the next decade will be to learn from past experience, both in Regent Park itself and in other locations and jurisdictions, to build on successes and rectify errors.

Notes

1 The words quoted were spoken by Egbert L.J. Perry, founder and CEO of the Integral Group, a real estate development firm that played a prominent role in Atlanta's redevelopment.
2 In 2015 the facility received a second award, from the International Olympic Committee (IOC) / International Association for Sports and Leisure Facilities (IAKS) Awards for Exemplary Sports and Leisure Facilities: http://www.mjmarchitects.com/?mid=award&node_srl=15398. (Accessed February 2, 2017).
3 As of 2015, the TCHC affordable rental rate for a one-bedroom apartment was $822/month.
4 One (non-tenant) informant who has closely followed the redevelopment plan put it this way: "[Critics] are going to label what's going on at Regent Park as 'social engineering'. It isn't that at all. Selling the land for development of market housing is simply the only way we can afford to rebuild the deteriorated public housing units."

References

August, Martine. 2014. "Challenging the rhetoric of stigmatization: The benefits of concentrated poverty in Toronto's Regent Park." *Environment and Planning* A 46: 1317–1333.

August, Martine and Alan Walks. 2012. "From Social Mix to Political Marginalisation? The redevelopment of Toronto's public housing and the dilution of tenant organisational power." In *Mixed Communities: Gentrification by Stealth?* Ed. Gary Bridge, Tim Butler and Loretta Lees. Bristol, UK: Policy Press.

Barber, John. 2013. "Condo cash was going to save Regent Park. Kiss that idea (and others) goodbye." *Globe and Mail* October 4, 2008.

Bloom, Nicholas Dagen. 2008. *Public Housing that Worked: New York in the Twentieth Century*. Philadelphia: University of Pennsylvania Press.

Canadian Broadcasting Corporation (CBC). 2014. "Regent Park catering collective cooking up community profit." December 31. www.cbc.ca/news/canada/toronto/regent-park-catering-collective-cooking-up-community-profit-1.2883755. (Accessed January 10, 2017).

Chetty, Raj and Nathan Hendren. 2015. "The Impacts of Neighborhoods in Intergenerational Mobility: Childhood Exposure Effects and County-Level

Measurements." Harvard University. (May). scholar.harvard.edu/files/hendren/files/nbhds_paper.pdf. (Accessed January 10, 2017).

Cohen, Mitchell. 2015. Personal communication. June 8.

Connelly Consulting Services, Tim Welch Consulting. 2004. *Options and Strategies for Realizing Affordable Home Ownership in Regent Park: A Report to the Toronto Community Housing Corporation*.

Daniels Corporation. ND. "Deposit and Down Payment Advantages at One Park Place South."

Daniels Corporation. 2015. Personal communication. July 20.

Fernandes, Stephanie. 2014. "Informal relationships in a newly mixed income community: A Regent Park case study." School of Planning, University of Waterloo, Waterloo, Ontario, Canada. Master's thesis. uwspace.uwaterloo.ca/handle/10012/8535. (Accessed January 10, 2017).

Gladki, John. 2014. "Inclusive Planning: A Case Study of Regent Park." In *Inclusive Urban Planning: State of the Urban Poor Report 2013*. Ministry of Housing and Urban Poverty Alleviation, Government of India. New Delhi: Oxford University Press of India.

Gladwell, Malcolm. 2015. "Starting Over." *The New Yorker* August 24: 32–37.

Goetz, Edward G. 2013. *New Deal Ruins: Race, Economic Justice, & Public Housing Policy*. Ithaca, NY: Cornell University Press.

Hackworth, Jason. 2009. "Political marginalisation, misguided nationalism and the destruction of Canada's social housing systems." In *Where the Other Half Lives: Lower Income Housing in a Neoliberal World*, Ed. Sarah Glynn. London, UK and New York, US: Pluto Press, 257–277.

Hume, Christopher. 2012, "Regent Park's splashy new aquatic centre." *Toronto Star*, November 23: E8.

Jacobs, Jane.1961. *The Death and Life of Great American Cities*. New York: Vintage Books.

Kelly, Sharon. 2013. "The New Normal: The Figure of the Condo Owner in Toronto's Regent Park. *City and Society* 25(2): 173–194.

Lefebvre, Henri. 1996. "The right to the city." In *Writings on Cities*, trans. Eleonore Kofman and Elizabeth Lebas. Oxford: Blackwell.

Mayor's Task Force on Toronto Community Housing. 2016. "Transformative Change for TCHC." www1.toronto.ca/wps/portal/contentonly?vgnextoid=4184a1f9b4a72510VgnVCM10000071d60f89RCRD&vgnextchannel=102d30787e87b410VgnVCM10000071d60f89RCRD (Accessed March 21, 2017).

McConnell, (Councillor) Pam. 2015. "Coming Soon! Regent Park Neighbourhood Association." *Newsletter* 17:2, 3.

NFB (National Film Board of Canada). 1953. *Farewell to Oak Street*. Grant McLean, Director. www.nfb.ca/film/farewell_oak_street. (Accessed January 10, 2017).

Rowe, Mary W. 2004. "Background on the Neighbourhood of Regent Park, Toronto." *Ideas That Matter* 3(2): 20–22.

RPCT (Regent Park Collaborative Team). 2003. "Action Plan Summary Report."

Saunders, Douglas. 2010. *Arrival City: The Final Migration and our Next World*. Toronto: Alfred A. Knopf.

Silver, Jim. 2011. *Good Places to Live: Poverty and Public Housing in Canada*. Black Point, NS: Fernwood Publishing.

Southey, Tabatha. 2014. "Reconsidering Toronto's Regent Park: Look Again, It's Where Canada Works." *Globe and Mail* March 14: F3.

TCHC (Toronto Community Housing Corporation). ND. "Rent at Toronto Community Housing." www.torontohousing.ca/rent/affordable-rent/Pages/default.aspx. (Accessed February 22, 2017).

TCHC (Toronto Community Housing Corporation). 2007. "Regent Park Social Development Plan: Executive Summary." (September).

TCHC (Toronto Community Housing Corporation). 2010. Regent Park: Building Great Neighbourhoods. Community Update Meeting. Powerpoint presentation. October 28.

TCHC (Toronto Community Housing Corporation). 2013. *Regent Park Revitalization, Housing Issues Report: Official Plan Amendment and Re-zoning Application for Phases 3, 4, 5, Lifting of the Holding Symbol Phase 3*. (September).

TCHC (Toronto Community Housing Corporation), 2014. Building and Investment Committee. "Affordable Home Ownership Programs in Revitalization Communities." BIC: 2014-60. July 17.

TCRC (Toronto Christian Resource Centre). 2015. Personal communication.

The Journey. 2015. Original soundtrack. Another Life Productions (SOCAN).

Toronto, City of. 2013. *Toronto Urban design Awards: Jury Report*. www1.toronto.ca/wps/portal/contentonly?vgnextoid=5b8e235bce0a1510VgnVCM10000071d60f89RCRD. (Accessed July 22, 2016).

Toronto Real Estate Board (TREB). 2015. "Historic statistics: Toronto MLS sales and average price." www.trebhome.com/market_news/market_watch/historic_stats/pdf/Historic_1509.pdf. (Accessed January 10, 2017).

Toronto Star. 2014. "Regent Park is Making New Waves." February 14.

Vale, Lawrence J. 2013. *Purging the Poorest: Public Housing and the Design Politics of Twice-Cleared Communities*. Chicago and London: University of Chicago Press.

10
Looking to the Future

In common with St. Louis's Pruitt-Igoe and quite a few other large-scale housing projects of its day, the first Regent Park enjoyed a "honeymoon" period in which everything seemed to be working according to plan. Visitors came from far away to admire and learn from this (apparently) well-ordered community. But within less than a decade more critical voices drowned out the praise. Even enthusiastic promoters of the development such as Albert Rose became disillusioned and focused their attention on Regent Park's failings rather than its successes.

In 2015 the new Regent Park appears to be flourishing. Many of the faults of the former development have been addressed. Resettled tenants are, for the most part, pleased and enthusiastic about their new housing, and the private market for condominium units looks healthy. The drab and barren streetscape of previous years has been replaced by a lively assortment of retail and recreational facilities. But is this another honeymoon? Will Regent Park remain a model that offers positive lessons to planners in other jurisdictions? Or will critics, a decade hence, be seeing it in a different light, just as earlier generations revised their vision of the first Regent Park?

In reviewing the findings of previous chapters, we assess some of the qualities that make the new Regent Park different from (or similar to) its predecessor. The achievements of the past decade must also be compared and contrasted to revitalization efforts elsewhere. Regent Park today is a work in progress, and it may be especially useful to relate it to efforts under way in other jurisdictions—New York, Chicago, Amsterdam—in order to predict what the future may hold for all of them.

Inclusive Planning

The first Regent Park was planned and built in the 1940s and 1950s with little regard for the wishes and concerns of the affected community. City-wide volunteer organizations such as the Women Electors' Association, The Toronto Welfare Council and the Citizens' Housing Association campaigned vigorously in support of this major housing proposal, but with little representation from the neighbourhood. This was a top-down initiative—part reformist/philanthropic, part political, but it did not emanate from the Cabbagetown community. Toronto's experience in this respect was little different from the urban renewal efforts of that era in many other jurisdictions in North America.

In contrast, the TCHC began its 2002 Regent Park redevelopment effort by investing thousands of person-hours in community consultation. The workshops and community meetings that were held served as a forum for assessing the wishes and concerns of Regent Park residents. The tenants' input confirmed their attachment to the neighbourhood and desire to continue living there after redevelopment, and provided suggestions and guidelines that helped to shape the 2003–2004 revitalization plans. Even so, it would be an overstatement to suggest that the *initiative* for redevelopment came directly from the community. Community members had, over the previous two decades, urged the city and province to renovate their homes and neighbourhood. Some had taken part in previous efforts to redevelop portions of Regent Park. But the timing and outlines of the 2002 proposal came mainly from TCHC. The difference from past practice was that now the corporation was actively seeking the residents' advice and cooperation.

Senior planner John Gladki, who has been involved in every stage of the revitalization effort, underscores inclusive planning as a key factor in Regent Park's redevelopment: "[S]uccess relies heavily on support and commitment from residents to make it work" (Gladki 2014). The planning exercise was inspired in part by earlier successes in such Toronto neighbourhoods as Trefann Court or St. Lawrence (Chapter 2). Specific features of the 2003–2004 revitalization plan were added or modified in response to the workshops and meetings that were held. TCHC's efforts to consult and include the affected community were more far-reaching than those of most planning bodies in Canada or the US. By way of contrast, Robert Chaskin and Mark Joseph have faulted the Chicago Housing Authority for taking what amounts to a window-dressing approach to community involvement: "… to engage 'community' principally as a target of intervention rather than as a unit of action, emphasizing planning, design principles, and the primacy of development professionals rather than mobilization of community-level actors, processes, and resources" (Chaskin and Joseph 2015, 218).

On the other hand, programs in certain other countries (e.g., Amsterdam's Bijlmermeer and Slotervaart districts) seem to have gone much further than Toronto in encouraging grass-roots initiatives to transform public-housing communities (Saunders 2010, 300).

While it is true that TCHC has continued to seek community input throughout the stages of construction, the residents' comments in our project's interviews suggest that these efforts were not always successful. Not all Regent

Park tenants were aware of the many meetings and proposals. Rumours that circulated through the community were sometimes distorted and troubling. Many residents remained suspicious of TCHC and pessimistic that they would be able to return to their neighbourhood. The first stages of relocation were described as chaotic and, to some residents, demeaning, as tenants lined up before dawn without knowing what to expect. At a later time, when new housing became available, negotiations with TCHC personnel were described by our respondents as sometimes difficult or confrontational. As well, some tenants were bewildered by blueprints and unable to visualize the apartments that they were being offered. By the time residents were permanently resettled, most of these issues were resolved. Through trial and error, the relocation system has been improved and many of its problems corrected in subsequent phases of redevelopment. But it seems likely that some of these difficulties could have been avoided altogether if the TCHC had dealt with them in a more proactive and consultative way. The blueprints problem, for example, could have been anticipated, and tenants could have been given other kinds of information such as three-dimensional drawings or computer simulations of living space.

Consultative planning doesn't (or shouldn't) end when a "final" revitalization plan has been approved. Inevitably, any plan will evolve over time—hopefully in positive ways. Community input can help monitor progress and promote better results. But true consultation entails more than public meetings and information sessions. TCHC's leaders and planners recognized this principle at the outset of the Regent Park initiative, but their successors—over a decade of turbulent politics and high administrative turnover—have not always adhered to it. At its best, TCHC—with the energetic support of the Daniels Corporation and local officials such as Councillor Pam McConnell—has been attentive to the wishes and needs of the community, as with the accelerated planning and implementation of the central park and athletic fields. At its weaker moments the agency's staff has seemed to revert to top-down and bureaucratic modes of management that produced poor results in the past. The longer-term success of the Regent Park experiment may hinge on whether this tendency can be overcome.

Public Private Partnership

In 2016 the New York City Housing Authority, which provides housing for more than 400,000 tenants, is said to be facing a $17 billion (USD) backlog in overdue repairs to public housing (Kimmelman 2016). TCHC, with about 40 percent as many tenants, might consider itself fortunate: Its repair backlog is estimated to cost a mere $2.6 billion (CAD). But in neither city, nor in any of the jurisdictions surveyed in Chapter 3, are higher levels of government prepared to provide financial support on the scale that was provided half a century ago. Local bodies must come up with new ways of covering their costs. Public Private Partnership (PPP) is one possible solution that is being attempted in Regent Park and in many other cities including New York, Chicago and Amsterdam. Housing authorities or equivalent agencies can sell or trade land or development rights to private-sector partners as a way of raising needed funds.

The oft-expressed fear that goes with such partnerships is that private developers' interests may supersede those of subsidized tenants. In Chicago, redevelopment of public housing sites resulted in drastic reductions in the numbers of replacement units available to low-income renters—a possibility that the Regent Park plan, with its promise of one-for-one replacement and a guaranteed Right of Return, has rejected. But replacement alone does not guarantee that market considerations will not take precedence over tenants' wishes and needs. When, in 2013, TCHC proposed a 50 percent increase in the number of market units in Regent Park, critics were concerned that this would change the character of the neighbourhood, inundating the RGI residents in a sea of middle-class owners.

Toronto's partnership has, to this point, provided some major benefits for the wider Regent Park community, with the developer taking a role well beyond construction and sale of condominiums. In addition to creating the Daniels Spectrum as a centre for cultural activities, the Daniels Corporation has helped to mobilize support from major donors such as Maple Leaf Sports and Entertainment Foundation to build a hockey rink and other community recreational facilities. Daniels CEO Mitchell Cohen has put great emphasis on respecting and listening to the members of the RGI tenant community. A very public example was the musical show described in Chapter 9. If the mixed-income community envisaged in the Revitalization Plan comes to pass, the developer's engagement will deserve some significant part of the credit. Housing authorities in other settings may not find such a willing and enthusiastic partner, but in drafting redevelopment plans they should pay attention to ways of encouraging this sort of participation. TCHC's initial proposal to work with multiple partners instead of a single firm looks, from this perspective, as if it would not have produced such positive results.

Social Mix/Income Mix

Robert Chaskin and Mark Joseph, whose study of three Chicago neighbourhoods found little evidence of positive effects of social mix, conclude by suggesting a series of measures that might, in another setting, produce better results.

Measured against this list, Regent Park may offer a greater prospect of success than the Chicago cases. For example, Chaskin and Joseph note that commercial development in the Chicago sites was postponed until after housing was built and occupied; in Regent Park it began in Phase 1. Parks in the sites they studied were located on the periphery of communities, and there were few places "that welcome shared use, such as stores, coffee shops, recreational facilities, and schools" (Chaskin and Joseph 2015, 235). In Regent Park, the central park and aquatic centre plus a series of other community facilities are already in operation. The authors also suggest "moderating social distance" by offering a range of rental and purchasing options that will attract an economic spectrum of residents, instead of polarizing a community between well-to-do owners and low-income tenants. Unit design, they note, can also be used to moderate social distance (ibid., 231). In all these respects, the Regent Park redevelopment has at least made a start in the recommended directions. But more could be done, in the remaining stages, to reinforce these beginnings. Certainly the number of shared social spaces can and will be increased. The economic divisions between renters and tenants are already somewhat blurred by subsidized mortgages and market-level rentals, but TCHC—unlike the New York City Housing Authority—has to date done little to attract "working poor" tenants of slightly higher income. The condominium buildings appear—though we have no reliable statistics—to house a large proportion of renters, but this is not necessarily conducive to social integration, since turnover is likely higher in this renter population.

With respect to condominium owners, Chaskin and Joseph observe that owner-occupancy is more likely to promote stability in a community. Non-resident owners may be more likely to treat their properties as investments to be kept or sold according to changing markets. TCHC and other housing authorities might do well to explore incentives that would encourage a higher degree of owner-occupancy. Unit size may be relevant here, since—to date—most of the new condominiums in Regent Park are single-bedroom or two-bedroom, more attractive to households without children. Children are, in general, more likely than parents to socialize across socio-economic or ethno-cultural lines. If they are enrolled in school (and if they and their parents are pleased with the school), a family will have more reason to remain in a neighbourhood. These possibilities are reduced if the available housing is not well suited to family living.

Regent Park differs from most US public housing communities in its racial and ethno-cultural mix. The high proportion of immigrants has more in common with some European sites, but whereas Amsterdam's Biljmermeer and Slotervaart each has one predominant ethnic group (Surinamese and Moroccan respectively), Regent Park's population is diverse, with Bengali, Tamil, Chinese, Vietnamese and Somali as the most numerous language groups in 2011; almost 27 percent of residents were of South Asian descent, over 17 percent were of African ancestry, and 12 percent Chinese. In our interviews, residents maintained that relations among these many populations have been friendly and inclusive. But the use of multiple interpreters in the community consultations and in subsequent community meetings suggests that there are still divisions among them. Encouraging closer interaction and mutual understanding will be another challenge that the neighbourhood and the service-provider groups will face in the coming years.

Previous immigrant populations in Toronto (as in many other localities) have tended, over a generation or two, to develop skills and accumulate resources that allowed them to resettle away from the sometimes disagreeable conditions of the inner city. We may anticipate that within another decade or two, some of today's renters—whether in RGI or market-level units—will be looking for market-priced housing. In the interest of sustaining a viable community, planners today should perhaps be asking whether the supply of family-sized market units will give upwardly mobile households the option of remaining within Regent Park.

Chaskin and Joseph's list includes a number of other suggestions, which can be summarized under two additional headings: social development and community building.

Social Development

Regent Park's history, at least since the 1960s, has been defined by the persistence of poverty, and the same has been true of most public housing in Canada and the United States. Chaskin and Joseph echo the judgment of many other planners and critics that housing alone cannot solve the problems of poverty or remedy the structural factors—such as unequal education and lack of employment opportunities—that reinforce and perpetuate it. They recommend that housing redevelopment be complemented by efforts to build human capital, create employment opportunities and address the social needs of low-income residents. Particular attention, in their view, should be given to programs directed toward youth.

In these respects the Regent Park Revitalization Plan and the associated Social Development Plan appear to have anticipated the Chicago study's recommendations. The Toronto proposals envisaged a multi-faceted community service effort to coordinate the work of municipal and non-profit agencies—providers of various kinds of social services. This work was to be coordinated by a Stakeholders' Table that included representation from the neighbourhood as well as from the affected agencies. But a recent report (RPSDP 2016), based on interviews and focus groups with several hundred residents as well as service providers, raises doubts about the effectiveness of these initiatives. Residents, it found, were unaware of the existence of the Stakeholders' Table, while service providers were critical of it for failing to provide focus or promote concrete outcomes. Residents expressed "compelling concerns" about shortcomings in housing and employment programs, as well as about poor communication with TCHC and the Stakeholders' Table. And the organization that was supposed to provide ongoing input from the neighbourhood—Regent Park Neighbourhood Initiative—is defunct. Efforts to replace it have begun, but at the time of writing they had not come to fruition.

The report concludes with a series of recommendations to address these problems and "enable the meaningful participation of community residents and… collaborate with all stakeholders, including residents, to advance social development and social inclusion" (ibid., 4). If Regent Park is to achieve the goals and fulfill the hopes that were expressed a decade ago, the relevant agencies will need to refocus their energies and redouble their efforts.

On a more positive note, RGI residents who participated in different stages of the planning process have sometimes found this to be an eye-opening and empowering experience. Shauna Brail and Nishi Kumar, who interviewed residents in 2014, quote several examples:

> You just felt like, "Well, I don't have anything to bring to this game." And [someone] said: you do, you have experiences they don't have. You have information and knowledge… that they can't read in their books, they can't get in their classrooms, they're not gonna get in their office. They don't know what you know… Put Regent Park around the table. You can learn all that while you're there.
>
> … all the skills that I mentioned that I find I have, they're all from these programs… So in having meaningful conversations, then you're better able to vocalize what it is that you believe in and what you see as wrong, what you see as right. And that all helps to build the person that you will become, and you are.
>
> (Brail and Kumar 2015)

Design for Community

Design flaws of the original Regent Park have been discussed and dissected for decades. The old community was off the grid of city streets, unwelcoming to outsiders and isolating its own population from the rest of the city. Many of the criticized features have been addressed in the new plan. The street grid is restored, houses are oriented along streets instead of being surrounded by unregulated "dead spaces." Shops and recreational facilities have replaced the single-use zoning of the past. In our interviews, returning residents welcome many of these changes, but are ambivalent about the street grid, with some fearing that it will make the neighbourhood more vulnerable to criminal incursions. Young people are nostalgic for the now-paved "Boardwalk" where they once congregated.

The aforementioned report evaluating the Social Development Plan (RPSDP 2016) repeats similar comments from residents and service-providers. While the new parks and other recreational and cultural amenities attract praise, residents identify an important gap in the community design: open, unprogrammed, informal spaces. They want green zones, trees, and places in which groups can assemble without renting or booking meeting space. The new plan, they observe, lacks areas where residents can gather naturally, spontaneously, without pre-planning and organization. The new community centre, which opened in February 2016, will address some of these wishes and needs, but the residents' comments point toward other needs that may not be met by present plans.

Jane Jacobs, writing close to the end of her life, eloquently described immigrant neighbourhoods that have grown up across North America in recent decades: "Newcomers are enlivening dull and dreary streets with tiny grocery and clothing stores, second-hand shops, little importing and craft enterprises, skimpy offices and modest but exotic restaurants" (Jacobs 2001, 4).

What distinguishes these spaces and uses from the often-sterile environment of planned communities like the old Regent Park is their spontaneity and unpredictability. Paradoxical as it may seem, *spontaneity doesn't just happen.* Unless the designers, builders and stakeholders of a new community leave some space for unregulated and unpredicted uses, they will miss an opportunity to create a vibrant and close-knit community. Compare this to Douglas Saunders's description of Amsterdam's rebuilt Slotervaart district:

> Amsterdam decided to make it a place that looked good to someone arriving from a village. People were moved closer together… because of the belief that higher population density is better for social cohesion and prosperity. Zoning restrictions were all but eliminated, so that retail, light-industrial and commercial services could be mixed up with housing.
>
> (Saunders 2010, 295)

In Saunders's account, density, diversity and flexibility have combined to produce a vibrant urban culture to replace the sterile modernism of Amsterdam's former public housing. The planners and managers of Regent Park could do more in this direction.

One more aspect of successful redevelopment in Amsterdam, New York and Toronto's St. Lawrence neighbourhood is inclusiveness. If residents can take an active role in managing and regulating the spaces where they live, the chances of cooperation across economic and ethno-cultural lines will be greatly increased. This can take the form of self-management in autonomous housing cooperatives. It can find expression in a residents' council or a parent-teacher, home-and-school association. In Amsterdam and New York residents have formed street patrols to deter antisocial behaviours. In the new Regent Park, apartment owners have a voice in their condominium associations. TCHC has a system of elected tenant representatives in its buildings, but their role is not nearly as far-reaching as that of a co-op or condo board. The revitalization plan called for an inclusive Regent Park Neighbourhood Initiative to become a voice for all residents, both market and RGI, but this organization has now been disbanded. In order for a vibrant and cohesive community to flourish, TCHC and the City should consider devolving real responsibility to neighbourhood groups. Without true decision-making powers, such groups will be seen by residents as empty shells, window-dressing or rubber-stamping instead of bringing the communities together in common purpose.

The Best Laid Plans...

Reviewing the history of public/social housing in various cities and countries over the past century, we can see it reflecting major political and social trends of the various eras—for example, post-World War II reconstruction and prosperity, economic uncertainty of the 1970s and neoliberalism in the 1980s and beyond. But historical contingency has also played a role in determining the success or failure of any one initiative in this field. A good example might be Chicago's Parkside (former Cabrini-Green), where the market crash of 2008 occurred just as new condominium units were coming up for sale. This caused at least one developer to file for bankruptcy, and produced chaotic disruption for others. Some units intended for market sale were redesignated for RGI occupancy (Vale 2013, 296). Critics thought the same might happen in Regent Park, but the Canadian real estate market held steady and resumed growth soon after 2008. This favourable market has worked to the advantage of Daniels Corporation, which has (from all indications) had little difficulty finding buyers for new condominiums. As of early 2016, Toronto is still experiencing a real estate "bubble" that has increased prices city-wide by almost 35 percent since 2008. Phase 3 units in Regent Park are now being sold, but overall economic conditions at the moment of this writing are uncertain. If the real estate market should take a downward turn, the later stages of Regent Park could be severely affected.

On a quite different plane, Toronto's municipal government has gone through more than one cycle of turbulent change, including the late Mayor Ford's much-publicized efforts to "end the gravy train" in city expenditures. The fact that the Regent Park revitalization program was able to go ahead more or less as planned is perhaps remarkable, but to carry it all the way to completion will still be a challenge for the next generation of TCHC administrators. Their work will be, in some measure, defined and constrained by two critical external reviews, both released in the winter of 2016. The Mayor's Task Force on TCHC has recommended a drastic overhaul of that agency. Meanwhile a recent review of the Social Development Plan (RPSDP 2016) has pointed to a number of shortcomings in implementation of the recommendations that were made almost a decade ago. Both reports point to challenges on the near horizon that may shape the ultimate results of the Regent Park experiment.

The comparators we have used here—Chicago, New York, Amsterdam—are all, like Toronto's Regent Park, works-in-progress. Each in its way has offered promise of a better outcome in public housing than the older regimes have delivered. But none will magically overcome all the associated difficulties. The same is true of smaller-scale initiatives such as self-managed cooperatives, which have flourished in some localities but not in others. Human nature being what it is, there will be no "one size fits all" solution to the issues associated with poverty and community building. Ten or twenty years hence, the positive and negative achievements of Regent Park and those other efforts will stand out in clearer relief. For the moment, Regent Park seems to be offer grounds for cautious optimism.

References

Bloom, Nicholas Dagen. 2008. *Public Housing that Worked: New York in the Twentieth Century*. Philadelphia: University of Pennsylvania Press.

Brail, Shauna and Nishi Kumar. 2015. "Community engagement and leadership after the mix: The Transformation of Regent Park." Paper presented at the annual meeting of the American Association of Geographers, Chicago. (April).

Chaskin, Robert J. and Mark L. Joseph. 2015. *Integrating the Inner City: The Promise and Perils of Mixed-Income Public Housing Transformation*. Chicago and London: University of Chicago Press.

Gladki, John. 2014. "Inclusive Planning: A Case Study of Regent Park." In *Inclusive Urban Planning: State of the Urban Poor Report 2013*. (Ministry of Housing and Urban Poverty Alleviation, Government of India) New Delhi: Oxford University Press of India.

Goetz, Edward G. 2013. *New Deal Ruins: Race, Economic Justice, & Public Housing Policy*. Ithaca, NY: Cornell University Press.

Jacobs, Jane. 2001. "Time and Change as Neighbourhood Allies." *Ideas That Matter: A Quarterly* 3: 2.

Kimmelman, Michael. 2016. "How to Build Affordable Housing in New York City." *New York Times* January 25, 2016.

Mayor's Task Force on Toronto Community Housing. 2016. "Transformative Change for TCHC." www1.toronto.ca/wps/portal/contentonly?vgnextoid=4184a1f9b4a72510VgnVCM10000071d60f89RCRD&vgnextchannel=102d30787e87b410VgnVCM10000071d60f89RCRD. (Accessed January 10, 2017).

Regent Park Social Development Plan: Community Engagement Report (RPSDP). 2016. January 26.

Saunders, Douglas. 2010. *Arrival City: The Final Migration and our Next World*. Toronto: Alfred A. Knopf.

Vale, Lawrence J. 2013. *Purging the Poorest: Public Housing and the Design Politics of Twice-cleared Communities*. Chicago and London: University of Chicago Press.

Appendix

Research Methods

This book reports on results of a qualitative survey, carried out by Laura Johnson with the help of a team of graduate students and research assistants, tracking the experiences of a sample of 52 Phase 1 households through displacement, relocation, and resettlement. The household was the main unit of analysis for this study. A linked survey of young people's experiences of Regent Park redevelopment interviewed youth from some of those households as well as some others from the community (Johnson and Schippling 2009). Multiple interviews were conducted over a six-year period with adults and youth from those 52 households to document the original tenants' views about the redevelopment process.

Interviews were also conducted with key informants from the local community, including representatives of the housing authority, the private developer, the school board and numerous local community organizations.

This section reviews the methods used in the study. The redevelopment began in 2005; this research started in 2006. In a longitudinal study design, households were interviewed multiple times to collect information on the tenants' views on the processes of displacement, relocation and resettlement.

Sample

The study used a volunteer sample of 52 households out of the total 380[1] households that comprised the redevelopment's first phase. Since the researchers did not have access to a sampling frame, participants were recruited through a volunteer sample combining various means including: an intercept survey conducted in public places within Regent Park; door-to-door screening survey of occupancies to be relocated in 2007 due to a change in the phasing of the redevelopment; posters and flyers recruiting participants, placed on local neighbourhood bulletin boards in numerous locations in the local community (e.g., the lobbies of residential buildings, the local public library branch, social agencies, and retail establishments). Participants were also recruited by means of referrals from local social agencies and community services, and "snowball" referrals from other participants. All respondents were promised anonymity, but a few key informants agreed to be quoted with identification. In the chapters of this book, names and other identifying characteristics of study participants (including residents and most key informants) have been omitted. Identifying details have been omitted or altered to protect confidentiality.

The youth subsample of 29 young people (ages twelve to twenty years) started with youth from the sampled households. This group was expanded by asking participants to refer others ("snowballing") and by referrals from local youth-serving social and community agencies. Some of those community agencies distributed a flyer about the project via email to their clients/members on behalf of the research project, describing the study objectives and providing contact information for any who wished to consider participating. Some youth participants were recruited by contacts made by members of the project team attending a Friday evening drop-in program at a local community centre. Agency staff introduced the researchers, and invited youth from relocated households to speak with the researchers about the study, and about possibly participating. Several youth were recruited in this way. Several households were recruited into the household sample based on initial contacts with youth from those families.

The population of Regent Park, and of the study sample, is ethno-culturally diverse. In recent years Regent Park has evolved into an immigrant reception area (TCHC 2007). Prior to the start of redevelopment, the Regent Park neighbourhood had a higher population of immigrants, visible minorities, and people whose first language was neither English nor French, than the Toronto metropolitan area as a whole. The top five languages in Regent Park, other than English or French, are, in descending order of frequency: Chinese, Bengali, Tamil, Vietnamese and Somali (City of Toronto 2008, 2).

Ethnicity/ancestry for the households in the study includes, by region of origin or descent: South Asian, African, Southeast Asian, European, Caribbean, Latin American, Middle Eastern, and Native Canadian.

Data Collection and Analysis

Personal interviews were conducted in participants' homes or other location of their choice, including project office space within Regent Park or a quiet study room in the local public library branch. The great majority of the interviews were conducted in participants' homes; this was useful since many of the interview questions dealt with aspects of the home environment. Interviews were semi-structured and generally lasted approximately one hour. Participant households were given an honorarium in the amount of $50 per household per interview in recognition of the time involved—usually an hour. Most interviews were conducted in English; translators were used in some cases where participants expressed a preference for an interview in another language. Interviews were transcribed and coded according to key themes as identified in the research questions. Interview transcripts were analyzed with NVivo software to identify and explore main themes.

With participants' permission, interviews were generally audio recorded; a minority of about 25 percent were also video recorded. Videotaped material was used to produce two documentaries: *Breaking Ground* (2007) and *Growing Up Regent* (2009), that were presented to study participants as feedback, to obtain their reactions to findings and solicit further input on the continuing research.

Key informants were generally interviewed in their own offices, or in the research project office. The project interviewed about 20 key informants; several of these were re-interviewed at various points as the redevelopment progressed. At a relatively late point in data collection, interviews were also conducted with three additional figures, who played major roles in the development of this project. Derek Ballantyne, the founding Chief Executive Officer of Toronto Community Housing Corporation, is credited with the idea to redevelop Regent Park, and played a formative role in it. John Gladki was the senior planner throughout various stages in the redevelopment. Mitchell Cohen, President and Chief Executive Officer of the Daniels Corporation, the private developer partner, has been actively involved not just in the construction or the sale of market units, but in overall planning and community-building. All of these latter expert informants agreed to be interviewed with attribution.

In addition to the structured data collection, Laura Johnson used participant observation methods to gather further background on the redevelopment. She regularly attended community update meetings organized by the housing authority for the tenants. She also attended some less formal "town hall" type meetings organized by residents' associations. Along with her University of Waterloo graduate students, Laura participated in workshops and attended various celebrations of openings of buildings and programs. In summer and early fall 2014, shopping at the farmers' market was an opportunity to greet some of the people she had met in the community, and a way to keep up to date with redevelopment progress. The Regent Park community holds a number of public events—such as the opening of a Cabbagetown Regent Park Museum Exhibition, the Regent Park Film Festival, the Sunday in the Park summer festival and workshops of the Regent Park Village of Storytellers Project. Some, like Sunday in the Park, are longstanding annual events that form part of the community's tradition; that festival marked its 25th anniversary in 2016. Others, such as the storytelling workshops, are new, and attract new audiences. All of these are events that provided the authors abundant opportunities to follow the re-emergence of community in the new Regent Park.

Member Check

To assess validity of research findings, qualitative research frequently shares preliminary results with participants, as a means of member check (Charmaz 2014, 210). In this regard, at several points in the data collection and interpretation, efforts were made to share preliminary results with participants, and to engage them in discussion of those findings. Focus group discussions, conversations based on screening documentary video from the study, and workshops to discuss research themes were among the methods used to obtain participants' views of the redevelopment process. As background to these discussions, printed summaries of research results were distributed to participants, as were DVDs of rough cuts of documentary videos produced based on the interviews. Distribution of those materials also served as a way of updating project records on residents' addresses and contact information.

Limits of the Research

This study has been conducted, for the most part, without the active participation of the housing authority, Toronto Community Housing Corporation. The Corporation has provided informal assistance including, for one period, office space within the Regent Park complex and, in one instance (covered by a formal memorandum of agreement) a confidential exchange of limited information about sample characteristics. But the identification and recruitment of the study sample for this research has been done independent of the Corporation, which declined, on grounds of confidentiality, to provide a sampling frame (listing names and contact information of all Phase 1 tenants). Since the 52 respondent households were not chosen randomly, they cannot be taken as a representative sample of all who were resettled at this time. Comparison of the study group's characteristics with the TCHC's published statistics on the entire population of Phase 1 households indicates close correspondence (e.g., on housing outcomes). Nevertheless, the lack of access to household-level information about the full population represents a limitation of this research.

Language of the resident interviews represents another possible research limitation and potential source of bias. The large and diverse immigrant population in Regent Park means that many of the residents have only limited English language fluency. While the research team had some multilingual capability, there were numerous instances where we had to rely on interpretation services. Sometimes teenage children in an immigrant family household agreed to serve as interpreters; sometimes independent interpreters were hired. Limited interpretation resources represent another potential source of bias in this research.

Note

1 Slightly higher figures—ranging as high as 418—are given in some TCHC publications for the total number of households displaced in Phase 1.

References

Breaking Ground. 30 minute documentary video. Appended to Richard M. Schippling. 2007. "Public Housing Redevelopment: Residents' Experiences with Relocation from Phase 1 in Toronto's Regent Park Revitalization." Master's thesis, School of Planning, University of Waterloo, Waterloo, ON. uwspace.uwaterloo.ca/handle/10012/3028. (Accessed January 10, 2017).

Charmaz, Kathy. 2014. *Constructing Grounded Theory*. 2nd Ed. London, UK: SAGE.

Growing Up Regent. 27 minute documentary video. Appended to Laura C. Johnson and Richard Schippling. 2009. *Regent Park Revitalization: Young People's Experience of Relocation from Public Housing Redevelopment*. Ottawa: Canada Mortgage and Housing Corporation, External Research Program. (June). NH18-1-2/50-2009E-PDF.

TCHC (Toronto Community Housing Corporation). 2007. Regent Park Social Development Plan: Executive Summary. (September).

Toronto, City of. 2007. Social Policy Analysis & Research Section, Social Development, Finance and Administration Division. "Regent Park (72) Social Profile #1, Neighbourhoods: Age & Gender." (December). www.toronto.ca/demographics/cns_profiles/2006/pdf1/cpa72.pdf. (Accessed December 10, 2011).

Toronto, City of. 2008. Social Policy Analysis & Research Section, Social Development, Finance and Administration Division. "Regent Park (72) Social Profile #2, Neighbourhoods: Language and Ethnicity." (July). www.toronto.ca/demographics/cns_profiles/2006/pdf2/cpa72.pdf. (Accessed September 25, 2015).

Index

Page numbers in **bold** denote a figure; page numbers in *italic* denote a chart.

9780367667825